D1743872

disunified aesthetics

LYNETTE HUNTER

DISUNIFIED AESTHETICS
situated textuality, performativity, collaboration

McGill-Queen's University Press
Montreal & Kingston | London | Ithaca

© McGill-Queen's University Press 2014

ISBN 978-0-7735-4185-6 (cloth)
ISBN 978-0-7735-4186-3 (paper)
ISBN 978-0-7735-8959-9 (ePDF)

Legal deposit first quarter 2014
Bibliothèque nationale du Québec

Printed in Canada on acid-free paper that is 100% ancient forest free
(100% post-consumer recycled), processed chlorine free

This book has been published with the help of a grant from the Canadian
Federation for the Humanities and Social Sciences, through the Awards
to Scholarly Publications Program, using funds provided by the Social
Sciences and Humanities Research Council of Canada. Funding has also
been received from the University of California, Davis.

McGill-Queen's University Press acknowledges the support of the
Canada Council for the Arts for our publishing program. We also
acknowledge the financial support of the Government of Canada
through the Canada Book Fund for our publishing activities.

Library and Archives Canada Cataloguing in Publication

Hunter, Lynette, author
Disunified aesthetics : situated textuality, performativity, collaboration /
Lynette Hunter.

Includes bibliographical references and index.
Issued in print and electronic formats.
ISBN 978-0-7735-4185-6 (bound). –
ISBN 978-0-7735-4186-3 (pbk.). –
ISBN 978-0-7735-8959-9 (ePDF).

1. Canadian literature (English) – 20th century – History and criticism
– Theory, etc.   2. Canadian literature (English) – 21st century –
History and criticism – Theory, etc.   3. Aesthetics in literature.
4. Performance in literature.   5. Ethics in literature.   6. Creation
(Literary, artistic, etc.) in literature.   I. Title.

PS8071.4.H85 2014   C810.9'357   C2013-907605-0
                                       C2013-907606-9

Set in 10/13 Warnock Pro with Futura, Cyntho Pro, Arial, and
Times New Roman
Book design & typesetting by Garet Markvoort, zijn digital

contents

part one | situated textualities

part two | performativity

part three | collaboration

My scholarly life, mainly in the United Kingdom and in Europe, but increasingly in Canada itself, has a long history in parallel with the growth of Canadian studies. I immigrated to Canada in 1961 and lived and worked in the country until 1973, returning every year for several months from the late 1990s to today. While it is not unproblematic, I self-identify as Canadian and am grateful to the country for giving me the opportunity to do so. I have been involved in the usual academic administrative work of establishing centres for Canadian studies, creating undergraduate and postgraduate curricula, and facilitating greater public understanding of the arts in Canada. But the key motivation of my commitment to the verbal arts in Canada is that I found in so many writers a challenging and engaged interaction with language, society, and culture. This interaction formed a wide cultural range including areas such as First Nations studies, feminist philosophy, and political theory – to name a few – and their intimacy with poetics and aesthetics. Canadian writers have always made it possible for me to value ways of living and knowing that are not usually heard or recognized.

With this book I am attempting to bring together the essay form and performance critique, in other words written and embodied modes of critical engagement with other people's writing. From 1994 to 2007 I created a series with seven performance art pieces attending to Canadian writers that toured internationally. They usually took one to two years' work to script, score, rehearse, and produce, as did the later typographic "performances" that could be referred to as "concrete criticism" by analogy with "concrete poetry." One of the greatest strengths of Canadian writing is its ability to morph genre and catch us unawares in new places, new thinking. The critical approaches to the writing and the visual and performance art in this book have been long-influenced by this tradition, and I hope will contribute to it.

The combination of making value for ways of living and knowing that are unheard, along with the context of generic morphing that opens up processes for collaboration, is key to the exploration here of a disunified aesthetic that is founded on the participation in art-making by anyone who wishes to engage. It is a combination that underlines the work that art does in creating agency and enabling change and is part of an ongoing conversation about the need for more differentiated public participation in politics.

acknowledgments

I would first like to acknowledge the writers and collaborators who have made this book possible by making art with which I could engage: these include the writers around which the essays cohere, but also the many others who have corresponded on the performances and been part of the Canadian studies world which has nurtured the text. In particular, I would like to thank Shirley Chew, past-chair of postcolonial and commonwealth studies at the University of Leeds, and Frank Davey, among other things, editor of *Open Letter*, for their mentorship.

The first six performances were directed by Peter Lichtenfels, and the video editing undertaken by Alex Lichtenfels. They, with Andrew Lichtenfels, are the main reason for the book, having provided me with argument, discussion, conversation, and joy. The studies I have undertaken with Catherine Bates, Susan Billingham, Danielle Fuller, Caroline Fyffe, Judy Halebsky, Armando Jannetta, Sheila Latham, Mark Leahy, Jill LeBihan, Stephen Morton, Jeffrey Orr, Sarah Poulton, Gillian Roberts, Cristina Savioli, Emma Smith, and Karma Waltonen have been inspirational to these explorations. The research here could not have been completed without the help of many people, too many to name, but in particular I would like to mention Peter Kulchyski, who has been more than generous with time and friendship, and Marta Dvorak and Susan Rudy who were instrumental to these essays and with whom was created the "Women and Texts / Les Femmes et les Textes" conference held in 1997 at the University of Leeds.

The Canadian government has helped in the production of many of these pieces, especially the performances, not only through the guidance of Vivien

Hughes at the Canadian High Commission in London in the 1990s but also through travel grants and programs supporting visiting artists, without which Canadian creative work would not be recognized outside the country. I would like to thank the government of Quebec for its extraordinary support in this area. In addition, I would like to thank the Arts and Humanities Research Council of the UK for support toward performance, and in particular the University of California Davis for support toward publication.

Some of the chapters in this book are based on previously published essays. I would like in particular to thank Susan Rudy for permission to publish our jointly written essay "Labour Notes." I would also like to thank Frank Davey for permission to publish some material in chapters 1, 4, 8, and 9 that was previously published in part by *Open Letter*. Marta Dvorak's tireless work on behalf of Canadian literature in France gave me the opportunity to think through, write, and perform parts of chapters 3 and 7. For material in chapter 5 I would like to thank Anne Collett, editor of *Kunapipi: Journal of Postcolonial Writing*, and for material in chapter 6, Louise Forsyth, the editor of *Nicole Brossard: Essays on Her Works* (Montreal: Guernica, 2005).

The process of working on the printed book has been rewarding. Ryan Van Huijstee has been extraordinarily inventive at finding solutions, as has Garet Markvoort, the designer for McGill-Queen's University Press. I remain in awe of the copy-editing skills of Kate Merriman, as I am of Joselle Miller who indexed the book with critical intelligence and care. Above all, I would like to express my gratitude to my editor Jonathan Crago for his belief in this experiment.

Finally, I would like to thank most of all those who gave permission to include their responses to the performances, and all those writers whose texts have inspired these performances and the associated essays.

disunified aesthetics

introduction

There are a number of voices in this book and its attendant web-based performances.

Over the past fifteen years I have developed a series of written commentaries on contemporary Canadian literature that have worked in varying ways with performative counterparts. I have pursued pressing questions about aesthetics and ethics, and in doing so I have also pressed the essay form into different generic shapes the better to address those questions. I have great respect for the essay as a genre, yet for me its traditional form at times leaves out much that I would like to be taking into account with the people who are engaging in conversations around these issues. This is not to say that for all people the essay has the same problems, but for me, with my particular background, developing an essay in association with a performance has opened out the landscape of how and what it is possible to think.

Even this introduction has distinctly different voices: that of the book-builder and editor shaping the contexts for the essays and performances, that of the personal history working in a conversational mode honestly to address the way in which academic inquiry is so often embedded in daily life, and that of the philosopher critic trained specifically to analyse, critique, and, I hope, mark out points and potentials for agency and change.

OVERVIEW

The simple rationale for this book is that I believe that dominant theories of aesthetics no longer respond appropriately to the political ecology and claims on cultural power of people in Euro-American nation-states today. Aesthetics is a field still rooted in universalist modernism and a unified "aesthetic" where very small numbers of people produce, commodify, and consume objects called "art."[1] Yet nation-states and their ideological discourses have changed the range of citizenship, and global economics is constituting nation-states and their citizens into transnational networks. These changes have fundamentally dislodged notions of universality and over the past fifty years have problematized ideas not only about relativist aesthetics but also the normative and responsive ethics of liberal culture and society.

The book walks step by step along a path in Canadian culture that studies resistances and alternatives that delineate a disunified aesthetics, based on the processual and partial, and rooted in complex modes of collaboration. This disunified aesthetics opens out the participation in art-making to anyone who wishes to engage. To this extent it is quite different from the normative implications of traditional aesthetics, and potentially alterior. However, traditional aesthetics is not going to go away, given its rootedness in commodity culture, and I am also interested in exploring how disunified aesthetics relates to nation-state culture and in raising questions about policy and support for this radically democratic mode of art-making.

The essays offer studies of twenty-first-century aesthetics in the context of recent Canadian writing. The book can be read as a series of insights into the literature and poetics of the last two decades, or as a book that tells a story about moving from a traditional view of the relation between the artist, the art, and its reception to a more radically democratic view of aesthetics and ethics. Either way, the chapters are structured like essays, many of which relate directly to performance art pieces I have scripted and produced internationally over the past fifteen years. The performances are key to the aesthetic theory being explored because, at a crucial point in the development of the theory, they act to coalesce the aesthetic experience of criticism itself. The performance critiques for the first seven chapters are available in a simple recorded version on the web. For chapters 8 and 9, which are present as typographic and visual art on the pages of the book, the website material offers a record of the process of the materials that went into the printed text. The website materials are not essential to the essays except in the case of the final chapter, "Roget Falls in Love." However, the documentations of the performances enhance and can open out the implications of the written critical discourse, and their connections raise particular ethical questions about the interactions of critic, text, and artist. The kind of engagement thrown forward by the performances, and increasingly present in the written essays, underwrites not only a disunified aesthetics but an engaged ethics.

The book is in three parts. The first three essays are relatively conventional and run in tandem with three performances. These early performance critiques, as I have called them, were constructed to work allegorically so that they comment in indirect ways on the texts they explore, and each essay attempts a critical reading of the text allegorically treated in the respective performance. The second group of four essays has a different stance with respect to the performances. Here the performed critiques and the critical writings have either far closer or far more separate lives. Each performance stands on its own as a unique critical exploration, while the essays move toward performed writing. With the third and final group of essays the performance critiques and the critical writing coalesce into performative critical writing on the page, quite literally so in one case. These final chapters transfer concepts of the physical performative to the typographic, becoming a kind of "concrete criticism."

Parts one, two, and three are each prefaced by a commentary on the kind of exploration of aesthetics that is taking place and the ethical questions and implications that arise. After each individual essay in each part there is a short piece of contextualization that provides information about chronology, about sites of production, and other material elements of the textual production. These discussions, which follow each chapter in the book, relate the chapter to the performance critique that accompanies it on the website. The purpose of the discussions is to provide more context for the performances and to suggest ways in which the two modes interconnect. For example, the performance "Can a Man Be a Woman?," devised for a Strasbourg conference, also played in Huddersfield, Leeds, London (Ontario), and Toronto. It found itself with quite distinct audiences and the performance critique varied depending on the audience interaction with the performance of that day. These ending pieces also attempt to prompt thinking about the relationship between the performance critiques and the critical writing, and refer specifically to elements from the performances that the readers of this book can access via the website.

AESTHETICS, ETHICS, AND LIFE: A PERSONAL BACKGROUND

When I spoke to the editor at McGill-Queen's University Press, Jonathan Crago, he asked me whether I had considered the ethical impact of the performances in comparison with the ethical understanding that exists between the critic, the reader, and the writer of the text. My considered response to this was to say that with an essay the form is generically defined, the participants are educated into a particular kind of response, while with a performance critique there are no generic expectations.

I was thinking about the formation of the critical essay in the early nineteenth century when the genre was remaking itself. One element that surfaced then, and remains with the essay today, is that part of the ethical relationship between the critic and reader presumes that they both understand that what is written is the critic's opinion, not a "truth" that has to be agreed upon, but a certain set toward the text which the reader is invited to share. Yet because the performed critique has as yet no generic expectations, its form takes you by surprise, involves you more, alienates you more, wraps you into the opinion delivered by the performance or into the significance being made by the performer. At the same time, there is also often a suspension of the usual skilled interaction with criticism because – despite movements such as conceptual art – performance is thought of as an "art form." What emerges from the performance critiques is a different way of thinking about the criticism, possibly not a "critical opinion" but more engaging, although I suspect that as more people become familiar with the performance critique as a form, they will develop appropriate critical skills.

One of the publisher's readers of this book asked, acutely, whether "performance critique" was connected in any way with "fiction theory." Fiction theory, a phrase developed by the group of *Tessera* editors in the late 1980s from the earlier French-language "fiction théorique," attempts to reclaim fiction from representation (Godard et al. 1986). Rather than reproducing the allowable systems of ideology, it is "a corrective lens which helps us see *through* the fiction we've been conditioned to take for the real" (Marlatt 1986, 9). The *Tessera* collaborative provided insight into a longer tradition of women writers' deconstruction of ideological norms through formal experiment.[2] As Barbara Godard put it: "Fiction theory: a narrative usually self-mirroring, which exposes, defamiliarizes and/or subverts the fictional and gender codes determining the re-presentation of women in literature and in this way contributes to feminist theory" (Godard 1986, 10). "There is, in fiction theory, also the focus noted by Marlatt that ... fiction *theory* deconstructs these fictions while *fiction* theory, conscious of itself as fiction, offers a new angle on the 'real,' one that looks from inside out rather than outside in ... it enters a field where the 'seer' not only writes it like she sees it but says where she is seeing from" (9).

In the same chronological period, feminists involved in the situated knowledge analysis of science and technology – Donna Haraway, Hilary Rose, Sandra Harding – were arguing for "strong objectivity," a perspective usually particular to those practising scientists from outside the then Western white male constituency who could recognize the limits that normative science took for granted. The *Tessera* collaborative understood that this kind of knowledge, which reflects on its own positionality, has immediate effects on the medium of its communication. One of the main effects of the *theory* in fiction theory is that it generates "fiction that contains within it a feminist examination, even self-consciousness, regarding the material of the text, the language" (Gail Scott 1986, 11). And as Kathy Mezei reads from Nicole Brossard, it is "a theory working its way through syntax, language and even narrative of a female as a subject, a fiction in which theory is woven into the texture of the creation, eliminating or trying to, distinctions between genres, between prose, essay, poetry, between fiction and theory" (Mezei 1986, 7–8).

Fiction theory explores the possibility that writing from the positionality of women with a consciousness of theory can not only deconstruct ideological codes but produce different and non-hegemonic knowledge. To do so it has not only to engage in critique of content but also to engage in making alternative critical forms of communication. This insight is central to the discussion of situated textuality introduced in *Critiques of Knowing* (Hunter 1999) and is developed much further in the present book. But more clearly impelling "performance critique" as it is used here are both the concept of "installation," developed by Nicole Brossard (Brossard 1984) and the topic of the previous volume of *Tessera* "Writing as Reading/Reading as Writing" (1985), which is of course intimately part of fiction theory if not foregrounded as such, and the topic of "collaboration" that coheres the thinking of the *Tessera* editorial collective ten years later. The editors' introduction to *Collaboration in the Feminine* (Cotnoir et al. 1994), appropriately a series of commentaries rather than a collectively digested text, offers words key to the studies that follow in this book: difference, passion, disagreement, separation, and the importance of speaking and acknowledging such particularity within collaborative work. When I started to build these performances, I called them lecture performances, then quickly turned to theory performance, and finally, after four productions, to performance critiques. In each case "performance" is present partly and predictably to call attention to the process of the formal qualities, but more to remind everyone taking part that everyone *is* taking part, that it is a collaboration.

Other critics have attempted to move into performance critique. Not all take the act of performance as formally demanding in its own right. Some use it not as performance, but to produce physical metaphors like a rebus. A good strategy, but it is different from the kind of performance I am producing. Still other critics have adopted some of the devices to produce performance that is apparently there to mine the relationship of spectator and performance through generically known models. For example, a PhD student who attended "Can a Man Be a Woman?" in Huddersfield and who went on to fund her final PhD years lap-dancing, on completion, turned the experience into a lap-dancing performance, which was successful for a brief period in the 1990s and toured several artistic and educational locations as a performance critique. Again, this is a potentially interesting strategy, but not what is happening in these performances.[3]

At the same time, there is the ethical relationship between the performer and the person who created the text on which the critique is based, between performance critic and the person who made the text under critique (whether written, played, scored, painted, i.e., in whatever medium). The first performance critique I undertook, "Can a Man Be a Woman?," was devised for the Strasbourg conference mentioned above, celebrating the works of Robert Kroetsch, whose book *The Puppeteer* had been published a couple of years earlier. Not much criticism had yet been written about the book, but I wanted to discuss the way that the text took gender theory and used it as a technical field, severing it from its material base in experience. I was concerned about this being forced into a series of statements that could become reductive and offensive, and wanted to construct a form that would allow for an experience generating a range of allegorical responses and varied discussion. Indeed, unknown to me, Aritha van Herk had created a conference paper that was equally concerned to engage the audience in a different genre for criticism, as she constructed and read a poetic critique.

I did not want to upset Robert Kroetsch personally, especially at a conference rightly celebrating his significance as a writer. The form devised enabled a strong critique that generated recognition of problematic issues in the book as well as foregrounding the ways in which those issues were possibly helpful but also possibly unhelpful to readers considering gender issues. I do not know how Kroetsch felt about the performance, for he was very quiet during and after it, but I do know that the group for whom I was performing found the piece provocative and disturbing.

At a later conference in Oviedo, during which I performed "I'm a Very Dirty Critic," I remember talking to him about the way that several people there complained about that performance. His response was simply to say,

"If you can't take the heat, get out of the kitchen." I have often wondered whether this was also a comment on his own reaction to my Strasbourg performance, and whether I had, through my performative attempt to open up engagement with his novel *The Puppeteer*, only made matters worse: either insulting him with a naive reading, or creating an unwanted vulnerability, or offending him with the possible critiques.

Was I crossing an ethical boundary with this genre? Both in relation to the audience for the performance critique, and in relation to the maker of the text under exploration? In an essay I wrote in the late 1990s, I distinguished between normative ethics and responsive ethics, the latter being attentive to difference (Hunter 2001). I would now add to these a third: engaged ethics that necessarily uses a wide variety of strategies to engage its audience into the many particularities for which neither responsive nor normative ethics has vocabulary or recognition. I talk about these distinctions in some detail in the following section.

The initial performance critique genre I was devising did not work within a normative ethics, but attempted a responsive interaction with its audience. Over the decade or so during which the performances were produced, it became apparent that this ethical-aesthetic relationship was not appropriate to working with people and texts that were so diverse that they were literally unrecognizable from a liberal perspective: they live "alongside" hegemonic systems. Continental philosophers have consistently gestured toward such an alongside in politics. Levinas calls it being "otherwise" (Levinas 1998), Derrida refers to "d'ailleurs" or "elsewhere" (Derrida 1993), the later Foucault generates ideas of "beside" picked up and elaborated by Sedgwick (Sedgwick 2002). Performance allows us to put some flesh onto these gestural bones through more detailed work on the "alongside." Apart from the work on this word in my own criticism, other performance critics such as Alan Read (Read 1993) also use the word "alongside" to call upon the energy generated in performance. Exploration of the ethical dilemma that much of our lives is unseen by hegemony and outwith normative ethics led to the delineation of an engaged ethics and disunified aesthetics that I outline in what follows. The key to such work is to acknowledge that difference does not exist before we make it. With all due respect to the work of Emmanuel Levinas, who argued that ethics was not about making the self a better person but about the recognition of the "other" (Levinas 1998), an "other" does not exist until we make it so.

If someone falls outside the ethical understandings we hold, they do not exist outside them naturally, but have been placed outside by us. This is usually what happens with normative ethics, and in responsive ethics we engage with others on the basis of our relations with them. Yet with engaged ethics we learn that we make these differences in our interactions with other people. Because we make these differences, we also have to take responsibility for them, learn how to value them as parts of our own lives even when they do not fit our understanding or beliefs. Performativity, and in this case the kind of performative critique I have attempted to develop, foregrounds the process through which we "make other," but simultaneously, because we ourselves make it so, we change ourselves in the process. The difference we make lies within us, and we value it even when we do not agree with it or understand it. In this making of difference, the position is quite separate from the liberal toleration of difference which has an important place in nation-state politics and society but which does not offer much agency for change.

Engaged ethics is often perceived as a challenge to normative ethics because it does not take the assumptions of that ethics for granted – yet this kind of resistance is the action of responsive ethics. The action of engaged ethics is not particularly concerned to set up a challenge at all, more to work on the situated context at hand, in the moment, beside or alongside – and performativity is well placed to offer strategies and devices that can effect that work. Whether effective or not, the later performance critiques in which I have participated have been attempts to reach out to the audiences/readers and make some thing of our jointly engaged collaboration with the text.

One of the central factors that went into the early performance critiques was, quite honestly, that I wanted to remain friends with the writers and also retain a critical edge toward their work. The first time I wrote about a "live" writer was just after completing my doctoral work in the late 1970s, when I was thinking through Michael Ondaatje's *Billy the Kid*. Engaging with Canadian writing has nearly always been for me the experience of writing about live people, and hence always a different kind of ethical relationship from writing about Shakespeare. From the 1970s to 2003 I lived and worked in the UK, teaching and doing research on, among other things, Canadian studies. I was in the position of inviting many of the outstanding writers in Canada to Europe, and since part of my philosophy is that life is too short to write about the work of people whose writing I don't like, and even though I could not invite all of those I did, I usually tried to invite those with whose texts I'd fallen in love.

At the same time, I consistently wrote theatre and performance reviews which were quite direct and definitely not worried about the fact that the people being critiqued were alive and well and probably still involved in the production. Perhaps I was concerned with writing about live *writers* because I was personally invested in writing, but not in the theatre. And those genre expectations were, again, different: in a theatre review you usually come right out and advise the reader whether to go to the production or not. It is part of the style that readers expect, given that the production will probably be playing only for the next few days or weeks. With a critical review of a book, it is rare to find someone saying, "Don't read the book." One offers a more distanced critique, possibly because the text will be around for a number of years.

Perhaps this difference in expectation is why the performance critiques have garnered many more reactions than the accompanying essays.

This relationship between the critic, the artist, and the text fascinates me. People have said to me that the performance critiques are problematic because the writer has the right to expect their text to remain "as they wrote it." I suspect the comment signifies that, in these performance critiques, what you do with the text is not conventionally bound up. I see no difference in kind between a performance critique and a written critique, only in generic expectation and education. Both performer and essayist spend a long time with the text. I usually spend one to two years either developing performances or writing essays, and am struck by the devotion of critics who write about a text more than once. We interact with the texts as material objects in the world – indeed if the writers were not alive the relationship would be just like our relationship to Milton, or a picture on the wall, or a vase, when we are unconnected to the artist. Keats was troubled by this disconnect with the dead artist and explored its ironies in "Ode on a Grecian Urn" and what that urn tells us about its maker if the reader-critic will take on a material engagement.

People in general have a fascination with the writer or artist that stands in for the critics' involvement with the live text in front of them. In a sense, this fascination is not surprising if we think historically. It used to be that critics and writers knew each other, often reversing roles. Today, with the huge critical industry supported by the university structure of many democracies, critics far outnumber the "recognized" artists and many never meet those whose work they critique: so the biographical fallacy was born. Yet the so-called biographical fallacy has morphed into acceptance as long as the artist is cast as a socially produced and contextualized being rather than an essential subject.

The structure of a critical education leads the individual critic to spend a very long time with the text. A doctorate, for example, may result in the critic spending four years or more with one or two writers and their texts. This is what we learn how to do as we make those texts our own in the process. Writers often do not understand the dedication and commitment that is shown toward their creations, and miss not only the devotion of the critic to the virtual friendship, but also the amazing energy released when their creations come into contact with the engaged reader. The performance critiques have the effect of bringing this energy right into immediate recognition/visibility/feeling.

Nevertheless, I once learned an important lesson from the writer Joan Clark. I had been travelling in 1989, trying to regain some sense of where Canadian literature had been or was since my previous foray in 1982. Air Canada lost my luggage and I ended up staying at Joan Clark's house. She fed me, clothed me, and introduced me to many wonderful Newfoundland writers. A year or so later, the Scottish Arts Council was thinking about bringing her over on their exchange fellowship and talked to me about what I might be able to arrange in England. When she arrived, I wrote asking them if she would come south, saying I knew her personally and would be happy to arrange a small tour. They wrote back saying "no," and copying me her letter to them in which she said she did not know me and did not understand the request. The point is that I did *not* know her personally. I knew her work and had spent two years reading everything she had written, and I felt as if I did. She kindly reconsidered and visited later in the year.[4]

In the theatre, however, people still know each other. Theatre critics are frequently acquainted with the artists on whose work they comment. Perhaps a similar sense of acquaintance, this virtual friendship between critic and writer, has been kept alive for me partly by the poetry reading circuit in Canada in which I was active in the late 1960s and early 1970s, both as an audience member and as a performing reader – reading work of my own but more often of others. Just so, the presence of writers-in-residence at universities when I was doing my early training put me literally in the same room as many of them. They were my community. Listening to their work, getting carried away on the surge of their energy and skill, was probably my impetus into making critiques in the first place.

The different generic expectations of the theatre may explain why I had also over-stepped boundaries when I became involved a decade earlier in helping The Traverse Theatre in Edinburgh prepare Michael Ondaatje's script of *Billy the Kid* for the stage.[5] I had by then given a paper on the book (1978) and read all I could of Ondaatje's work. I ate and breathed it for a while, teaching it to others and spending months rereading it. When The Traverse asked me to act as dramaturge, which in the UK means adjusting the text for the context of the production in question, I leapt at the chance. Having persuaded everyone that the words were unassailable, the key problem was that The Traverse could afford only five actors, including one woman, when the script called for six including two women. I edited the text to double the women, not thinking about the poetry writer in this theatrical context, and to be honest, because I was already so familiar with the text. The director and I visited Ondaatje the following summer and in our brief conversation about the production I talked about the doubling. He was taken aback. Although he courteously did not lose his temper, we could see that this was a major issue that my familiarity with the text, and the theatrical context, had completely erased.

Spending time with the text is like having a relationship. We have to figure out whether it's us or the text putting up the resistances. We need to locate those points at which we make the text different from ourselves, points that we come to value and over which we obsess. It's what I call the critic's work in being in love with the text.

Generically, the performative critical writing toward which these essay-performance interactions move is no different in kind from the performance critiques, except in the education we give and receive about the possibilities for a reader's engagement with the text. Given that, there are ethical implications. The performance "What Is an Honest Man and Can There Be an Honest Woman?" was given at a conference celebrating Frank Davey's contribution to Canadian literature (Hunter 2006), and focused on the poetry of Daphne Marlatt. Edgily performative, the final section offered re-readings, literally, of several poems from *this tremor love is*. I had re-laid out the poetry in question in different typographic designs. But in reading this material aloud, it was eerily near to Marlatt's text and many people thought I was reading her poetry, and she was present at the reading. Well, I was reading her poetry – in the sense of critically engaging with it – but I was also reading it out loud, and if the listener had not already been familiar with her text, they could be forgiven for mistaking the one for the other., I now acknowledge that despite my attempt to honour her work, this was a mistake, and there is no visual recording of that performance. The experience prompted me instead into typographic experiments and what I am calling performative critical writings. With grace, Daphne Marlatt allowed me to duplicate my typographic work in print, and I am deeply grateful.

The performative critical writing generated by the performance critiques is simply a rethinking of critical style so that it can more actively engage its readers in thinking about the text. The form prompts us into different interactions with the text, the writer/artist, and the reader/audience, just as the performance critiques that focused on engaged ethics and aesthetics attempt to do. I see the writing as related to a long tradition in Canadian literary-critical circles, from early experiments by bpNichol to Frank Davey's recent website postcards.[6] Perhaps the movement is due to the tradition of writers-in-residence, but whatever the underlying contexts, it is the case that, during my many years working on Canadian literature, this kind of poetic criticism has been perceived as particular to Canada. Today, more and more people around the world are writing this kind of creative criticism, partly, I suspect, because it is so full of energy.

In the 1990s, I attempted to build a learning journal process that incorporated performative writing into the work of students studying Canadian literature. An associated book, co-written with Rebecca O'Rourke (Hunter and O'Rourke 1996), encouraged students to find a performative voice for their criticism. In retrospect, having used the techniques now for many years, I would say that only about 20 per cent of the students who did it really enjoyed it. It was far more difficult than writing a conventional essay, and yet the other 80 per cent, who resisted it in various ways, always came to appreciate it for what it was even if they never undertook such writing again – and I had to warn them that other teachers might not approve. But that 20 per cent really took to it, and I still hear from many of them.

There clearly are ethical questions raised by both the performance art critiques and the performative writing that may well have wider implications. I have been lucky enough to have worked on texts by writers whose generosity has been astounding in this regard, to the point where some writers have asked me to create performance critiques rather than a traditional essay. Mistakes have been made, but on the whole the work has received positive feedback. Most vitally, the performance critiques, whether as performance art or concrete criticism, attempt to make it possible to engage aesthetically from diverse positions. Starting from a viewpoint that discards a universalist aesthetics, they increasingly explore ways of enabling a reading of the text open to moments of difference. This has entailed disturbing not only the normative but also the responsive ethical agreements between critic, reader, and writer. An engaged critical ethics treats the writer with respect and as another kind of reader. And the reader is an active participant in making a text for themselves. In engaged critical ethics, the writer/maker remakes the text with the critic and often many other readers, makes the new differences that build a disunified yet collaborative aesthetics.

AESTHETICS, ETHICS, AND RHETORIC: PHILOSOPHICAL BACKGROUND

We learn much about different kinds of ethical strategies by looking at the rhetorics of aesthetics. To do so, I would like to distinguish between the rhetorics primarily attributed to an aesthetics of performance, which focuses on the audience, and those primarily attributed to an aesthetics of rehearsal, which involves the initial makers of the art object. Much of this book opens out the different rhetorics of these activities and their interconnection with a disunified aesthetics and an engaged ethics. Here I offer a short introduction to the concepts that underlie the philosophical framework of this study, and which will be developed in detail throughout.

"Performance" is to the live arts as publication is to the written in a print society. It is the moment at which the on-going process of rehearsal ceases in order to enter culture. To enter culture necessitates some kind of hegemonic recognition, and Western liberal nation-states have devised many gatekeepers to such opportunity: for example, publishers and the apparatus of editors and publishers' readers, or in theatre the artistic director and the dramaturge. Both have to deal with boards of advisers who oversee potential risks and benefits. Some of the mechanisms are embedded in the capital-intensive mode of production of Western "art" in which so much time and material goes into pre-publication that there needs to be a safeguard to ensure that that this will be rewarded by income from the cultural performance. As a result, many of the mechanisms are hegemonically political, in that what gets performed or funded is what the producers know will satisfy audience expectations and generate income. This I call an aesthetics of "enough." Some of the mechanisms challenge hegemony within limits that it can tolerate, often dissatisfying a proportion of the audience. Yet other mechanisms make available performance that lies right on the edge of what "makes sense," nervously hovering in that porous border area where things can just be made out as present yet incomprehensible, and sometimes get recognized. The moment of recognition is what I call the moment of "fit," the moment in which the apparently chaotic suddenly coalesces into cultural sense.

In "rehearsal," whether it is the acknowledged rehearsal of the performer or the often unacknowledged rehearsal of the writer, the process of making art involves fundamentally different rhetorics of aesthetics that work at least partially alongside hegemony. Furthermore, for many people today, the making of art takes place in groups of people who have come together not necessarily to transgress hegemonic structures, but to make differences that have radical potential for change. This is particularly important in societies where diverse populations have not only systemic common grounds to transgress but also quite separate experiences outwith hegemony. In rehearsal, because performers work together to generate affect and action that is appropriate to the moment, each apprehension or awareness of another person is an opportunity to make difference, a moment we experience because we think we know them "until" we can no longer make sense of them. In that making-different we change our own self, because the making of something radically different necessarily generates in the person doing the making some thing that was not there before, makes it present. Because the performer is changing their self, the work is vulnerable, and they know and/ or choose these changes more easily in groups that have come together to support precisely this kind of work. These like-minded groups offer collaboration, or rehearsal, that enables them to do this work so that they change, become present in a different way, and in the process prompt those around them to make further differences and change their selves. But at times, the moment of until generates an abyss, a sensory experience of "nothing," an impossibility of difference or the impossibility of the sensory experience of making sense. Until is one way of re-thinking Derridean "différance."

The aesthetics of rehearsal, of "nothing," and of "alongside" that move to presence, engage ethically through the moment of "until" and materialize through the moment of "ar(rest)."[7] I would argue that the experience of engaging with presence in the performing of that ar(rest), those moments when incomprehensibility opens up rather than closes down, brings the audience into the world of rehearsal. Part of the movement of this whole book is to merge rehearsal and performance and to think about the relations between art-maker and audience, writer and reader, which come into being.

Another way of putting this:
Enough: all that needs to be said has been said, and what is not said cannot be said.[8]
Fit: not all that needs to be said has been said, and what has not been said is said.[9]
Alongside: the unsaid is made in the making of difference, which is an unending process of making present.[10]
Arrest: what has not been said is said, yet that saying renders further unsaid.
Until: what has not been said is made present, and then we have a choice.[11]
Nothing: the not-said cannot be said and what is said is nothing.

These different kinds of aesthetics illuminate different kinds of ethics, for ethics is not only related, as it is traditionally, to rhetoric and persuasion but also to feelings, the sensible realm of aesthetics. From the point of view of the rhetorics above, a normative ethics is one that is "enough": it can be described in detail by rhetoric. Responsive ethics, which attempts to change normative ethics and get it to "fit" differently, uses rhetorics of relation, opposition, resistance, and partiality to do so. But the point at which rhetoric and aesthetics meet, arguably in epideictic rhetoric and/or poetic, is in the articulation of what has not been said and the feelings and energies that generate further recognition of people and things unsaid by society. This point anchors the need for change rather than fit, and requires an engaged ethics. An engaged ethics deals with diverse populations and marks the moment at which each individual body recognizes its ecology within the sociopolitical context through its feelings and senses, whatever the medium in which these work – from words to dance, to visual art to music, and so on.

A lot goes on within an aesthetics of rehearsal. Somewhere a person or people find themselves in an ecology that releases energy/energies. I call this process, after Nicole Brossard, "installation." At that moment many things can happen. Those involved can move, among other actions, to a self-bound capturing of that energy, or to collective identification or relational give and take around it, or to changing the self or others into it, or to continue making the differences among or between the people in collaboration alongside hegemonic structures. I use the word "gift" to signify the possibility of making a difference that distinguishes the last. Only with a gifting willingness to recognize that one cannot know a person, a thing, a context, can we experience "until" and begin to make that recognition into a valued difference. And to value the differences we make is a step along the way to a sense of extended self-hood, that one is in an alongside ecology with others, a collaboration that generates all kinds of art-making. Because the gifting generates sensible, bodily feelings, it is inextricably part of changing the self in the process of making the difference, and it releases extraordinary energy.

The process of rehearsal winds around some of these makings that work alongside sociopolitical systems, inflected by them but not primarily interested in them, so rooted are the processes in the particular ecology they are making. Rehearsal reiterates these makings, and not everything is kept for performance. Some makings are held to be more helpful in a particular ecology than others because most art-makers want to involve others, to enable these makings to engage more people in the possibility of recognition and change. So the choices stabilize in different ways depending on the situated contexts for the production, the society, culture, politics, geography, history that make up "until" – about which more will be said below. As the rehearsal moves to performance, or begins to involve an audience, these makings and decisions can happen over a range of renewed gifting, or of need, or desire, or control – each with quite different aesthetics – that can build on just one energy release or continue to generate many. We cannot predict how long these makings will go on, how long they will generate presence. It depends on the people participating and their collaborative process.

Directors, composers, or choreographers are often there precisely to enable more rather than fewer "makings" and to guide choices about what to hold on to, to act as a bridge to the particular ecology within which the production will perform.

Although initial generative energy comes from that alongside collaborative gifting, if the recognition of difference is self-evidently understood to pre-exist an interaction with another in a manner typical of normative ethics, even the aesthetics of rehearsal can become one of exclusion. Normative ethics underwrites a universalist aesthetics based on identifying with the people in the performance either as a fellow worker or as an audience, as if we are all "subjects," that is subject to hegemonic norms. The focus on identification being "enough" implies that what is not said cannot be said – hence anything different should not exist. Something "not said" is not behaving correctly. It does not belong. From my perspective this kind of rhetoric is one of evasion, self-delusion, and repression (Hunter 1984).

However, it is also common to find a general understanding that difference does pre-exist interaction with others, yet that understanding has many other forms than the normative, forms that involve different kinds of ethics. An ethics of "fit" holds that what has not been said can be, and fractures into many aesthetic positions. There are those who believe that what has not been said is the "not-yet-said": this typifies relativist and relational aesthetics[12] that work on the elements that universal aesthetics has not yet articulated but that can be made to fit into its plan. There are also those who take the what has not been said as "unsayable" in the current sociopolitical conditions, and offer resistant and oppositional strategies to aesthetic fit.[13] And there are those who consider the what has not been said as, baldly, the "not said" of conditions that would undermine the culture and society: these often work on an aesthetics of partiality that excludes anyone not already within the conditions of that "not said."[14]

These latter kinds of aesthetics of fit delineate different kinds of ethical relations within a hegemonic structure – usually set within that of the Western, liberal democratic nation-state. They each turn to a kind of sympathetic willingness to recognize difference as a problem that can be solved by tolerating its identity, changing its identity, or secluding its identity.[15] These aesthetics require an understanding of the underlying assumptions and principles of hegemonic structures, and can express themselves in terms of exchange, relationality, martyrdom, sacrifice, donation, torture, refashioning, conversion, and so on – all strategies that to some extent make the self "like" the other, or establish a self in relation to, in resistance to, or in exclusion from the other. In a sense, these aesthetics often reverse the power of "universalist" aesthetics (an aesthetics of the empowered who define themselves as "universal") by delineating the "other" as the empowered, and ethics as responsive.

At the same time, because performance can also make possible to an audience the moment of "until," that gifting that the presence made in rehearsal takes into performance, the audience may also open up to the possibilities of making difference. Audience members, or readers, who recognize that difference does not pre-exist their making of it, enter an ethics of engagement. Experiencing "until," the non-identity with others, is registered by the senses in ways that we often do not articulate. But when the moment of recognition occurs, when we realize we have made difference, that change has happened in our self, there is a coalescence that not only generates intense somatic and energetic feeling but also puts into process the making of value. If we have changed our self, we need to value the change. To recognize is to know it is there; to value it is to articulate it within the ecology of our lives, including our alongside lives, to take responsibility for it. In one way, this is the initiating experience that can become an aesthetics of fit, yet is simultaneously an engaged ethics, from which the hegemonic deployments of fit often follow.

One key centre of aesthetics that does not relate in any way to normative ethics or hegemonic fit is that of "nothing." The philosophers and critics who have turned to Afro-American pessimism would claim that the commodification of the black American body underlies the entire civic structure of western liberal democracy and is most evident in the stresses and strains, the violence and elimination practices, of the United States.[16] It is not simply that these bodies are not-yet-said or unsaid, they cannot be said. In this they agree with those who have an aesthetics of "enough." However, whereas that aesthetics believes that all that needs to be said has been said, the advocates for "nothing" believe that all that is said needs to be swept away, and that what cannot be said is only impossible to say because what is said is said. I respect this position, especially because it describes a stance that believes that what is said can be swept aside to release different sayings. In this I find a most hopeful address to agency. However, I, and this particular book, are clearly part of the civic structure involved in this commodification, and perhaps for this reason I have always chosen to act on the premise that, faced with not being able to sweep hegemony away without destroying my self, I can sweep aside.

Once an audience is participating in the production, the aesthetics of performance becomes far more distinctive, and the rhetorics of "enough" and "fit" come to the fore. I call this process "constellation." Yet there is a fascinating growth area of what I would call situated aesthetics, derived yet distinct from the work of situated epistemologists. The distinction lies in the element of text that situated aesthetics brings to epistemology. Understanding that knowledge cannot be knowledge without a communicative medium, situated aesthetics adds the element of textuality to a philosophy that is largely focused on the social structures effecting different kinds of knowledge. Situated knowledge is interested in the ways in which knowledge is constructed by groups of people who find themselves in particular sites that are tangential to hegemonic systems. One of the appealing aspects of situated knowledge is that it attempts to account for agency in overdetermined systems of knowledge. Situated aesthetics adds a necessary element that insists on the exploration of the textuality of that knowledge (Hunter 1999). A group of people in a particular site may not necessarily produce situated knowledge. Instead, they may simply duplicate the structures to which they are tangential. The only way of distinguishing between such groups is to explore the textuality of the knowledge that is produced, and this is an aesthetic question.

Scientists interested in the situated often gesture to the storytelling abilities of the arts. Humanities scholars often gesture to the collective nature of the scientific method. But neither in itself can guarantee a situated textuality. The marker of the situated occurs as the rehearsal moves to performance, as alongside (or tangential) moves toward fit. A situated aesthetics maintains an interaction between the two so that the unsaid that has been made in the process of rehearsal, in performance renders new contexts, new ecologies, a new situatededness that renders further recognitions of the making of difference. Situated aesthetics insists on a rhetoric of rehearsal continuously engaged with rhetorics of performance. It creates a constant sense of "until" in performance, that one has said what needs to be said only until one knows there is something more to be said.

Audiences extend the interaction of aesthetics and ethics. At times they are excluded from the energy of "making" yet swept into identifications that satisfy. At many other times they are seduced, challenged, unnerved, co-opted. And at others wholly engaged. Engaged audiences do not always wholeheartedly embrace a performance. As Brecht suggested, devices to get an audience not to identify, not to feel "enough," not to "fit," are often alienating. Often stories that encourage audiences to tell their different stories to themselves and each other, or allegories, are intensely engaging – offering the audience its own way of participating in an ongoing rehearsal. This kind of participation generates a disunified aesthetics.

Today, when audiences are increasingly diverse and aware that universal aesthetics, or the aesthetics of the empowered few, do not apply to them, some people have become more open to the idea of a disunified aesthetics (Hunter 2011). It does not concern them that other people have different engagements with an art object or text, indeed, it is a source of aesthetic value to make those differences in an ongoing process. The experience is an opportunity to learn about a different kind of engaged ethics alongside the normative, and one not predominantly concerned with either the norma- tive or hegemonic responsiveness. Other audiences, or the same audience seeking a different feeling, may be more partial, or more market-targeted, or more niche consumer, or more "mass." In a sense, an audience rehearses the sociocultural energies of the alongside, the until, the fit, or the enough. And many audiences stabilize their responses depending on their political ecology in a relatively unselfconscious way.

Critics, however, work to foreground the integration into, the impact upon, the involvement – or not – with the society, culture, politics. A large proportion of critical work articulates the kinds of participation of an audi- ence in, or its response to, the performance, but increasingly critics also at- tempt to articulate that submerged iceberg of work that is the rehearsal, the performers', the artists' activity. Critics usually abide by a set of normative ethics that holds that aesthetics are not involved in criticism. Nevertheless, we all recognize when there is an aesthetic impact, and as increasingly more critics attend to the rehearsal, generic criticism is called into question. It is difficult to have an opinion about energy. Criticism could hold to normative or generic procedures quite happily in a period in which the people in the critical circle were from a coherent enough sociopolitical background to make that unified aesthetic appear reasonable. Yet as more people claim cultural power, aesthetics has become disunified, and a critic involved only in generic response will limit their audience, and their audience's ability to engage. A central element of both performance critique and performative critical writing is to release energies in the audience and reader that will locate places where making difference is possible.

WHAT HAPPENS NEXT

The critic's work on the performative aesthetics of rehearsal has provided me with just this one way of re-thinking the ethics of critic, reader, writer, and text interactions. If a disunified aesthetics is emerging in response to the radically diverse concept of democracy that many political scientists have been articulating,[17] then the critic's opinion is only one way to act. A critical opinion used to be couched comfortably against a universalist aesthetics. Today critical opinion is most effective within sociocultural hegemonies within a relational aesthetics that tolerates different opinions or within various resistant aesthetics. However, the critic could instead take on the activity of enabling many readings, rehearsing the process of a reading that could indeed turn into opinion once it moves into performance, but whose value comes more from the points of making difference that become available, the collaborative processes of reading that happen. Each of critic, reader, and writer, of performance critic, audience, and artist, begins to make their own points of difference in a collaboration that generates ways of valuing those differences in others because they are in ourselves. In other words, the critic's position with regard to the reader, text, and writer is as a collaborator rather than an opinion-maker. The experience of critical engagement is a process of learning about agential skills and the possibility for change through aesthetic collaboration.

In what follows, I offer nine instances of my exploration of this critical activity, all of which are experiments, and experiments are learning grounds. Because they describe an arc of learning, the essays are set in the chronological order in which they and their associated performances appeared. The first three are concerned primarily with fit and the problems with enough. The middle four pursue elements of fit and of alongside. And the final three are situating themselves in a place where they attempt to make possible alongside collaboration rooted in the arrest of "what happens" and the felt presence of "until." "Happen" derives playfully from the Greek "haptic" or touch, as well as the Sanskrit "hap" or chance which is neither arbitrary nor fated. Chance touch reminds us of the somatic elements of performance in all media, and I hope that what happens next makes sense.

part one

SITUATED TEXTUALITIES

ART IN THE AGE OF THE FRANCHISE

The essays and performances in this first section are concerned with what Art and aesthetics mean in the enfranchised democracies of the twentieth century. They explore the relation between the critic and the text within an aesthetic paradigm focused first on the way in which the state permits a "subject" certain representations that make the individual recognizable within ideology, and second on the ability of "art" to challenge these allowed images of subjecthood. The artist in liberal social contract states has been consistently employed, directly or indirectly, by people with money and property central to the power of the state. Their work has indeed been challenging, but historically, the materials they produced that have been valued as "art" have focused on disrupting and transgressing the representations permitted to those in power. This is a value-generating activity that has changed culture and society throughout the modern world. The modern artist has been able to facilitate shifts in the treatment of women, of people of colour, of the working class by creating things that have not been imagined or said before, by articulating a vocabulary for ways of life that were not central to propertied white males who defined the parameters of society. But this relational aesthetics has been undertaken from the position of those men and is unable to imagine those things that do not belong in the privileged world even from their own situatedness outwith[1] that world.

Modern art has worked with the concepts of disruption and transgression, of eruptions through the representations satisfying the conditions of subjecthood, eruptions that are valued as art when they crystallize into cultural recognition. I suggest in these three opening essays that crystallization occurs through a sense of satisfied criteria, or *enough*, or through a sudden sense of *fit*. As the first essay on *The Puppeteer* (1991) by Robert Kroetsch suggests, that recognition of fit often carries an adrenalin charge of joy, and "beautiful" art maintains a relation with its cultural environment that makes possible the continual triggering of fit through mimetic performance. Mimesis is a contested word. In this book it calls both on Plato's belief that no telling or re-telling can be ideal, and on Aristotle's subsequent thought that a response to a text can re-tell that text through a particular body, acquiring a different materiality in the process of the performance. Performance that attempts to represent, to deliver ideological representations, is not mimetic but replicative or commodified, aiming at just *enough*/just at *enough*. Insofar as each of us is constituted by hegemonic structures and particularized by our separation from them, mimetic performance will simultaneously generate enough representation to contextualize art and enough separation to provide the surge of energy that accompanies the sense of fit.

The essay is a beginning. It confidently lays out a critique of pomo[2] thinking and relational aesthetics as the domain of the relatively empowered, those who work within ideological systems, unable to change them and afraid of the implications of leaving them. The reading of Kroetsch's work that it offers follows critiques that end in *enough*, in *fit*, and in the performativity of alongside work, setting the scene for the extensive study of situated knowledge, standpoint theory, feminist ethics, and situated textuality that follows in the second and third essays, chapters 2 and 3. *The Puppeteer* raises issues about theory tourism, about appropriation of voice, about the ethics of criticism, and takes steps toward understanding the separateness of people's positions with regard to the state, the way groups outwith ideology manifest themselves, and the incomparability of positions.

Chapters 2 and 3 offer a guidebook to the philosophical underpinnings of the exploration of aesthetics that occurs in the later chapters. Drawn from writing that took place between 1994 and 2002, but based on performances scripted and performed first in 1995 and 1996, these chapters offer the written essays that accompanied those performances, and then proceed to critique the theorization in light of conceptual developments in situated knowledge and situated textuality. Situated knowledge contributed a powerful analytical tool to feminism in the 1980s and was part of a larger concern with women's ways of knowing, black feminist thought, indigenous feminism, and standpoint theory – among other epistemologies. These and other approaches generated a profound critique of the way the ethos of liberal hegemony sets itself forward as responsive to challenge while its structure retains devices that ensure a necessary ignorance of any and all lives that cannot be recognized because they put in question the sheer existence of the civic state. It is too simple to say that these epistemologies grew out of the woman's movement slogan "the personal is the political," but they are anchored to the same impetus that inspired it: that not all politics are the politics of the state, that we are not in an "overdetermined" culture that denies us agency, that we have the energy and ability to create alternatives, to value difference and change society from the basis of non-subjected positionality. These insights lead directly to a concept of disunified aesthetics.

CRITICAL BACKGROUND

Since the 1960s many feminists have drawn on linguistic (Wittgenstein, Bahktin), cultural (Benjamin, Foucault), and working-class (Lukacs, Williams, Hall) traditions to articulate the ways women, and by analogy other people less empowered with respect to the state, make values for their lives. In contrast to discourse theory, these values may or may not be recognized by the state, let alone change it – they sometimes do, but that may not be the point. A set of highly articulated theoretical approaches arrived in the 1970s to 1980s, from feminists specifically drawing on "situated knowledge" and coalescing their work in social studies of science and technology (Haraway, Harding, Hartsock, Rose). One of their greatest achievements was to expose the way that women doing science change not only the way science is done but the outcomes of that science. This notion of knowledge alongside the hegemonic generated not only Harding's "strong objectivity" – that the knowledge of work not primarily concerned with the hegemonic was far more able to see the strengths and weaknesses of that hegemony because it was not invested in it – but a sense of "objectivity" or "object position" to complement the use of "subjectivity" and "subject position" in discourse theories. Since Western modern science has often been held up as the defining structure of political science, this critique has had far-reaching implications.

During the same period, a rather different group of feminists began articulating "women's ways of knowing" (Belenky et al. 1986). Working with similar key insights, Dorothy Smith, who laid the groundwork in the 1970s for thinking about the "everyday" as knowledge, carried out studies that looked at the ways women know things that do not fit the rationalist, isolated, and autonomous elements that give credibility to knowledge in Western nation states.[3] These thinkers managed to talk about tacit knowledge and women's "intuition" as learned skills from a materialist rather than phenomenological perspective, and paved the way for the concept of practice as a mode of knowing that addressed in a detailed manner the specifics of how women's actions can change what is known.

The engagements with epistemology ran parallel with other disciplines also developing theories of knowledge and experience alongside the hegemonic such as black feminist studies (Spillers, Hill Collins), philosophy (Lennon and Whitford), rhetoric and gender (Code), and rhetoric and the arts (Hunter). Hortense Spillers argued in "A Hateful Passion, A Lost Love" (Spillers 1983) that Toni Morrison's Sula is a radical characterization, a discursively exceptional concept that comes from outside sociohistorical understandings and portrayals of African-American women. Four years later, she pushed this insight further in "Mama's Baby, Papa's Maybe" (Spillers 1987) saying that in order to understand the African-American woman, a distinction has to be made between "body" and "flesh." Flesh is a "zero degree of conceptualization" that never "escapes concealment" by discourse (67). The flesh of the slave is always necessarily erased by discourse; it never can become a body. In *Black Feminist Thought* (1990), Patricia Hill Collins argued for a partial epistemology, knowledge and communication that was specific to particular experience – here of African American women. The central stunning thought she advanced was that it did not matter if people from outwith that particular group did not agree or did not understand the logic and positionality. Situated knowledge theorists had argued that "objective" or marginalized experience led to different kinds of knowledge, but they also expected these knowledges to be recognized and understood. Hill Collins suggests that it is possible, if not necessary, to have knowledge that is not universal.

These developments posited that rather than take an in-place occurrence, such as "women in science," a group of people were actively attempting to build an environment for themselves outwith hegemonic institutions that would encourage the kinds of change, practices, and processes that would value black women's lives. The move was perceived at the time, and still is, as an exclusionary measure. Ironically, Hill Collins articulated to many non-African Americans the central plank in what became Afropessimist philosophy. Philosophers such as Saidiya Hartmann (1997) begin with the fact of partial knowledge but argue that there are no conditions in today's liberal humanism that can allow for the valuing of the African American woman's body, that in fact the civic state is built on the necessary treatment of that body as if it is a commodity rather than a living being that contributes to the world.

Kathleen Lennon and Margaret Whitford built an influential collection, *Knowing the Difference* (1994), which established an advanced standpoint position in the introduction, and drew on philosophers such as Sabina Lovibond and critics interested in life-writing such as Liz Stanley. The collection laid the ground for a non-reductive conceptualization of standpoint theory that pulled it away from authenticity/identity politics and combined it with insights from situated knowledge analysis. Extending this ground from ethics into rhetoric, Lorraine Code began with philosophical alternatives to the liberal state dependence on rational logic, and examined the implications of rhetorics more appropriate to varied contexts of gender. To contextualize the thinking in the present book, it is helpful to know that I learned from these thinkers and contributed a modest analysis of the rhetoric needed to communicate situated knowledge as a process and standpoint positionality as alongside, technically a rhetorical stance rather than a tactic or strategy. I call this situated textuality, initially studying the links with allegory and more recently developing it into a theory of performativity.

During this period from the 1970s to the 1990s, several other groups of critical thinkers began to work on how to recognize values necessarily concealed by discourse and build viable structures alongside hegemonic institutions. Feminists, discourse studies scholars, and gay-lesbian-bisexual-transgender thinkers hammered out the concept of queer studies as precisely a place that was agential with respect to hegemonic structures. Curiously, the first wave of this philosophical and critical endeavour was co-opted so quickly into cultural imperatives that its potential situated value was subsumed – as had been the white feminist academic movement before it – into those hegemonic structures. Second-wave queer theory, like 2000s feminism, has struggled through the fittingness of the last wave, feeding phoenix-like on the parts still left out.

One of the fallouts of the split of the women's movement at the end of the 1970s was the space made in academia for a Western recognition of the feminism emerging globally. This feminism was not concerned to assimilate into existing power structures, but to a) critique them and b) suggest alternatives (Andalzua, Mohanty, Alexander, Russo, Torres, Wieringa, Bannerjee). These writers were writing from non-G8 women's experience, profoundly critical of Western liberal democratic structures, and offering different ways of knowing the world. At the same time, people within indigenous communities were beginning to speak of traditional knowledge systems as examples of knowledge-making in communities where individuals were not conceptualized as fully autonomous and rationalistic. One of the contributions made by this field of epistemology was a recognition that the way the knowledge is articulated is imbricated with the knowledge itself (Elders, Maracle, LaRocque, Profeit Leblanc, Vizenor, Owens, Kulchyski). The medium of the transmission of knowledge and its textuality is part of the kind of knowledge being transmitted.

Feminist and other political philosophers of the 1990s regrouped around epistemology and the concept of knowledge arising from difference. If isolation, the autonomous, and the rationalistic define a concept of epistemology as unified and universal, and women (and people similarly unfitting) do not belong there, then where they might belong is by definition not unified, non-autonomous, non-rationalistic, and not universal. These thinkers asked what this kind of politics would look like and carved out alternatives (Benhabib, Young, Yuval Davis), focusing on how to re-think the individual as non-autonomous and not isolated, by studying how we make the public and political differences with which we live.

In the meantime, during the 1990s and 2000s, many people began to develop some of these ideas into other areas. For example, the work on women's ways of knowing contributed to the development of tacit epistemology in crafts such as silver-smithing and cooking, and into computing science. Judith Butler's shift from "construction" to "constitution" and the notion of the abject could be seen as part of this environment. Uma Narayan's work on "De-centring the Centre" attempted to join feminism to a global awareness of women's positionality with respect to governance. If situated knowledge is particularly helpful in reminding us of those not seen/heard/touched by the state, situated textuality helps us recognize that we make difference, that difference does not exist before we make it. Taking a cue from traditional knowledge systems, I would argue that situated knowledge does not remain situated if it is not textualized/performed in particular ways that draw on performative presence: that there are rhetorics more or less appropriate to a particular time and place that encourage or do not encourage people to recognize the knowledge they are making and to take responsibility for it.

From the late 1990s and through the 2000s, there has also been pointed critique of the study of "others," who are made "other" by our own definitions. The "abject," for example, is a label used by those relatively empowered to put upon those who one thinks do not fit into the sociopolitical system, yet those so labelled may well consider themselves full and whole living beings. Gayatri Spivak's recent move to redefine subaltern studies not as the study of the relatively empowered, or of those the relatively empowered "make visible," but as work with those not heard/seen/touched by the state, and the ethical re-positioning that this generates, is a good example of how situated knowledge plays out when exposed to insights from black feminist and indigenous studies. Spivak's attention to the processes and practices again underlines the importance of textuality.

The development of Afropessimism (Marriott, Sexton, Wilderson, Keeling) is an analogous move that positions a group of people completely outwith the hegemonic civic state in order to demonstrate that liberal states consistently fail to face the basis of civic structure which is the non-humanity of the black body. Most Afropessimists, as the name implies, currently focus politically on the impossibility of the black body in a valued civic space, rather than the possibility of being a reconceived black body outwith the hegemonic (and this reconception may be impossible), or a civic space redefined by a valued black body. A corollary to Afropessimism is found in some of the work on terror/ism (Mbembe, Agamben, Morton), in which terror becomes the performance mode allowed to certain people by the civic state. Analogically, other work on necropolitics uses similar arguments, for example, on starvation as a political strategy (Anderson).

Work on new democratic rhetorics runs parallel to these moves: in other words, current studies that do not give up on democracy but attempt to re-conceive it differently from liberal social contract democracy. Central to this analysis is the focus on rhetoric, on the interaction of people that is materialized by the way they engage in communication, the way they perform as non-autonomous beings. The turn to affect by a number of aestheticians is also one possible way of thinking about the integration of self and textuality (Sedgwick, Brennan, Ahmed) and of energy rather than power. The interest in collaborative art-making (Kwon, Kester), the increasing deployment of "ecology" (Code 2006) in its scientific definition of imbricated interactions, and the growing attention to presence in performance (Phelan, Foster, Lepecki) have provided a helpful focus on presence, process, and practice before they give way to cultural fit. More recent performance critics are, however, not "mourning" the in-the-moment quality of presence but celebrating it as the site for a disunified aesthetics with, among others, interactions that can re-define selfhood and collaboration in the particular.

My own progress through this critical and theoretical history is contained in the performances associated with these essays. The turn toward performativity as a vital tool for political analysis results from the intertwining of the essay and the performance in this book. In many ways, the essay "Opening," on *The Puppeteer* by Robert Kroetsch, sets out the groundwork from which I began. It establishes definitions for the relation between the critic and the text within an aesthetic paradigm focused on the banal representations of the state and the ability of "art" to challenge these allowed images of subject-hood. The second and third essays in this collection are woven into the conceptual history/critical background just outlined. Chapter 2, "Trying to Say," contextualizes my concern in the early 1990s with ways in which the legitimated critical approaches for dealing with texts from communities "marginal" to hegemonic structures failed to speak to the point of the readers with whom I was working as a teacher and researcher. This experience led us, and me, to recast "marginal" – as in: on the periphery of hegemony – as "alongside" – as in: the situated positioning of a valued world not primarily responding to the hegemonic. The performance associated with this essay casts these two approaches as aesthetics à la carte, and aesthetics in the kitchen. The shift is told through an initial taking up of situated knowledge and post/neocolonial theory during a course on Canadian women's writing, and is then critiqued from the growing awareness that not all "alongsides" are positioned the same way with respect to hegemony. That awareness alerted me to the need for an understanding of the textuality of the situated knowledge.

The second of these two essays, "Listening," the third chapter in the book, re-contextualizes my use of situated knowledge within standpoint theory's focus on difference, and follows my realization that difference is made: it does not pre-exist somewhere where we find it, but is created by each individual. The implication that this had for my theoretical development led me to take up issues being articulated in African-American feminism and in First Nations traditional knowledge, and resulted in a performance and paper on the work of Lee Maracle (1996). Here that analysis is followed by a further critique of the assumption that anyone can understand any other alongside, or that strategies helpful to one will necessarily be helpful to another, assisted by commentary from recent Afropessimism: there is no comparability of terrors. It then turns to advice I received from Inuit elders about how to learn to listen to other cultures. This took me to issues of presence and performative engagement that encouraged me to redefine situated textuality as a rhetorical stance.

1 Opening

Robert Kroetsch's *The Puppeteer*: Being Wedded to the Text

Three strands are gathered into the following critique: a commentary on textual ethics of readers and writers, a discussion of certain aspects of gender studies, and a concern with the domestic. All three find particular focal points in *The Puppeteer*, Robert Kroetsch's novel published in 1991. This text elaborates on various dilemmas experienced by people within relatively empowered groups: groups which, like anyone with an interest in capitalism, enfranchisement, and nation-state democracy in Anglo-American Western countries, learn to repress and discard a lot of daily life, and yet be also self-conscious that they are doing it or they might miss a trick, lose out.

This is a group to which, as an academic critic, I belong, and with which the writer Kroetsch also has affiliations. The group is part of a cultural environment that defines the aesthetics of "enough" and of "fit" that are embedded into nation-state ideology. To function, the nation-state of the modern world has, since the seventeenth century in England, elaborated a systematic structure of power that many critical theorists refer to as ideology. One of the primary rhetorical devices it uses to maintain stability is "representation," and representations are the allowed images of the nation-state and its subjects. People who are classified as subjects within the nation-state are permitted certain ways of living and expressing themselves, and these are known as representations (Hall 1997). In Lacanian terms, representations make up the symbolic world.

When this system of institutions began to coalesce over three hundred years ago, it referred primarily to citizens of the state. This meant an exceptionally small number of people: white, Christian, propertied, educated usually in privileged "public" schools. The common background of many of these people, including their a priori definition as propertied, meant that representations were relatively close to what that group wanted to sustain. The representative democracy that came into being at the time was appropriate to the needs of this tiny proportion of the population. However, with larger numbers of people working their way into what became known as the middle class, and then the broad extension of the franchise in the twentieth century, representation became increasingly policed by the institutional structure of the state.

Nevertheless, in one sense citizens were still subject to the representations of ideology, about which there was little negotiation. I call this the ideology-subject axis, and its power goes one way: from ideology to the subject, generating the conceptual structure of crude Marxism and reductive Freudianism, alerting us to all that is repressed in that structure because it does not fit representation. The aesthetics of enough satisfies the expectations created by the representational structures that carry the nation-state. In contrast, fit is the moment that an artistic object comes into cultural recognition through performance. That recognition often delivers an adrenalin charge of joy, and "beautiful" art maintains a relation with culture that makes possible the continual triggering of fit. However, the twentieth century marks a shift in liberal nation-state power away from a small, socioculturally coherent group of people in power toward many and more diversified groups with potentially different recognitions of fit. Kroetsch's writing consistently presses on the cultural embeddedness of enough and the cultural eruptions of fit "until" they no longer deliver. Readers then have a choice.

The Puppeteer directly addresses the theorizing of sexuality that had been emerging from the late 1970s from critics such as Alan Bray, Eve Kosofsky Sedgwick, and Judith Butler who were informed by Michel Foucault's early work *The History of Sexuality*. Propelled by the AIDS epidemic, theorizing on sexuality in the early 1990s, particularly on cross-dressing, had moved a long way from where a "heterosexual" woman such as me might position herself because heterosexuality had become a monolithic word that stood in for patriarchy and nation-state ideology. Erotics, and the distinctions made by homoerotics and heteroerotics, had not yet made the alliance around non-normative sexuality enabled by queer theory. Most of the theoretical discussions assumed, naturally, that sexuality is not essentialist and focused on the social regulations of sexuality and the discourses that define it.[1] Yet they also moved quite fast into postmodern pluralities and the attendant ghosts of that analysis: all the things we forget to remember about the immediate society and about our daily life.

But sexuality is, like any other relation, involved in power. So what is the text of *The Puppeteer* doing as it gads through the field of contemporary gender theory glancing at transvestism, at homosexual society, at women's community support? To what extent is it exploiting the aesthetics of enough? Or using that pleasure in representation to generate the eruptions of fit? What is it doing when it concludes its commentary with two men dressed as women speaking to each other in a wedding that ends with death for one and transformation into female life for the other? Can a man be a woman? And what am I, a heterosexual female critic, doing with this male text? I have been trained for decades to think within a logic supposedly constructed by and for men, yet while I read these intimate explorations of male sexuality, can I be a man?[2]

Alibi, the novel against which I am reading *The Puppeteer* in this essay, can be read as an arch pomo (ahistorical postmodern[3]) discussion of sexuality. Pomo is one condition for the relatively empowered; in other words, I would argue that it is not of relevance to the powerful or to the disempowered.[4] It addresses that portion of the population that is self-conscious about its repressions, but embedded enough into ideology that it is reluctant or unable to change the institutional structure of representation. It is a condition of conspiracy theory, with its corollaries of paranoia and cynicism, as against, for example, utopia, a mode more favoured by the disempowered for its offer of hope. The rhetoric of pomo asks for the strategy of doublethink: Nietzsche's *ressentiment*, Freud's return of the repressed in neurosis, narcissism, or psychosis. In *Alibi* Dorf is the person who puts into action the policies of the powerful: remembering to forget.

While the voice of Jack Deemer in *Alibi* presents the clichés of Western capitalism and male heterosexual desire, Dorf is the character who produces what the capitalist wants through the other cliché, of masculinity – the rational, categorizing, and analytical mind. Against the background of male desire which also includes collecting, buying, owning, privatizing, ordering chaos, and turning knowledge into information, Dorf's "Pilgrim's Progress" is gridded within a framework of feminist theories where the male gaze is returned on to him by Karen; where the Oedipal family becomes the hunt for recognition that always eludes; where sexuality becomes multiple orgasm responding to the extended group body of a hermaphrodite.[5] In effect, the women in this novel are never "the Other"; they are simply without appropriate context and hence unpredictable.

Dorf's spa experiences, through the dislocating liminality of the tourist that is mimicked by the cultural tourism of the text's run through feminist theory, set him toward another male sexuality (Moore 1988). He becomes a man who works in and indeed constructs a man's world, but does not want to be there, there in an economically powerful world that has no significance. The versions of sexuality offered to Dorf gradually allow him to rescind power so that his culminating multiple orgasm is not something he does, but something done to him. Yet he is not allowed to retain the experience, and the text has him retreat into a hermit-like existence as if indicating that, if you take this kind of sexuality from the liminal back into the social, there is no place for it. The cynicism of this stand leaves Dorf's travels, and the commentary of the theorizing, enacting a series of deferrals of power – no engagements but no losses, simply deferral.

If the novel *Alibi* can be read as if it were a huge psychomachia offering two dominant versions of male desire and sexuality, buttressed by a variety of theories mainly from feminism but also from psychoanalysis and carnival, *The Puppeteer*, in contrast, is a novel without conspiracy. The narrator changes: it is no longer evasive but shuttling, not juxtaposing devices from a variety of genres but mixing voice and so dislocating the sense of a positioned speaker/writer/author. There is no disruption here but rather a braiding together of other voices between which a writer might shuttle. The characters change: Deemer is no longer without explanation, so Dorf has to take responsibility for his own actions. The pizza delivery is yet more evasion: a collection of beautiful icons incidentally difficult to bring together because they are immediately consumed, as opposed to the stasis of the Greek icons that comes to dominate the latter part of the story.[6] But the puppet performance that occurs at a central moment in the text is transformative, is different in kind. Deemer himself becomes subject to re-definitions. We watch the powerful become implicated in the web of self-consciousness; we see the neutrality of power foregrounded as the biggest evasion. And there is also the possibility that just when the powerful get implicated, it is an indication of their loss of power to somewhere else. In other words, with *The Puppeteer*, the two main centres of power in the novel genre, the narrative and characters displaying power, are made subject to it.

The problem of power in *Alibi* is underlined by the way readers can find in it an easy gender tourism, one that takes feminism and some work on the grotesque as the "Other" for male sexuality – significantly not taking on homosexuality or the popular or race. Yet this other sexuality is only an *Alibi*; Dorf is asked to leave the "other" world of the mud spa; he cannot re-enter the social community. This is not an actuality for him but becomes part of the long evasive strategy, the semiotics of which are similar to Rorty's ethnocentrism and yet not openly problematized by the narrative (Rorty 1991). The gender tourism is like Rorty's global bazaar where you trade pieces of culture and ethnicity, and here sexuality, yet where the real neoliberal economic power makes some traders, particularly white male middle-class traders, more equal than others. The potential connection with Rorty is especially troubling because of Rorty's appropriation of domestic tropes and the vocabulary of "care."

The Puppeteer is highly domestic, unusually so for Kroetsch, but rather than appropriation I would like to argue that readers can read it as pushing at the line where culture and ideology meet. Ideology functions by obscuring its grounds and culture by foregrounding them. The easier it is for culture to foreground, the more likely that it is dealing with something ideology does not need any more. When culture wrests some element from the veiling of ideology, manages to articulate it, we get the shock of the aesthetic, the sudden recognition of "fit," the ecstasy of something that seems "true" because it sits so neatly into the interstices of social life: what we call "beauty." Kroetsch talks of this through the concept of "notation" in "Frankfurter Hauptbahnhof," where notation is "a prediction / a saying (assaying) of / what will be said" (1989, 198) with echoes not only of bpNichol but of Walter Benjamin's ruins of allegory (Benjamin 1985, 181). Beauty tells us of images, ways of living, which have been wrested from ideological repression, but its occurrence signals the moment that the image or possibility is losing its power to change ideology.

The narrative that fears its own tyranny (Kroetsch's vocabulary) of representation, the text that tries to go further than "enough" (this essay's vocabulary), must occasion through notation, first, the ecstatic "now" of recognition: the cynegetic energy of the hunt,[7] the adrenalin surge of the poetic: the aesthetic. And second, it must occasion the "larger if not always enduring" (Kroetsch 1992, 181) experience of transformational vision: the reader's articulation which is the process of performativity. I take this to be not merely a transfer of responsibility to the reader but an occasion of mimesis that constructs the possibility of repetition and performativity that puts the reader into an engagement with an actual and a social immediacy. Mimesis is not a strict copying but a reliving of a text in the present and immediate body that necessarily materializes that text differently. In the "Hauptbahnhof" poem (Kroetsch 1989), the speaker defines himself by difference, provides a notation for himself in the form of a physical "double" (which/who wears a hat, which he never does), a notation that shuttles back and forth between the speaker and the spoken selves, offering an analogy for the shuttle between writer and reader.

The Wedding Dress Notation

In *The Puppeteer* Kroetsch is dealing with the line where culture and ideology meet on a version of heterosexual sexuality. I want to take just one image, the wedding dress, and follow through some of the narrative, generic, and cultural expectations involved in the rhetoric of the text, to a point where it could become possible to talk about whether the narrative semiotics are yet more gender tourism dependent on the aesthetics of enough – or not. The novel raises issues to do with cross-dressing, particularly the difference between transvestism and cross-dressing as they are emerging in theories of masculinity. More pertinent to my self, since I have chosen to be a heterosexual and also a feminist, I feel the need to engage with any notion of male heterosexuality that could move toward a feminist heteroerotics.[8] And what could be more semiotically obvious than the equation of heterosexuality with wedding dress.

The image of a wedding dress pervades *The Puppeteer*. Maggie writes the narrative to tell its autobiography, and a number of the dress's rhetorical functions are set up in the initial pages of the book. First, it becomes a way of deflecting significance. For example, when Papa B and Maggie first meet, she is wearing the wedding dress but has forgotten about it, and so she misinterprets Papa B's interest in her. He is recognizing the dress, not the person. Meanwhile, she is noticing his dress. The misinterpretations are a classic example of cross-purposes, let alone cross-dressing, perhaps a definition for marriage and wedded life. Or, for example, when Maggie and Ida and Josie go to the hotel at Deadman Springs, the reader has been led to believe that Deemer is after the dress, so that when Maggie hangs it up in the hotel, there is the suspense of wondering what will happen – will it be stolen, savaged, destroyed? But Jack Deemer doesn't want the dress; he wants Papa B/Dorf; and then we find that he doesn't want Dorf but Julie Magnusson; and then not Julie Magnusson but the image of god … and deferred desire becomes fetishized into the dress.

This reading is to allow the dress to work as a representation, to set up and attempt to satisfy narrative and generic expectations: we are even told at the key point of the visit to the hotel about the trout embroidery that is traced all over the dress, calling up the association with trout fishing – the lure, the play, the setting of clues as red herrings. Later, we discover that the beads and the embroidery are at times focused on the detail of a postage-stamp sized wedding dress caught in the swirl of other notes, at times the dress is the delicate colouring of the trout, at times the animal wildness, passionate and/or brutish, of the beaded images. Like the written words to the reader, the dress becomes a text made satisfying by each character for each character, whether it be Josie, Maggie, Fish, Papa B, Julie Magnusson, or Deemer himself.

Second, we find that the dress allows Maggie to "hear the story she intended to tell" (Kroetsch 1992). This is particularly interesting because Maggie has different discourses. She wants to write the autobiography of the dress – her husband corrects this to "biography," missing entirely the performative medium that is materialized by the dress – and Papa B says the dress can tell its own story. The ambivalence these different discourses instigate about the stance/position of autobiography pervades the narrative strategy. But the dress then complicates the rhetorical strategies it has allowed. When Maggie puts the dress on, her voice is infused by other voices, particularly Jack Deemer's, that intrude more and more as the novel progresses. At first the Deemer-voice can be recognized simply by the disjunction between a cynical narrative commentary and the bland reported conversation that Maggie uses as a character. For example, "Why didn't he get on with it, whip out a knife from under his cassock? The waiting was brutal. Like having a loaded gun for company. 'It's fresh. Want a croissant with your coffee?'" (9–10), the commentary being melodramatically out of place with regard to the speech. Deemer's voice also interjects overt comments that underline the braided discourse, such as the opening of chapter 2: "Maggie Wilder is writing this. Reading over her left shoulder, I become a loving supporter" (17). Maggie and others often seem privy to information they could never have known so that by chapter 3 this other voice says, "As you have no doubt guessed, I am Papa B's Jack Deemer" (30).

Deemer's voice, through Maggie, moves from an originating authorial voice that we don't trust because it presents itself as self-serving – at one point Deemer has Maggie dream about him – to a highly consistent character that is arrogant, prideful, and pompous. But we never figure out Maggie's voice: it is difficult for the reader to know what she will say or if she is the author of Deemer or a character of Deemer's mind. One of the strategies of narrative braiding is the subtle doubling of vocabulary. A minimal instance of this is found in the description, possibly from the Deemer-voice that foregrounds itself during the opening section of chapter 3, of Ted Bludgett, acting "with all his care and incompetence" (31). A few pages later, this vocabulary is replicated from a more Maggie-centred voice that refers to Bludgett's "careful or careless presumption" (39).

Another braiding strategy between Maggie and Deemer is worked into perceptual description. At the start of chapter 7 there is a backward and forward play between a clear recounting of Maggie's returning to Vancouver that is distanced from her own immediate voice through a use of reported speech, and a more loosely textured prose description of present process that mimics the qualifications and hesitations of the tired mind in its complex clause structure and phrasal interruptions: "Maggie made a cup of coffee and then decided to drink it in the bathroom upstairs while she prepared to collapse into bed. The door to the attic, she noticed, climbing the stairs, was open" (85).

The passage moves into distinctly Maggie-focused self-questioning, only to be suddenly interrupted by "I, Jack Deemer, would have given a million dollars to be in Maggie's place that late night" (86). Even more obvious a narrative device, but written with tight skill and delicacy, the whole of chapter 8 negotiates around Maggie's actions as the writer of this work. She writes down notes, makes lists, types as she thinks. In this process of the action of writing, she sometimes says the things she wants to say and sometimes does not, or at least the reader sometimes finds them and sometimes not. What we watch here is a writing about articulacy and about how much resists being said or simply elides under or into something else. Yet the text moves swiftly into Deemer's voice, focused through visual image toward much more defined and limited observation.

Although the narrative becomes more consistent toward the end, Deemer's voice continually intervenes and the writer foregrounds the intervention: for example, transferring Deemer's snide comments on his Greek dwelling as a "house" not a "villa" directly onto Maggie's recounting of seeing the dwelling a little later on (229). The interventions render the text ambivalent even to the point of confusing Maggie with Julie Magnusson (205–6). Yet the ambivalence never collapses the voices into one speech. Deemer and Maggie disagree about interpretation – for example, Deemer suggests that Julie Magnusson's pursuit of the wedding dress is set up to hurt Maggie, while Maggie "insists" that the remarks were meant for Deemer. Furthermore, in a broader narrative framework, the possible control over both text and reality attempted by Deemer, who "gives permission" to Maggie to be other people, is implicitly undermined by the complex ways that other characters textualize her, as in Karen Strike's photograph or Papa B's puppet. There are other attempts to control her life, from husband Henry Ketch; to

Blodgett, who is easily resisted; to Papa B; and possibly most interestingly to Fish, who both suggests and provides itineraries for her to follow as well as being the unseen supporter of her body in the photograph, and who is described by Deemer as "using" all the women although Maggie "was blinded by her own words" (183). Maggie's writing both articulates and obscures, even though it is possibly obscurity only from Deemer's point of view.

The story that Maggie intended to tell can perhaps only be told if she is wearing the wedding dress, since with the dress on by her own choice she becomes both the image of the "collected" woman that Julie Magnusson claims she became when she wore it when Deemer married her and the person who has dressed willingly for transformation. As the writer, she, a woman, is both subject to the patronizing comment of Deemer that she wants to make order out of chaos she regrets (245), but is also able to nurture him through to a possible change in the grounds for his actions by passing on to him the wedding dress. The former traps her into an aesthetics of enough that can be challenged by an experience of eruptive fit, but the latter indicates a moment where fit is no longer fitting. Perhaps Maggie realizes that wearing the dress will help Deemer not only experience the sociocultural fit of women but also its limitations. At one point Deemer says that Maggie wants to protect his life (198) and, as with many of his pronouncements, this one has elements that make sense: if she does not write, his living story cannot be told, his possible change cannot happen. Maggie is writing the present; her stories get written while waiting, and they become what she has to do.

Reader/Writer Relationships

In the process of writing this present, Kroetsch the writer has constructed a most extraordinary narrative voice that comes close to overwriting the writer. The authorial voice is displaced onto a character whose life is being written by another character. The second character (Maggie) is writing her own life, knowing that part of it is subject to the control of the first character (Deemer). The strategic first-hand autobiographical interventions made by the first character into the text of the second could only be made naturalistically if he edited her texts. But given the dominant motif, they could also be a sign of narrative cross-dressing: that the two characters are in the same narratorial place but behaving/telling/narrating as very different people who partially know each other but not entirely – even as most individual friends or companions partially know each other. The effect is a radical dislocation of authorial voice: not by way of the clear definition of narratorial stance which signifies position (Eliot), nor by the structural separation of say narrator from supernarrator or editor (Thackeray) or narrator from character (Orwell), nor by the location of narrative in character or between/among characters (Virginia Woolf), nor by the shifting of character into voice (James Joyce), nor by the multiple overlaying voices that comment on each other (Thomas Pynchon) or leave gaps for the reader to fill (Angela Carter), nor by the ironic strategy that erases a common ground and asks the reader to replace it (Leonard Cohen), nor by parody.

What happens in this writing is that generically specific concepts of author, narrator, and character are encouraged to shift their location, at times to braid together and at others to stand off against one another. Of particular interest is the focus on elements of modern autobiography, itself generically recognized by many devices and techniques held in common with the realistic novel with development of which it is roughly contemporaneous. Essential for current response to autobiography is a notion of authenticity: fictional device immediately dissolves the patina of intimacy that autobiography promises. Deemer's voice is established from the beginning by way of obvious visual imagism such as the Japanese print on the calendar, soon to be followed by the intrusions of the first-person direct address. In contrast, Maggie's voice could either be itself a character in a classic realist novel, or it could be a self-reflective voice narrating-in-process. The book opens with: "The pizza man. That was the first name for him. What made him look so silly at first, there on the porch with the rain behind him, was his hat" (1). The sentences could be reported internal thought or narrated present consciousness; only the register of the word "silly" weighs the reader to the latter.

Deemer's voice quickly acquires the clarity of an authorial stance related to fictional narrators, while Maggie's carefully constructed "authenticity" articulates expectations of the writer writing autobiography. Each voice ends by contesting the "origin" of the other. Deemer, bit by bit, with every contradiction and expression of cynical underconfidence, turns from author/observer/narrator into character, and is literally given a place/physical space in the story as this happens. Maggie, who presents herself as an autobiographical "I" from the start, with all the expected details of age, family life, and intent, acquires the apparent randomness of everyday acquaintance. This voice rarely makes authorial comments or self-regarding observations (but see 218). As the two distinct narrative positions braid together, the reader's response is continually called into question because it is rarely clear whether the fictional or the authentic is in play.

What gets distanced in the process is the notion of the writer of the book: readers are used to engaging with narrator-character overlay, even writer-narrator-character palimpsests. But when a text mingles two strategies with quite different truth claims on reality, even if we recognize the constructed work of those claims, it is difficult to disentangle those strategic bearers of the text to the point where the reader could assess response.

One example among many of the finely drawn line in generic expectation can be found in chapter 9, when the Deemer-voice comments on the fear Maggie feels when faced with Papa B's puppet performance. He says: "I am at seventy hardly an old man. Yet again men are the butt of the joke in many a performance. Senex something or other. But, old or not, I guessed what Maggie had not been able to guess about herself. She could not, that second night, bear the directness of the puppet's approach. One of the puppets was asking her simply to play herself, and Maggie found the assignment impossible" (122).

The passage opens with a topos of humility: the speaker is, at seventy, socially defined as old since he has his three score years and ten; so his claim to "hardly" be old is a sign of self-deception, immediately borne out by the elision of the word "old" from the next sentence which the third sentence's "Senex" makes clear is implicit. The half-aware, self-convincing self-deceiving technique is all too human. When we then move on to the next part of the passage, we are looking for similar ambivalence. However, in an authoritative contrast, not heralded or sharp but modestly modulated, we are told firmly that this character "guessed" something about the other that she did not know about herself. Not only is our response predisposed to accept this judgment because of the move from ambivalence to knowing authority but we have ourselves just guessed something about the speaker (his age) that he did not know himself. The ambivalence of the humility topos is precisely the kind of humanly recognizable self-deception that can mark an authentic voice, while the knowing if modest authority is more typical of the first-person fictional narrator. The reader's progress through the passage encourages a transference of trust, conventionally given to the authentic voice, onto the fictional, a transference that is without substantive reason. Yet our awareness of the character of this voice as arrogant and potentially deceptive/deceiving is not necessarily clear until much later in the narrative telling. This remains one of an accumulating number of pockets of response increasingly in tension with the reader's understanding that this authentic voice is not to be trusted.

But why should the reader worry about assessing their response to the mixed truth claims? Any reader can impose a clear critical line: for example, Kroetsch the writer constructs the character Deemer as a larger-than-life, highly defined "character" who is then made the narrator of Maggie's attempt to write autobiography: in other words, the structure of *Wuthering Heights*. But the text does not work this way. Deemer is affected by the narration of Maggie's autobiography, implicated in it and changed by it. Maggie is not only at/under his control. The reader's next line of response could be to take the implicit message of the contending truth claims and simply play exegetical games. Yet when a text addresses issues as important as gender, sexuality, and domesticity (household work), not to mention capitalism, logic, and beauty, to take the text as clever play is to reduce it to enough. In this predicament, the reader, who in any event may not want to impose response but undertake engagement, has to be able to participate in the context of the generic debate. The sign of the braiding of both the narrator and writer is their action of putting on the wedding dress, and in this sense I too, as the reader and critic, am wedded to the text.

The wedding dress is put on by both a man and a woman, and allows each to hear or tell a different story. Overtly, we read the story of the woman, but implicitly, by the end we have also begun to hear the story of the man – not the man who finds hermaphroditic bliss, but the man who remains until the end a "collector," the sign of capitalist masculinity, who is now collecting gender, specifically womanhood, in his pursuit of a woman's life. At the beginning of the writing, however, it is Maggie who puts on the dress, and the third primary rhetorical function that the wedding dress encourages is to allow a character/narrator not only to hear or tell but also to respond. For example, Maggie cannot respond to Papa B's puppets unless she is allowed to be someone else. At first she becomes Inez in the puppet story, the successful and powerful careerwoman. When she is asked to be herself, she runs out for two days only returning with the dress, which allows her to answer. At this point Maggie and Papa B sense the presence of a stranger – Deemer immediately and arrogantly suggests that it's him (123) – and this may be a stranger in the sense of a "third place," the difference and change that comes about when people choose to respond by engaging with each other. It is also a sexual response, but is focused not on penetrative heterosexuality but on the erotics of touch and breath and taste, the trying out of new names. And Maggie's response allows Papa B to tell his own story.

Maggie says that every autobiography is a decoy – even the autobiography of a wedding dress. Not deferral, which denies life, but decoys which allow us temporarily to try out difference and even, possibly, to change our lives. In this sense the entire text is a decoy: all artificiality, all articulation that permits externalization and communication is a decoy. It puts us and others off the track, partly because if you could say or re-present your reality you would be hunted down, partly because reality is impossible to re-present except through decoys, partly because the hunt for a recognition of reality which is the beauty of aesthetics is constantly misleading, and partly because the stasis of such recognition is in itself a decoy for the temporality of life. Decoys become markers of possibility, they sit at the place where enough is no longer satisfying and fit no longer brings joy, they perform bits of oneself, and have the potential to transform in the process.

In this text we cannot know who is the decoy, who the hunter; who is a decoy for the other's reality? can we recognize it? does it change them? or us? Maggie also says that you have only one life, so the decoys we make become that life; our performances become ourselves. Whether you read or write, the participation in the text changes reality. For Maggie, wearing the wedding dress changes her life: she puts on someone else and she does it twice. When she buys the dress she is told that it might bring bad luck, and she marries with a sense of the excitement of danger. What she finds is that the danger is the banality of ideology, of representational satisfaction. The second time, as a writer/maker/constructor, she does not just don the dress as a receiver of accepted significance, but she hauls it into the transforma-tive performance that allows her to challenge that significance. It allows her to respond and to change.

The wedding dress allows her not only to respond to Papa B but also to Julie Magnusson, and through the dress the two women exchange stories of the women they might have become. Maggie then moves the dress on to Deemer, and he does not know whether this is to frighten him or to reveal something. Deemer eventually puts it on as a disguise, in echo of the dress Papa B wore at the start, which he describes as a "discard" and Maggie (Deemer) hears as "disguise." And then these two male characters, the ver-sions of male sexuality in *Alibi*, each in a dress, face each other for the first time in the last pages of the novel, before Dorf "dies" and Deemer is left to roam the island with Maggie: he as a woman in the dress, shaving every day to look the part, and in search of the icon with the image of God as a woman.

There is in this the appalling possibility that Deemer is merely appropri-ating a woman's form because he thinks: maybe, if God is a woman, he had better be on the right side. It is just the trivial, banal kind of thing "he" would do. But it is also possible that, as with Maggie, Papa B, Julie Magnusson, the dress is transformative, not an enduring state but, like decoys, transform-ative. There are here no longer the pluralities of *Alibi* but in effect a notion of social practices. These not only culminate in the recognition of moments of cultural significance wrested from ideology but are also interrupted by moments of individual transformation which cannot usually be articulated as significant precisely because they partially dismantle signifying practices – can only be described – scripted out and away from significance.

The significance of wearing the wedding dress, away from which the performance scripts or acts, is quite different for a man and for a woman. The dress comes loaded with notions of female heterosexuality which it is one thing for Maggie to work through and quite another for Deemer to acquire. Maggie is working through to the other side of something that she is in the middle of, transforming sexuality into erotics; Deemer is trying out someone else's way of life, and we cannot do this casually because of the risk to them, never mind the risk to oneself. Furthermore, I don't believe it is possible for individuals to move beyond banal appropriation, or beyond recognition of significance, to transformative moments without a supportive community – so what in this narrative would that be?

Reading Choices: Remembering to Forget, or Re-membering

The ambivalence of the ending is a problem in the reading, focused by the potential in the text for reading for theory tourism in cross-dressing. I would like to consider three approaches to gender study through cross-dressing – fetish theory, the carnivalesque, and Kabuki – to sort out whether they can guide my response, and follow this by turning to the text's writing around domesticity. The final presentation of the two men in women's clothes could be a manipulative appropriation of transvestite theory, particularly the notion of two people living in one body. The basis of much male-to-female transvestite theory current at the time of *The Puppeteer*'s publication was as a power centre: that the moment of revelation occurs when the man can reveal that he is still a man despite the feminine (Simpson, 1992, 96). There are other problems, other potential abuses of power that had been theorized concerning the use of transvestism within homosexual communities, such as misogyny or the unselfconscious use of other cross-dressings – for example, a fashion in the 1980s for wearing Fascist uniform which had acute implications for Jewish or black homosexuals (e.g., Mercer and Julian 1988).

However, within queer theory at the time, there were other attempts to look at cross-dressing as positive, attempts that had not been made in theorizing of heterosexual masculinity. Writers such as Mark Simpson (1992) or Marjorie Garber (1992) concern themselves with such issues. Both writers focused on the fetish and discussed the very different positions held by male-to-female and female-to-male cross-dressing. The former is cast as perversion, for no one would want to be female, while the other is a fetishization of desire. Garber in particular theorizes each as a fetish in her attempt to look at the constructive practices of transvestism. The problem with fetish theory arises from its development out of the split between the symbolic and the imaginary in Lacanian versions of Freud, which renders it either as a commodification of the subject or with the dislocation of the subject into desire. As commodity the fetish is banal, potentially abusive, and "bad"; as desire the fetish is repetitive, it becomes desire on the move, in exchange, designer desire that is "good." Yet in effect, you can't tell the difference between commodity fetish and desire fetish, between an economy of the same or of different, without social context.[9]

Indeed, if I take the clothes that I usually wear – trousers, jacket, shirt, shoes – I could be seen as a walking fetish. But is this a neutral academic commodity, or clothes embodying back versions of masculine desire to a predominantly male academic audience? I, certainly, wore these clothes for many years as banality. In the British academic world where heteroerotic women are profoundly threatening, these clothes allowed me to neutralize or neuter, to denaturalize, indeed to denature or sterilize sexuality. Yet I am aware that this in itself could be seductive. The significance of cross-dressing is ideologically constrained but specific to social context.

A second set of ideological constraints for cross-dressing, different but parallel to the fetish, is that of carnival or the grotesque – particularly the clown, which is itself a useful institutional performance, as Deemer notes of Karaghiosi, the slave or fool become the master puppeteer (126). Do we read the ambivalence at the end of *The Puppeteer* as these two men trying to disempower themselves in standard carnivalesque style? This would be the defining pomo gesture of the relatively empowered at play – moving toward a relative disempowerment, a temporary displacement of power. Quite apart from the political implications of doing this by way of women's clothes (try thinking of the implications if clothes signifying a racially disempowered group had been used), the action is within a closed system. Theory on carnival presents it as preserving the conventional: either in a temporary release of disempowered anger; or, as carnival events are repressed during the eighteenth to the nineteenth centuries, in a policing of that anger (Stallybrass and White 1986); or as with Bahktin, in what happens to popular anger with the occurrence of enfranchisement and the supposedly equal access to power by all (Holquist 1981) – which popular access gets contained by sidelining it into "vulgarity."

The balance of relative empowerment/disempowerment is parallel to Bahktin's structure of monologism and dialogism – yet again it is very difficult to distinguish between the two. Monologic systems have rules and rules for breaking rules, and if we play the game according to the rules we're all right. Dialogic strategies are supposed to be more flexible, opening out into plurality where things can be repeated with a different design, even generating disruptive structures that can permit change. But it is impossible to know whether your dialogic engagement is not simply part of an unrecognized monologic structure. Only social context can make a significant distinction: all too often, especially with the clown, which is a fruitful device for academic institutional labour, you know you are only allowed to play the fool to the extent that the institution is prepared or able to bear it.

A third domain for cross-dressing theory, which is pertinent to *The Puppeteer* because of its relation to theories of rehearsal and the performative so important to the topos of puppets/puppeteer, is Kabuki. In specific, Kabuki theatre has the characterization of the onnagata. At first, Kabuki was a women's theatre, with women actors and writers, but when cultural and social centres of power shifted, the theatre was transferred into men's hands. The onagata is the male actor who plays the lead woman's part – although there are several training paths for different men's roles, there is only the one for women's. Yet the onnagata is not really cross-dressed but performing, and certainly not in the disguise needed by desire. The onnagata never, ever, takes his work home with him.

However, the novel also invokes an area of gender studies that at the time did not address sexuality: domesticity. The social context of domestic community support for Maggie's changes in life is provided initially by the women she meets: Ida, Josie, Inez, Julie. Several of these women, including Maggie but excluding Julie, are overt producers of daily necessities – clothes, food, communication. The wedding dress itself is recognized by Deemer as a work of labour, in the cumulative syntax of his description that he returned it "to the woman who had done the sewing and the beadwork and the embroidery" (31), and he is its consumer. In effect, most of the larger characterizations of the narrative are consumers: Papa B using the pizza delivery for his ephemeral collection of food icons, Deemer the arch-consumer/collector, even Maggie. And certainly most of the male characters such as Blodgett, George, or Henry are portrayed in this way. The women provide each other with a domestic/supportive community as they work, yet the men, who frequently consume in private, lack such a community, often only receiving support from other women. Papa B is an exception because the labour of his puppet theatre brings Maggie and then all her women friends together into a performative community; and like Maggie with the dress, Papa B then hands on the puppet strings to Blodgett. Most troubling, Deemer's wearing of the wedding dress seems to insist on Maggie's support and breaks up her earlier domestic group, as if the wearing of the dress by a man necessitates the loss of women's community.

Cross-dressing theory foregrounds the way that social context is vital for understanding significance; otherwise the rhetoric of the wedding dress will remain banal and appropriative. But part of the reading of this narrative is to do with the way that the sign not only affects the human being, but the way the change in the human being, the performed difference, affects the weight of the sign. Deemer wrests the wedding dress away from both heterosexuality and heteroerotic femininity, putting at considerable risk the women's communities around him; at the same time the act of wearing it reduces its power. Parallel to the de-mystification of the dress is the growing figurative emphasis on Artemis, the bear, the nurturer, the North Star, the big dipper, the arctic, Joan of Arc but also Diana the hunter. Julie Magnusson is all of these. Maggie sees "or rather realised that she had seen" – for again the event resists significance – an icon whose lips "whispered her a message" in the church built above the temple to Artemis. Like the male binary of Apollo and Dionysus, Maggie leaves the vision behind in the village of Appollonia on her way to Artemisia. In the process, she is able to pass the dress on, but also in the process she leaves behind the support of women with their domestic structures and becomes the nurturer; the dress becomes a travesty.

Given the overt gender politics of the narrative, these two uses of theory – the man putting on a woman's dress and life, and the woman recast not within domestic community but into the nurturer – could easily be read as a generalization, and generalizations raise acute questions of textual ethics. The questions could be rationalized by an analysis, for example, that claimed to recognize early cross-dressing theory as masculinist, and hence the novel's generalizations apply only to men. Or an interpretation that reads this cross-dressed man in search of Artemis as an inversion and interrogation of the cross-dressed men in *The Bacchae* who question Dionysus in an attempt to find out why women serve him: this man wishes to know why women support and love themselves. But the semiotics of the wedding dress tell against such exegesis, for the man puts on the dress only at the moment it has become a travesty.

Robert Kroetsch's work is seriously engaged with the history of ideas. His thinking deals largely in sexuality and gender against grounded notions of power, appropriation, ownership, private and communally held property; and it addresses a wide field of contemporary critical and philosophical concepts that may be used but also may be abused. A reader of the texts is faced with the same question as the critic: how does a reading use the literary text without abusing it? There is an ethics of textual engagement that we are expected to respect, which changes with the genre, canon, and literary culture of the writer or reader or text, and depends upon education, publishing, critical assessment, the whole long-term historical environment of the engagement.

The engagement has become so much more complex since the education system has increasingly extended entrance to social, political, and cultural power to people of different religion, class, colour, age, ability, and gender over the last few decades. The promise of the franchise, which supposedly extends to all equal access to power, is impossible in a liberal nation-state, and today there are many questions raised about the representative democratic systems which regulate contesting voices in terms of their current legitimation and struggle within this re-casting of power. Just so the enfranchisement of knowledge, which supposedly makes "knowledge" of equal access to all, in practice leads to people making knowledge in different ways that are not all acknowledged, to people making different knowledges. There are again contesting voices that raise questions of legitimation, struggle, and re-cast knowledge. Issues, including that of the "appropriation" of voice, raise acute ethical questions which derive in turn from immediate moral practices. Yet the ethical dimension, which implies that a standard of behaviour has been reached, is always dangerous because agreements about standards are made on the basis of particular grounds whose contexts will change from moment to moment.

This novel suggests that art also works in this way. The concept of the artist as a legitimate but unsettling figure within nation-state ideology has been part of the political structure of post-Renaissance Europe and its cultural colonies. Yet the aesthetic of beauty, the sudden recognition of fit we call truth that mediates significance to and fro between ideology and culture, is tied to the artist of relative empowerment. This person by definition has certain privileges and is part of an ideological structure that gives them power within culture. Complicit within, yet working to challenge the power of representations, the relatively empowered artist does wrest significance from stasis/the status quo of representation, both guided by and guiding the face of the state: neither remembering the construction of the status quo which would place the artist in the pomo position of seeing no significance outside the social, nor forgetting the construction and removing into a passive banality, but the simultaneity of remembering to forget that stimulates the aesthetics of fit.

With the enfranchisement of art, more people have become relatively empowered so that recognition of aesthetic truth multiplies into plurality. Relational aesthetics is tied to this sense that people from many diverse backgrounds can achieve aesthetic participation as long as they take up their newly found relative empowerment. But when people claim aesthetic participation, many do not have the degree of empowerment that defines the artist within the modern capitalist system of art. Hence the fundamental activity of the artist changes – no longer a spur or goad to ideology and the culture of the empowered, the artist can refocus on individual/group practices that recognize a range of positions of power and knowledge. Art becomes the place where we seek out strategies and stances that encourage us to remember to "re-member" to re-make, and hence where we can change. The transformative vision of performance carries no specific significance; it can only offer a way of mimetically rematerializing a particular reality that makes possible change through performativity. One can argue that this process of art-work has always been in place, and has typified artists from disempowered groups or artists working in political systems other than the nation-state. That it is possible is particularly important in the world Kroetsch's novel describes of increasingly global economics. This kind of art-making offers by analogy potential alternatives to existing structures of knowledge and power.

I would want to argue for this reading of *The Puppeteer* as a call to performativity because, although the use of gender theory and the domestic does, on at least one reading, raise questions about the ethics of taking on someone else's voice and life, the text also offers the potential for performative re-membrance that happens just at the point where the aesthetics of enough and of fit no longer function. It is striking how inadequate the seductive adrenalin surge of the theory junkie becomes with this text. Recognitions of fit are continually traversed by other stories that need to be heard, and which surface through the mimetic gaps of other performances, other autobiographies. My focus on generic strategies of narration, however sophisticated these strategies are, has excluded the story of Papa B, or the story of Blodgett, or the story of Julie Magnusson, or the story of Josie – all of which are also told, all of which play with other notions of sexuality and different approaches to community-building work. In stressing this reading I also stress not my ability to think and analyse "like a man," but my willingness to try the writing on in an attempt at domesticity. Being wedded to the text is loving work.

PERFORMANCE 1
Can a Man Be a Woman?

WEBLINK http://vimeo.com/18437659

"Can a Man Be a Woman? Robert Kroetsch's *The Puppeteer*"

1994   Université de Strasbourg (France), Conference in Honour of
        Robert Kroetsch
1995   University of Calgary (Canada), Calgary University Art Gallery
        University of Western Ontario, London (Canada), Graduate
        Studies
        University of Leeds (UK), Faculty Research
1996   University of Toronto (Canada), Faculty Research
        University of Huddersfield (UK), Graduate Studies
1997   University of Leeds (UK), Theatre Workshop, Graduate Studies
2001   Warsaw University (Poland)

"Can a Man Be a Woman?" is a performance piece that was conceived of for the Strasbourg conference celebrating the work of Robert Kroetsch, run by Héliane Ventura and Simone Vautier in 1994. I felt then, as now, that Kroetsch's writing creates texts that steal out on the leading edge of what is possible in the novel form. I was ambivalent about the topical matter he was using and wanted to critique this element while acknowledging that the formal textuality brought the topical fields into question anyway. This means that I felt the reader was set up to get the joke, and the joke was mainly against women, at the same time as a careful reader, one prepared to do a lot of work commensurate with the writer's work, would engage with something far beyond a joke.

This stance raised for me the ethics of the text: yes, it was possible to engage with a critique of patriarchy and liberal capitalist ideology, but most readers would probably read the surface text. Indeed most of my students were doing so and it was heavy-duty work to get to a place of engagement. Even when there, I wasn't sure that I hadn't simply put all this critique into the textuality of the reading experience – not that I have any concerns about doing so, but usually I feel fairly clear when it happens, and with *The Puppeteer* I was uneasy.

The production was deliberately thought of as a type of allegory for this unease. In this I was working with the excitement of having watched Bobby Baker's "Kitchen Show," which used the domestic topos to undercut any sense that transgression was heroic, and which celebrated the mundane at the same time as it grieved for its deadening valuelessness. I was trying to find a similar uneasiness to build a performance that would allow me to make a decoy of my responses, so that people watching, including Robert Kroetsch, would not quite know what to make of it. The audience would have to get involved in the strong through-line topic of gender tourism and,

I hoped, also experience unease. Kroetsch had visited and read at the University of Leeds where I taught, and I had attended a number of conferences where he did readings. Many people in the small audience at Strasbourg were Canadian literature critics from Canada and from Europe whom I had come to know and respect. I felt compelled to perform the piece and that I was in good hands if it all went wrong.

The script was written several months prior to the conference, and I went through six weeks of rehearsals with guidance from the director Peter Lichtenfels who saw some of the final preparation and gave helpful advice. The first performance did not involve a videorecording, and I was able to borrow a microwave oven from Héliane Ventura. Everything else was transported with me by plane and road to Strasbourg, in a way that I became familiar with defending at customs barriers during the next decade. The response was slightly stunned, but over the following hours most conferees came to talk to me about it and I realized that it had touched some chord in them. So I decided to do it again.

The next performance was at the University of Calgary Art Gallery in 1995, in front of a sophisticated audience of performance art scholars and other members of the public. I needed to engage with incoming visitors as well as the seated audience, and this brought an edge to the production as if it were occurring for the first time. Two further Canadian performances took place at the University of Western Ontario (1995), and later at the University of Toronto (1996), both in departments familiar with Kroetsch's work, and both offering far more response, possibly because my hosts had seen the piece in Strasbourg and been able to prepare the audience. I felt these audiences were far less familiar with the kind of physical theatre techniques used in Europe, and these strategies alienated some of the reaction.

The first UK performance was for an audience of my colleagues in a research seminar at the University of Leeds (1995), one response being a startled exclamation that I had taken off my shoes in front of the head of department, and another taking me to task for the exploitation of Kabuki in the penultimate scene. This latter, a comment from poet and critic John Whale, was one of the most insightful I received, because it picked up on just that level of theory tourism that I had been hoping to convey.

In 1996 I was asked to produce the piece for Huddersfield University, and here I was faced with an audience that had little or no knowledge of Kroetsch's work. The piece became more to do with critical performance – or as I casually suggested: how to keep an audience awake when you are talking to them about theory. This was the first videotaped production. Shortly afterward I performed the piece again for the Workshop Theatre at the University of Leeds (1997), in a performance that was intended to break some of the barriers between theatre and criticism. This is the primary version of the piece online, and incorporated the double-screens of microwave and videoplayer casting their baleful eyes on the process. The video playing a previous performance added a temporal frame that I brushed against, that reeled me in and out, during the live process.

The last production was at a retrospective associated with Warsaw University in 2001, in front of an audience highly experienced in seeing physical theatre but less so in the confines of the seminar room. Many in the audience did not speak English fluently, and the focus of this production was precisely on those elements of theatricality that engaged the audience. I felt that this production had finally left behind the issues of gender tourism and unease, and placed the text more firmly into a field where it lost allegorical nuance.

The essay is largely drawn from the script of the performance piece, and has been rewritten for this book to introduce the theoretical concepts that inform this opening section. It is one thing to put a video performance online nearly two decades later, tagging it openly as from a production in 1997. It is quite another to offer up an essay from material initially conceived in 1996 without trying completely to recast it, but this would eliminate the connections with the video performance. I cannot change the video but I could have changed much of the essay. The edited video from the Huddersfield production in 1996 gives a brief sense of how the performance shifted when produced again in 1997, but I have silently reworked the essay to provide coherence to the book overall while trying to retain its relationship with the video. The methodology involved in setting the essay next to the videotape record of the performance has largely conditioned the arc of this book as a learning curve.

2 Trying to Say

Women's Writing in Canada: I Am a Very Dirty Critic

This chapter carries out a series of critiques in the present of 2011 while exploring essays associated and contemporaneous with the performance "Cooking the Books" (1996–2000). In simple terms, I knew that there were things I valued that did not get talked about, that were crowded out by the representations that were supposed to satisfy me, that provided *enough*. I could see these values in the lives of many people and figured that if I worked on a range of them I would come up with ways of valuing. This is a common process in literary criticism and in the humanities in general: readers and critics go looking at times for similarities across a range of differences that will generate a vocabulary for something not yet said by any of them. At other times, readers and critics go looking for comparable experiences in books or visual art or other media, hoping the differences between and among them will generate common ground.

These actions are licensed; they produce results that are legitimated by the academic world and the intellectual media in Western countries. They lead to publications and radio shows, television debates and blogs. I found it possible to work with people in various groups who were doing the same thing. We shared a collective need to find ways of valuing at first within the group and then, once articulated, out into the surrounding sociocultural environment. For example, I worked with the scholar Margaret Beetham on valuing women's ways of living and working in the nineteenth century and would often move from long, complicated discussions with her out to papers and then essays that *arrested* our talk to put forward possible words and phrases that cast a contemporary light on these people's experiences, a light that helped push today's experiences into a new focus, a new sense of *fit*.

I saw the process as a political mechanism to get unsaid values spoken and acted upon. It addressed a need in the enfranchised communities of Western liberalism in the twentieth century and laid the basis for a responsive ethics. In these social contract liberal democracies there are many different people with many different and often unrepresented needs, who may claim power, hence there was a need to find out ways for them to do so. I was one of "them," but there were others who were not invested in my needs and had their own. "Them" is not a collective pronoun, it is a mixture rather than a solution.

In this exploration I first focused on my own need to get things said so that they became visible on the terms of my life, not all of which is inside or even primarily in response to hegemonic structures. This alterior work and world I call *alongside*. However, I also came to realize that working on my own values by making similar or comparable, for example, by making the complete effacing of women's culture comparable to the complete effacing of black culture, and even translating political mechanisms to others to "give them" tools, was to press strategies upon people whom I already recognized as separate from myself. What justified me in changing society *for* someone else – for example, getting someone a better job, improving someone's medical care? These strategies verge on the edge of paternalism, operate increasingly as assimilationist, and "give" someone more sociocultural power on my own terms.

Eventually I learned that another pressing component was not only needing to get something said, but learning how to listen. At first I applied the rhetorical techniques of similarity that had me searching through difference from the other for empathy, care, and the second person "other" of responsive ethics. But I then realized that difference is not there *until* we make it, and this is the heart of chapter 3. If we work to make our selves aware of the differences we are making, then we can begin to recognize that making and how it changes us. Listening while aware of the differences we make alerts us to the changes we are making in our selves and helps us to materialize the affect of others on our bodies. In like-minded groups, the ethics of alongside moves away from responsiveness and toward engagement. Rather than building a collective aim to say what has not been said, our colleagues become collaborators, supporting us in making differences to our selves that necessarily prompt them into that process.

Further, while we all make every other person different, there are no others that are fully our selves, there are differences we make in degree and in kind. And others make us different in degree and in kind. Those makings also need to be respected.

1   Aesthetics à la carte/Aesthetics in the Kitchen: From *Enough/Fit* to *Alongside*

Enough: all that needs to be said has been said, and what is not said cannot be said.
Fit: not all that needs to be said has been said, and what has not been said is said.

1.1   Cooking the Books

In the arts and its criticism, much recent work has focused implicitly or explicitly on the ideology-subject axis, on analyses and descriptions of ideology, or of the subject. More recently, critical theory, cultural studies, and English studies have challenged the determinist structure of ideology and turned to the discourse theory that circles around hegemony. If the power relations in the ideology-subject axis go only one way, the relation between hegemony and subjectivity is more interactive. Subjectivity, in the sense of the constituted individual that Stuart Hall (1997), and then Chantal Mouffe and Ernesto Laclau (1985) describe, is more fluid than ideologically constructed subjecthood. An individual's subjectivity is able to effect change in discursive structures of hegemony to the extent that the individual is compromised in the state. In other words, those changes will be adjustments, some with high impact. The gay-lesbian movement of the 1980s, for example, was successful partly because of the consumer power held by a portion of this demographic unit. The poor are rarely able to effect institutional change because they are not part of the hegemony that controls discursive exchange.

Canonical post-Renaissance artists in the West are the licensed transgressors of subject positions defined by ideological assumptions. The ideologically marked artist rarely produces work valued as "Art" that articulates the life of people excluded from the systematic because by definition this life has no formal representation and cannot be transgressed. Within the more flexible structure of discourse studies, the artist retains that sense of transgression and/or transcendence as they raid the underbelly of representation – no longer the hysterical place of the imaginary but the more seductive place of desire. Unrealized desires can be articulated, brought into discursive play, but the moment that they are, they cease by definition to be desire and begin to get co-opted into the hegemonic compromise.

With traditional aesthetics it is difficult to value aesthetic production which is not related to those in privileged positions of subjecthood or subjectivity, but which emerges from the domestic and other sociocultural places that raise issues of class, gender, and age, those of ethnicity and ability imbricated particularly deeply with class. My interest in reading and writing precisely from those locations has found itself literally lost for words. What activities can we put into play when reading texts relevant to our own day-to-day lives, but not relevant to sociocultural discourse? For me, this set of questions was focused in the 1990s by issues around household life and women's work in my own culture and that of women in other cultures around the world.

The discussion that follows is very much about pedagogy and how it could be informed by feminist theory on situated knowledge and the developments of situated textuality. When we teach texts that raise issues that are not part of the mainstream critical discourse, we have to devise strategies for dealing with the difficulties we encounter: the texts we find difficult when they ask from us different kinds of work; the texts that we do not find difficult when perhaps we should. For several years I worked on a course concerned with Canadian women's writing, and was struck by the ways students found it difficult to talk about the texts. This was not a problem of enjoyment. The texts made the readers cry, and laugh, and grieve. But these books were and are not about heroes and quests, with careful beginnings and endings, but about ongoing relationships beset by subtleties resistant to such analysis. My solutions started with the introduction of critical approaches that claimed they were there precisely to deal with the notion of difficulty and difference. What resulted was a gradual discovery of limitation, of the shelflife of *fit*, and of an initial concept of *alongside*.

1.2 Working on Canadian Women's Writing

I have written elsewhere and at more length about the texts we studied on this course (Hunter 1996; 1999, chapter 6), and provide here simply a summary of the issues. The course opened with a lengthy section on the work of Margaret Laurence, Alice Munro, and Margaret Atwood. These texts were ostensibly closer to the experiences of the mainly white British students in the room than many others, and could offer a handshake of recognizable structure and topic. However, when we tried to focus our discussions through available mainstream critical vocabularies, we frequently ended in silence. We lacked a vocabulary for engaged criticism through which we could bring these texts into our day-to-day actions.

Rather schematically, we read Laurence's *The Diviners* as a deconstructive text because her sedimented and layered narratives are particularly susceptible to being carefully taken apart. As responsible critics, we did not leave the pieces dismembered on the floor but attempted to reconstruct more appropriate strategies. Alice Munro's work is less open to such an approach, but provides continual and sophisticated segments of semiological analysis. Her stories have an apparently effortless ability to foreground normative behaviour balancing on the edge of the unacceptable and generating considerable ethical debate. The work of Margaret Atwood is especially open to structuralist analysis and narratological investigation. We would go further and subject the texts to poststructural study that opened the books out in unexpected ways and added texture to the text, releasing the acutely perceptive commentary on political narrative that her writing can achieve as it artificializes the apparently natural with surrealist and fabular devices.

In each case, the critical stance allowed us to make important analyses of hegemonic power, but we also found that they restricted us to thinking of the texts as transgressive. Our criticism became systematized into one or another subject position, discursively contesting and subverting its ideological representation, failing to deal with the messy details of domestic work as knowledge, and denying any value to the complexity of the lives of women.

Another set of texts on the course followed the development of a community of women writers in Canada focused around language and poetics: writing by, among others, Daphne Marlatt, Nicole Brossard, Erin Mouré, Gail Scott, Smaro Kamboureli. Language-focused writing is often difficult to open up to readers because so many people are taught that grammar and syntax are fixed and immoveable. Actively to learn about this writing, we returned to a feminist debate that occurred in Canada in the late 1980s about the unhelpfulness of "theory" to the women's movement. The students had to take on the psychoanalytic discourse that underlay the debate and was actively employed by several of the writers. Despite the complexity of other work on Lacan's "real" as radical, the main use of his interpretation of Freud's work is still frequently taken to reduce women to absence, loss, and lack. Brossard's work in, for example, *These Our Mothers* or *Mauve Desert* attempts to give women's voices different breath, stress, and hope. Reading through standard Lacanian discourse renders the language brittle and full of nicety. Using the approach to value Daphne Marlatt's writing allowed us to take the early poem *Steveston* and find sudden silences in the text that were apparently necessary, silences that, after the 1991 publication of *Salvage* in which she published the edited-out sections on women from the earlier poem, made chilling sense as material productions. But while the theoretical approach allowed us to locate the silences and appreciate the exclusion of women, it did not encourage us to talk about the reasons we had committed ourselves to working on these texts in the first place: for what we valued in the texts concerned itself with friendship between women and with an erotics that can inform any sexuality.

The psychoanalytic discourse derives from nation-states that have a social contract that by definition excludes women. "Woman" even becomes the marker of "other" that generates transgression by men. This "woman" is a fantasy, a representation made necessary by the structure of capitalism. It is variously an exotic other of untameable sexuality, a repository of moral and therefore individual and non-social opinion, a pre-symbolic location for desire that can be raided to gain inspiration for changes to male representation. But at root this "woman" is the invisible source of capital and civic structure. Its unacknowledged, necessarily repressed labour guarantees the excess needed to maintain the illusion of profit. Its horror is to be the shadow, not even the ghost, of liberal social contract democracy, to be the body stepped upon and tarmacked over by the grounds of the state, to be recognized only if she/it behaves "like a man" and then not recognized "as" a man but something monstrous, to be not-even-a-slave, unnamed and literally unnameable within the social contract of Western liberal democracy.

But women breathe, eat, bleed, sweat. They have lives that they make valuable to themselves. They may be "repressed" from the position of a liberal subject, but they are a body of people with the energy for making and ability to make that sustains a life worth living and is anything but repressed. The work on these texts made me, a white, middle-class Canadian teacher in the UK, angry. I became acutely aware of the worlds of value in the lives of the writers and their positionality outwith hegemonic expectations. I also realized that the critical discourse that was being used encouraged me to think of the non-hegemonic as simply not-there, whereas I wanted a vocabulary for beginning to articulate the not-said that the writers involved me in realizing through the performativity of their text.

A third area of texts on the course concerned writing about social violence against women. The writers had little in common and many were new to publication and to literacy; several writers were First Nations women, some of whom came from complex traditions of orature. The books explored issues ranging from child abuse and pornography to more systemic violence. The first reaction of most students was embarrassment – at the perceived naïveté, crudity, and ignorance of literary conventions. They were frequently so embarrassed by the apparent lapses in decorum, so trained in canonical patterns, that they could not read the books in any engaged way, they could not begin to hear the stories about violence.

Reading these texts, we developed approaches closely linked to genre fiction devices, those of sf and romance, of Mills and Boon, or fantasy, B-movie dialogue, and fairy tale, where one simply has to vary the proportion of device to find oneself in another genre.[1] The strategy did allow us to read the social violence. It saved the texts from dismissal. But again it missed the point because it encouraged us merely to put the violence away in a box. Genre fiction devices are the fixed structures precisely suited to ideological representation. They work contentedly with an aesthetic of enough. They are not intended to be transgressive, hence they tended to give the impression that the texts were descriptive and analytical rather than critical, even that they were not "literary." They allowed us to engage only with the descriptions of social violence, not with its agency.

This concerned me and we turned to the more responsive strategies that we had used to open up some of the previous writers. There were still many points of embarrassment that could not be analysed away and that the genre fiction analysis did throw forward. We were able to choose to go back to these points as most acutely locating the tensions and difficulties around issues of social violence. In Jeannette Armstrong's *Slash*, for example, in working out what to do with the apparently romantic ending, we had to deal with the fact that for "us" the possibility of hope for the community being described was futile. Hence the ending felt ridiculous. Yet we had to acknowledge that this difference of view was rooted in a racist perception of another culture as one necessarily and tragically failing, despite the insistent portrayal of contemporary First Nations political agency as hopeful and positive. Gradually, through the labour of working on textual resistances, the discussion became a study of the pressures we were putting on the text to fit the representations we understood. In this and other similar debates, the difficulty of these textual elements put us in the middle of working on the problem, working with the writer on a more appropriate way to articulate the social violence, ways that involved us in learning how to value and respect a position outwith the usual relations of ruling power.

In each of these communities of writing, of genre, of canon, of reading, here put forward as examples, the legitimate aesthetic approaches for criticism presented the writer as transgressor, a single individual making little impact on the larger structures of ideology and unseen/unheard by those structures if it did not transgress at all. The reader too became a represented subject, at best allowed a subjectivity by hegemony on whose behalf the writer transgresses. Language itself was cast as an issue of (in)adequacy:

the notion of language as inadequate to representation, which underwrites and sustains the universal/relativist divide in criticism in the arts (Harding 1986, 245; Hunter 1999, chapter 5). Inadequacy implies that there is a fullness or adequacy that language can achieve, just as the concept of relativism implies a universal. Relational aesthetics attempts to use relativism to imply relative-to-other-relatives, a plurality rather than a universal. However, both pluralities and universals fail to acknowledge the way they activate radical differences that make it impossible to hear people outwith the relations/universals. Language is not inadequate to the relations or universals. It simply has the limitations that we bring to it and it will always communicate and engage, as will any medium, depending on how we use it.

The process of employing many mainstream critical approaches to writing by women left us – the readers in several years' of classes, both women and men – feeling deprived of agency, unable to discuss some of our responses, to articulate the things we found difficult to value yet immediate to our lives. The tacit we were trying to put into words was not a set of assumptions, nor the repressed that ideology would rather we forget, the shadows of representation that silently embody the subject. Rather, that tacit was lived experience that had not been spoken, recognized, legitimized by mimetic repetition, agreed to, valued, and acted upon – the tacit that we all have to work on within the limitations of language.

1.3   Feeding on the Text: Listening Responsively to Say What Hasn't Been Said

The theories of situated knowledge that had emerged first from the feminists working on the everyday (Smith 1987), and then those theorizing science and technology (Haraway 1988, Harding 1991, Hartsock 1983, Rose 1994), provided us with one theoretical framework to acknowledge the various non-hegemonic worlds of the writers as "alongside" and not there to satisfy or fit cultural expectation. Yet these theories came mainly from the social sciences and had little concept of textuality – little feel for how the communication of the situated knowledge could inflect the kind of knowledge it was. Understanding that knowledge cannot be knowledge without communication led us to work on the concept of situated textuality. For example, some authenticity politics can sound like situated knowledge, yet its static rhetoric of identity can also bend it toward crude standpoint theory. Situated knowledge is "in process" and needs a textuality that sustains that process. Significantly, theorists advancing standpoint theory (Lennon and Whitford 1994) in the 1990s turned to ethics and to textual strategies to ground situated knowledge in process.

Throughout this period, a book by a group of Yukon Native women elders *Life Lived Like a Story* (Sidney et al.) became my "impossible to read" writing, as well as my "impossible to teach" book. The text is transcribed by Julie Cruikshank from the oral accounts of three Yukon Native women elders, Angela Sidney, Kitty Smith, and Annie Ned. When I first read it I felt like a Swedish literate from the eighteenth century, someone who could recognize and even say a word from a page, but for whom it had no meaning. I would not have continued to read it had it not been put my way by someone I trusted. Yet as I read and reread it, minute repetitions began to cohere around certain words, give them significance. This work was labour intensive, part of my daily life. I could bring an armoury of strategies to it, yet when I did so, I found myself commodifying the work. Instead I attempted to work with the recursiveness of possibilities. Not with the repetition at the foundation of cliché or even of opposition, but possible words and phrases that you say to others when trying to articulate a response and sometimes they pick them up and return them to you or say them on to others, and in their reiteration the words and phrases leave traces that can net together and form a common ground on which to say our feelings.

The work is difficult to do on one's own, although it is possible with just the pages of the text and some social and historical understanding, yet it is far more valuable to do it in communities of readers and writers. Writers do this kind of thing all the time but readers do not, and this is a major problem with Western aesthetics. I was lucky enough to work with three communities of people similarly committed to building different ways of situating texts.[2] Through engaging with their activities, I began to build reading communities in the classroom by introducing personal diaries and then learning journals. The students learned how to work with others and began to use parts of their lives to articulate the critically unsaid in the texts in an explicit manner. They also began to assess the available literary tools in terms of their relevance to the work rather than allow themselves to be determined by their historical specificity – for example, they avoided "ironizing" for the sake of cultural fashion.

The procedure, which is by no means the only way of learning to position oneself so that the text can trust us, asked the students to read as if the texts were able to help them value aspects of their own lives. By doing so, we were explicitly making a connection to the work in auto(bio)graphy that emerged in the 1980s to 1990s, which implicitly makes a standpoint critique that can contribute to situated textuality. But we were also asking the students to be aware of the rhetorical stance by which they were engaging the text.

It took me a long time to find it, but listen to Annie Ned talk about these things:

Long time ago, what they know, what they see
That's the one they talk about, I guess.
Tell stories – which way you learn things.
You think about that one your grandma tells you.
You've got to believe it, what Grandma said.
That's why we've got it.
It's true, too, I guess –
Which way they work at moccasins ...
Which way they make sinew ...
Which way to fix that fishnet ...
Some lazy women don't know how to work,
Don't believe what old people tell them.
And so ... short net! (Sidney et al., 313)

In gesturing toward my negotiations with the text, I am talking about a process of situating, engaging in situated textuality. It is a practice that readers can take on to position themselves alongside hegemonic discourse, and it raises questions about why we would want to build a community with any particular text. It raises questions about the ethics of aesthetics: whether it is à la carte or in the kitchen. Textuality, literature, and art-making in general are not only concerned with language as inadequate, and with creating more adequate representations whose transgressive moments of birth are beauty as "fit": what I call aesthetics à la carte. Textuality is also concerned with distinction, boundary, language as limited, and working on those limits. This latter aesthetics in the kitchen is the hard graft of the recognition of repetition and coherence, of syntactic, morphemic, semantic, and narrative restructuring that always occurs between at least two people, often more, as words, phrases, and stories are repeated back and forth across a gap of individual difference until we find we have netted together a workable common ground.

As I worked with the different textuality of these women writers I felt the aesthetic joy of shared common ground, a joy akin to finding someone who retains a memory in common with one of your own, and common memory, whether found or worked on, is the basis for all collective action. Marilyn Frye speaks of blocking expected patterns so that "In the consequent chaos, they slide, wander or break into uncharted semantic space" where one can see the things "denied, veiled, disguised, or hidden by practices and language that embody and protect privileged perceptions and opinions" (Frye 1993, 108). Pattern perception, similar to what I have called repetition and coherence, includes the ability to be astounded by the "ordinary," to recognize patterns that do not "fit," and to press at the "limits" of pattern (109). In these movements we make meanings and form non-homogeneous communities brought together by story (110).

The experience of shared common ground in aesthetics à la carte is a shock of infringed selfhood because it is premised on isolated heroic action that someone else has suddenly got hold of: therefore, it is a beauty that should only happen once, should be rare and unique and somehow less valuable if in common. But working on language as limited is quite different in tenor. Although it needs courage, it has no heroes. There are no guarantees that there will be a result, or that a result will be valued by anyone else. This aesthetic response is precisely that of shared common ground; to pursue my domestic topos, it is aesthetics in the kitchen, a phrase that tells you a lot about my life, starting with the probability that I have one – a kitchen that is. The shock of shared common ground viewing language as work on limits is a shock of the recognition of common work, of shared value, it has hope written through it.

2   Critique: From *Alongside* to *Ar(rest)*

Alongside: the unsaid is made in the making of difference which is an unending process of making present (Frye 1993).
Ar(rest): what has not been said is said, yet that saying renders further unsaid.

2.1   *Situated Knowledge, Standpoint Theory, and "Alongside"*
There is little effective critique of the writer or of the reader as autonomous.[3] Throughout my own early criticism, I made theoretical investigation into ideology a self-conscious focus for my work as a researcher and then as a teacher because of a need to expose the discursive assumptions of the liberal capitalist societies whose literary products I taught. Yet as I became increasingly interested in writing that grappled with lives not recognized by hegemonic structures as valuable, whether in domestic settings, from family relationships to issues of age, colour, and bodily ability, to worlds of sociocultural otherness, it became apparent to my students and to me that we lacked a critical vocabulary with which to discuss and value these texts.

The set of questions I drew up to open discussion on these issues in a later class ran like this:

How to explain why things change within a determinist framework: ideological or hegemonic?
One answer:
  to gain power and knowledge that effects change
  i.e., how to put yourself into the framework.
How to change things within a determinist framework by assimilating?
How to change things within a determinist framework by compromising?
How to change things within a determinist framework by remaining outside?
Is changing things within a determinist framework agential?

There are three signal factors in the rhetoric of Western liberal social contract democracy:
  1 isolation
  2 the autonomous/universal self
  3 rationalistic structuring
Isolation guarantees that alternative ways of doing things or of thinking do not impede on the space controlled by a specific governing state. An a priori fact of the autonomous self encourages individuals to think that they are unique and therefore essentialized, and at the same time underwrites the force of representation to mould all individuals in the guise of universal man. Rational, "if-then," tree-structures of logic that move from a wide base to ever more reductive parameters can exclude random factors that challenge the self-evident logic of the isolated state.

A corollary to these three elements is the idea of language as (in)adequate to the representation of reality. Because "reality" is always already there, determining life, representations become the inadequate attempts to satisfy our knowledge of the real. The modern artist, as the licensed transgressor of these representations, heroically dives into the imaginary or risks desire to bring back into the symbolic, into articulation, aspects of representation that have eluded communication because they are inadequate to enough, and cannot/do not want to generate fit. The power of such production occludes the fact that we have few cultural ways of recognizing, let alone valuing, elements brought into textuality from outwith representations and their shadows, from an alongside world inflected by but not primarily interested in the hegemonic.

Most feminist thinkers have attempted to engage with these questions, and most feminist readers and critics have taken on the problems of (in)adequacy. Many have opted to set the questions about "How to explain why things change?" within a determinist framework of the ideological or hegemonic. But I am more concerned here with feminist critics and philosophers, scientists and political scientists, interested in situated knowledge and advanced standpoint theory who have asked instead: How to position outwith power and knowledge? With that framework – to position outwith power and knowledge – my questions then became:

Some things perform as if they are not determined.
How can things perform as if they are not determined?
What things perform as if they are not determined?
Does performing as if you are not determined mean that you have agency?
What is agency?
Is agency constrained by hegemony?
Is agency able to operate completely outwith hegemony?
Are there different kinds of agency?

How about reconceptualizing agency as non-individual?
How about reconceptualizing the individual as non-autonomous?

Situated knowledge proposes "the situated" rather than isolation, and the non-autonomous person interacting with the "concrete other" or the "second person other." By "situated" I intend the kind of work we do in fairly small communities or groups of people, often quite intimate, where we hammer out ways of living together and talking about events that mean a lot to us, but for which we often have no words, no way of communicating. This work is quite different from the work we do when we take up subject positions within nation-state ideology, or when we work discursively to challenge or oppose those positions and try to shift them. Of course, a situated practice is contingent on the others, as they are on it, but it is still quite different. "Situated" itself is frequently read as "in a location," whereas epistemologically it signifies "in process," a becoming. Nevertheless, in order to talk about the elements of a situated knowledge, it is necessary to think of it as having particular materiality, hence the concept of "arrest" or "a rest": that we have to choose to arrest the process of situating in order to make decisions and take action. This is the rhetoric of its textuality. Unlike rationalist structures, situated textuality is always in process and devises a range of strategies for creating moments of arrest, as well as for reminding us to put the situating into movement once more.

Rather than focusing on what is forgotten in the civic state, which has led to vocabulary that is often unintentionally disparaging – the mimic men, the subaltern, even most brutally the "abject" – several philosophers contributing to situated epistemology have focused on what can be re-membered by re-positioning alongside the state. The word "outwith" is a pivotal key to this discussion. I was surprised when a colleague told me that there was no term "opposite" to "with," since the Scots dialect has a long and helpful use of outwith. The OED lists a definition under "preposition" as, "a. In a position or place outside of; situated or located outside of; beyond." At times taking on the more familiar significance of "without," outwith also signifies the place not included within the boundaries. Not exactly beyond the boundaries as if that could be a place "to go to," but not imaginable, not sayable, not recognizable within the boundaries defining the place where you are.

The work of "outwith" is recognized in several theoretical discussions as "otherwise" (Levinas 1998), "elsewhere" (Derrida 1999, Minh-ha), "beside" (Sedgwick 2002), and "alongside" (Hunter 1984, Read 1995), and comes close to Doreen Massey's work in *For Space*. I use the term *alongside* in this essay to signify those ways of valued living that are not recognized, in other words outwith and not heard, seen, or smelled, by the state.

2.2 Responsive Ethics, Feminism, Gender, and Political Theory

Early philosophical work in the field looked not so much at the structures and strategies of alongside but at the negotiations between ruling and non-ruling power. One of its central concerns was how to move from the particular situated communality to public action. These issues generated an intense interest in ethics because they took up the accepted position that ethics is related to the way individuals interact with the public that is the state. Seyla Benhabib outlines the concept of the "concrete other" as a process that ties people into responsibility rather than relegating justice to an "ideal consensus" (Benhabib 1992). The concrete other "signifies the *unthought*, the *unseen*, the *unheard*" (281). Sabina Lovibond distinguishes between a private self and a "real" self that develops into an organized or centred self in negotiation with a shared public community that allows us to attribute meaning and value to "difference" (Lovibond 1994). In contrast, Jane Flax brings the public and private selves together into intersubjective citizenship through justice; she says that when one recognizes "differences as well as mutuality one is forced to negotiate with others and to see the boundedness of one's claims as well as one's mutual responsibility for and dependence upon the character of the 'we'" (Flax 1992, 207).

Studies on feminist ethics worked across the supposed split between epistemological and materialist approaches to gender and ethics: epistemologically based ethics puts pressure on the way canonical ethics exclude so many people, and materialist ethics focuses on substantives such as trust, care, and empathy (Bubeck 1998; Walker 1998, 17ff). Bringing together these two traditions was central for a situated ethics, an ethics based in particular practices, whether the urge was to define an ethics interacting with a hegemonic state or to articulate the values of a group alongside that hegemony. There is a remarkable consistency in what people were trying to do with a situated practice of ethics. The central impetus came from recognizing the diversity and plurality of access to ethical debate as opposed to the restricted and self-selecting basis of canonical ethics (Code et al. 1991, 15–23). Many people were trying to find alternatives to normative ethical standards based on a priori grounds that claimed absolute truth or at least neutrality: an ethics that by convention used selective access, held restrictive practices on the concept of "rights," and offered profoundly inappropriate representation to everyone else. Instead, the alternatives attempted to develop a responsive ethics not based on a rhetoric of similitude but on one of difference (Benhabib 1992; Young 1996, 38–59). Rather than tolerating or hiding elements that do not "fit," a rhetoric of difference involves negotiating procedures that move toward sharing some values, respecting others, as well as the possibility of personal change.

Political theory concerned with gender was another area concerned with these issues, probably because politics and ethics are inseparably intertwined, not only with each other but also with rhetoric. We cannot have one of the three without the other two.[4] Work in political theory was sprung into action by the same impetus, the diversity and number of people who can now claim access to democracy in Western liberal states. Political theorists began looking at the implications for the nation-state democracies in which many of them lived and the kinds of citizenship and problems of representation that have resulted (Walby 2011). Particularly interesting have been some of the strategies for deliberative democracy, which offer modes to participation to people conventionally excluded from political power through different ways in which they can be heard and which listen to the different modes of communication they use (Benhabib 1996). This kind of work by political theory and ethics, both often impelled by gender issues especially in the way that alternatively gendered communities have been excluded from discussion for so long, pointed to narrative, anecdote, story, autobiography, analogy, and other similar genres, and claimed their rhetorical efficacy for inclusion.

The argument, as we well know by now, runs something like this. Democratic structures of social contract liberal humanism were established for a small, relatively coherent group of propertied, white, Christian men. Their singular achievement, to deflect the destruction of a culture based on physical force into the controlled aggression of capitalism, went hand in hand with national imperialism and the growth of state institutions, and in England and the United States with the party political system of oppositionality that is inherently conservative. From the nineteenth to the twentieth centuries, when a large number of nations extended the franchise, there were suddenly many different interest groups, with many radically different needs, claiming political, social, and cultural power. Proportional representation has been one attempt, among others, to resolve the anomalies that have arisen. But "democracy" has frequently not answered this challenge, resulting in civil unrest, coups, revolutions. As Mouffe and Laclau argue, groups new to liberal democracy have to articulate their needs because they have not been heard before.

The writing of Benhabib and others with whom she has worked is particularly helpful here in combining procedural democratic strategies with substantive issues in rhetoric (Gould 1990, 272; Mansbridge 1996, 48) into a "responsive" universalism (Benhabib 1996, 339) – the political theory that underlies her responsive ethics. To encourage the procedural aspect of ongoing engagement, many writers have been concerned to elaborate the idea of "differentiated public spaces" (Habermas 1991), in other words claiming that public space is not only institutional, governmental space but also, for example, environmental (Benhabib 1996, 87) or ecological. It can involve Parent-Teacher Associations, trade unions, voluntary women's communities (Mansbridge 1996, 56), healthcare providers (Joshua Cohen 1993, 147), and so on. Significantly, these are places where people who are motivated by concern but not necessarily trained in formal debate or other institutional techniques can go to discuss, argue through specific issues, find ways of articulating their concerns, and eventually put them to larger policy making bodies. These spaces allow for the practice of a situated ethics working slowly in small groups. Habermas terms similar public space "civil society" (1973); Nancy Fraser calls it "subaltern counterpublics" (Fraser 1992). In these kinds of public spaces a well-articulated position can gain a hold, give legitimation to the group, and make it easier for it to be heard next time around (Joshua Cohen 1993, 156).

I agree that this aspect of deliberative democracy is a helpful strategy, even though it is energy expensive and puts enormous pressure on small groups to justify themselves. But it raises another question: institutional structures are always ethically normative. "Ethics committees" have been formed and integrated to deal with the problems that normativity raises in obvious places such as national medical associations and even the British civil service. How, then, does a small group using situated ethics interact with an institutional structure with normative ethics? The whole point about the former is responsiveness and ongoing engagement, and the defining feature of the latter is corporate stability. This leads to my second concern that, from this perspective, every situated articulation, whether it be in art-making or policy group, has to be partially normalized before it can become politically effective (Wolin 43–4), and the moment it does so it becomes co-opted out of the responsive and situated and into the hegemonic. Fundamentally, these are strategies that encourage groups of people who are building alongside worlds to assimilate those worlds into hegemony, to search for fit.

Central to anchoring the procedural or ongoing aspects of deliberative democracy and resisting co-optation are words and phrases such as "narrative" (Code 1995, 155; Young 1997, 60–74), "dialogue" (Jean Cohen 1990, 89), "expression" (Lovibond 1994), and "articulation" (Mouffe and Laclau, 113).[5] Each begs the question of how situated need is translated into the sociocultural and how, when this happens, it can resist being normalized into the discursive and hegemonic, let alone the symbolic and representational. Some political theories have claimed that story or narrative or even rhetoric in themself resist co-optation (Walker 1998, 66; Young 1999, 60–74). But as rhetoricians have always argued, whether a strategy is more or less likely to be co-opted has to do with historical particularities (Code 1994, 60; Hunter 1999, 162–76). For example, Margaret Walker's insights in her extensive discussion of narrative collaboration (112–27), which produces a self that is a "layered, nested, and 'ensemble subjectivity'" (117), may not have been co-opted in the reception of the "slave narratives" to which she refers (127). However, the production of any kind of subjectivity indicates that co-optation has occurred to the moment of entering sociocultural fit.

The political philosopher Iris Young has argued that there are discursive modes that can resist co-optation. She suggests that "storytelling" rhetoric and "greeting" are possible models of resistance. A counter-argument asks: what happens if we don't understand the story? I would answer that not understanding is a valuable first step in recognizing differences that we have to work on – the danger of story lies more in its normative power. A second counter-argument says that greeting is too affective, yet as Young notes, greeting involves the whole etiquette of valuing others, respecting them, showing care toward them. A final counter-argument attempts to displace rhetoric in favour of the law because the former is manipulative, but the structure of the rule of law is precisely a form of judicial rhetoric.

2.3 "Ar(rest)," Assimilation, and Rhetorical Drift

Nevertheless, I would like to begin to problematize any claim for genres and strategies that resist co-optation, and to consider a particular rhetorical event: the drift from the responsive to the normative. The situated "textuality" we developed in the classes I held and among the groups of like-minded people with whom I worked tried to take issues of co-optation and rhetorical drift into account in thinking about ways in which different voices can be listened to and included in current political and ethical conversations.

Although I do not think that Young foregrounded the historical constraints on the modes she proposed, I would agree with her that the rational and argumentative, agonistic, forms of the debate[6] are usually learned in privileged situations. Therefore, they privilege certain people over others, put in place a restrictive practice that inexorably makes normative other modes of articulation. If we could find a way of validating non-rational logics or structures, many people currently excluded from participating in political and public discussion, in the arts and culture, would find them more accessible and would be able to contribute. We could then start dealing with difference as a resource, not as an obstacle.

Lorraine Code looked at the rhetoric of responsive process and how it can be communicated through a storied epistemology that develops responsibility for others through empathy, non-rational logic, and an argumentation of gossip. Empathy becomes a "nuanced mode of knowing" through which we learn respect for others so that we can engage responsibly with them (Code 1995). The point for Code and Lovibond and Benhabib[7] is to treat others as the "friend." In Code's words, this is to respect people as a "second person" not "third person" individual. In Benhabib's, it is to recognize and confirm someone as "a concrete, individual being with specific needs, talents and capacities" (1992, 281), to treat them with friendship, love, and care. Second-person ethics is central to the feminist ethics project because the strength of commitment that brings one together in both commonality and difference is based on trust and friendship (Code et al. 1991, 23). Yet Code developed this into a consideration of ethics within alongside groups, taking seriously that "the personal is the political."

Nevertheless, as Nancy Fraser suggests in the context of politics, we cannot simply turn to a set of communicative devices and offer them as solutions to the issue of articulation (Fraser 1992, 119, 121). For example, Julie Cruikshank, who has worked for many years with Yukon women in northwestern Canada, speaks of the way that storytelling is a legitimate and valued way of organizing political action within the Yukon First Nations. She also notes that the same strategies are beginning to play a role in larger policy debates (Sidney et al., xv), at times in an attempt to manipulate and control. When mediated to southern Canada by television, these attempts may appear successful, convincing those viewers that the politicians are trying hard to understand the northern constituents, and this is a not inconsiderable political achievement in itself. However, the structure of oral storytelling in the north is so complex and culturally specific that among northern viewers, the politicians (happily) appear naive and opportunistic.

Situated ethics do not become normative simply under institutional pressure. If the work of situated textuality has to find a moment of *ar(rest)* in order to shift toward hegemonic articulation, it is also open to a well-recognized rhetorical drift toward *enough*, and for good reason. Situated practices take energy, time, and commitment. If another case arrives that looks similar to one in the past, and if we have fewer resources, we are likely to work by analogy and try the past strategy on the present case. If that works, we may be led inevitably into repetition until someone shouts and screams that it is not appropriate for them – and then they are lucky if we hear them because we may have lost the skill of listening to that voice.

Perhaps the situated articulation is forever lost to larger groups? Conceptually, perhaps we need to recognize that the "situated" is precisely that. Once "heard," the situation is different. But, most urgent, we have to resist the pull into thinking of the interaction between large and small political publics as one in which the situated ethics is engaging with another system that has "normative" as a need that will automatically flip arrest from articulation into co-optation. The normative is not a need. It is a position that underwrites coercive stability, that maintains the shift into the inexorably normative terrain of state structures and policies, that make the situated impossible.

2.3 Situated Textuality?

It is not enough to have a differentiated public space that produces the initial articulation of a need that has never before been heard. We need differentiated public voices with rhetorical strategies to maintain the situated textuality that enables articulation, and we need more engaged audience strategies to ensure they can be heard. But given the difficulty of being effective, of finding a way of being "heard" without becoming normative, or at least losing situatedness, how can the particularity of situated voices enter discourse? A large part of the answer lies in education. We still live with an education system that was initiated by white, male, Christian, and propertied people, and we have been educated to listen to the situations appropriate to them. Nor am I suggesting that these situations are without value – but in practical terms it is impossible to learn to listen to the situated particularities of everyone, so we need to make choices about where we will direct our energy.

An analogy can be made with the resistant voice, one that has informed poetics for centuries and by definition resists the normative. Despite the proportional relation between resistance and size of audience – the more the text resists convention the smaller the audience – people seem always to have recognized the value of training themselves to engage with resistant words and practices: either resisting subjectivity or responding through the discursive challenge, neither of which are to do with the work of articulation itself but with the recognition that an articulation of something previously unheard has taken place. Although most critical response has hitherto been with poetics produced by privileged people, there is no reason why we should not carry out this kind of reading for voices that are different. It would require learning how to listen as a resistant practice within a personal and situated context appropriate to ourselves, and none of us can do it for all voices. But we can do it for some. Which voices we work with depends on situated practice, time, energy, and commitment.

However, resistant work, like responsive ethics, may not be enough; we may well need not only to counter the representations in place within discursive systems but attempt to value the articulations that are being made while we do the work. Situated practice on texts will not take place with a focus on either hegemony or indeed ideology. Ethical feminist practice must know the situation of the text appropriately, hence its epistemological strategies must be prepared to work outside of hegemonic plausibilities (Code et al. 1991, 15). Or as Daryl Koehn puts it, for feminism to better carry out respect for an ethic of care and trust, it must not limit itself to identifying specific issues but engage in a dialogical interaction with the situation – by which an interaction of respect for difference seems to be signified (Hunter 1999, chapter 6). Situated work often doesn't know what it will say until it's said. Much situated art-making does not lack value; it simply needs other ears. Many of us can hear, we are trained as critical thinkers to do so. But we often also publish in print media that address a large community of normative readers. As a result, our work, as mine in the course I describe at the start of this chapter, talks explicitly about why much situated work fails rather than engaging in situated textuality that generates its own values through work on the syntax, vocabulary, grammar, and structure.

The claim being made by situated knowledge theorists was that responsive ethics can only be sustained within communities of situated knowledge interacting with public institutions, and (implicitly because of the rhetorical drift toward co-optation) the communicative devices needed to keep the situated knowledge situated are story, anecdote, autobiography, and similar messy genres that somehow elude that co-optation. I would challenge these claims by noting, as would any skilled reader or audience member, that no genre is by definition resistant to co-optation, although there may be some that are more or less co-optable in any specific sociohistorical time/place. There is no way of guaranteeing that the moment of arrest that makes possible social agency will not drift into consensus, then corporate, then authoritative/determinist structures. And as a corollary, responsive ethics is not enough, whether it defines the relation of the alongside within or outwith hegemonic structures.

What situated textuality can offer is a reminder about the presence of people working in the process to generate a textuality in the first place. Presence signifies here the actions that make up the process of situating knowledge by building a textuality. It is not metaphysical presence but material presence that makes up engaged collaborations of ongoing interactions. It cannot predict what it will make, only how it is made, making it technically a rhetorical "stance." It provides the energy for generating the grounds on which situated knowledge comes to a rest when it needs to intervene in and disrupt hegemonic representation. But if those grounds become recognized, then by definition they enter fit and achieve topical status. The history of rhetoric tells us that a topic may be employed to challenge, resist, support, or subvert (and many other) hegemonic norms, but the topic can have no sociocultural effect without being recognized. The only moment of social agency in the movement from presence, to situated textuality and the knowledge grounds it articulates, to sociocultural topic is the moment of *arrest* in which the grounds emerge into discourse and either rearrange the web of communication, or get co-opted into fit, or are simply not seen or heard. But the process of presence is agential in its own right in the lives of those working outwith hegemonic structures and can prompt us to re-engage with the alongside.

PERFORMANCE 2
Cooking the Books

WEBLINK http://vimeo.com/18439744

"Cooking the Books: Reading Canadian Women's Writing"
   1996   Oviedo Universidad (Spain), Conference of the European
      Association for Commonwealth Studies

University of Calgary (Canada), Visiting Professor
Trent University, Temagami (Canada), The Idea of North
Conference
University of Leeds (UK), Theatre Worshop, Graduate Studies
1997 Beilingries (Germany), Conference of the German Association
for Canadian Studies
2001 Warsaw University (Poland)

"Cooking the Books: I Am a Very Dirty Critic" was first performed in 1996 in Oviedo, Spain, at the conference for the European Association for Commonwealth Studies to which I had been invited by Isabel Carrera. The piece was built on the energy of despair with current postructural and neocolonial theory, and largely influenced by the food performances of Alicia Rios. I had attended and given two papers at the conference "Food and Performance" run by the Centre for the Performing Arts in Cardiff in 1994, where Ms Rios had taken over the top floor of an adjacent building and created an enormous garden shed with plants made of various foods, and wines and water in the watering cans. I was amazed and thrilled not only by the skill it had taken to build the entire event but by its scope, its ambition, its in-your-face confidence in the value of food as sculptural material, and by its honouring of ephemerality.

"Cooking the Books" requires careful preparation, in a manner similar to television cookery shows that always have the "next stage" handy: "I have one right here." It also requires a kitchen to prepare the materials just before the performance, and Isobel Carrera was willing to lend me her kitchen. The sugar cookery of the middle section is particularly tricky, and I have never been skilled in this area. Creating the sugar sheets needs careful work at high temperatures (240–50 °F) and I had an accident that raised substantial blisters on the thumb and palm of my left hand, requiring a quick visit to a local pharmacy. But all the food was prepared in time and transported to the conference.

The performance generated a wide range of responses. In the audience were a group from South Africa who were horrified by the waste of food and of books. Like them, I had grown up with injunctions to be careful of books and spent most of the rest of my life respecting and restoring them. I did not tell the audience that all the books had been reclaimed from a store that was about to pulp them, nor did I detail the careful reconstruction of the covers and some inside pages that had gone into their appearance – a reclamation that in a curious manner predicted the reclamation from the cooked goods that ensued. The food used was made up of industrial ingredients such as dried eggs and package recipes. It would have tasted appalling, but I recognized the horror at the waste as an unintended but fortuitous development.

Other responses confined themselves to asking, as did many audience members at performances in Leeds (1996 – the source of the videotape record) and Calgary (1996), about the significance of specific recipes as metaphors for the literature I was reading. One Belgian scholar was upset that I had put all these "dirty" foodstuffs over a beautiful linen suit. Another teacher commented that the delivery made the performer appear to be priest-like. Yet another student complained that in the question and answer period I "smelled." I had ceased to be concerned that people did not respond to the performatives in the physical theatre in the way they would have to literary performatives, and built these installations because their entertainment value allowed me to articulate things that were precisely not-yet-said.

During that year I also performed this piece at a conference run by Trent University, "The Idea of North." The conference took place in a retreat in Temagami Provincial Park, over a mile from the parking area. It was a testing experience but one that allowed me to perform in a small room with a small audience, completely changing the effects and affects of the interaction. The installation took place right next to the kitchen and became much more integrated and intimate. It slowed right down and worked on a personal level with the conferees, all of whom I'd had the chance to speak with over the preceding day. The intimacy made it far easier to be distant. Someone's dog ate the food. The audience didn't have to "like" my performing persona, which in any case was so physically close to them that its extravagant overlaying of book images and food images (for example the "apron" which is in fact a printer's apron) was much more evident.

The final performance of the piece was at the Warsaw retrospective of my work in 2001. Once more dealing with the difficulty of the medium, the cooking of food, I found myself in a small apartment let loose on how to prepare these specific dishes in another setting. The installation taught me a lot about how people live their lives in various parts of Europe and North America, how they negotiate their day-to-day sustenance, what kitchen implements they consider necessary – for example, at least two places did not have a whisk. And the experience prompted arresting consideration of access to foodstuffs, of what passes for "normal" in food preparation, of the different types and levels of skill in preserving, preparation, cooking, and presentation of food.

The written materials informing chapter 2 were a struggle. I wrote initial drafts that informed some of the ideas for a conference presentation that emerged from the meeting of the German Association for Canadian Studies in Beilingries in 1997 (Hunter 1998). My experience of giving the paper was based not on performing it but on showing a videotaped record and speaking to it. The result was unnerving. I discovered that I focused almost entirely on the liberal constraints of political systems rather than on the possibilities in alternatives. I then sat down to write the "alternative" story that focused on the not-yet-said, but once complete I could not place it with a journal. Much of that second work inspired later versions of chapter 2 and other parts of it emerged later in a completely different form (Hunter 2001). I was beginning to understand the value of the performances. They could combine and articulate things that otherwise were elusive. They performed knowledge that was embodied rather than verbal.

3   Learning to Listen

Indigenous Women's Writing in Canada: Presence, Rehearsal, and Performativity

I had moved from knowing that putting aesthetic experiences into boxes got us nowhere – it was an explicit assimilation – to working in like-minded groups of situated knowledge and standpoint epistemology in which we attempted to build vocabularies from the differences we each found. In this process of situated textuality, we were netting together grounds where they had never existed, arresting that moment of work and putting it out into sociocultural structures where occasionally it achieved fit. That fit then went in many different directions, sometimes toward beauty, sometimes toward disruption, sometimes toward representation or the articulation of desire, but many times it simply went unheard, a bothersome tick.

The process of situated textuality, arrest, and fit, led me to understand the political and ethical implications in responsive ethics and the problems of rhetorical drift into assimilation and co-optation. At root, responsive ethics is responding to hegemonic structures and is pulled into the agonistic rhetoric of which Mouffe and Laclau speak so eloquently in *Hegemony and Socialist Strategy*. Recognizing the assimilationist tendencies that are embedded in rhetorical drift, I became anxious about using and exploiting the differences we found in cultures and positionalities not part of the alongside groups I was helping to build: this was yet another process by which we saw "them" as assimilating into our own world.

I was learning that the way situated textuality works with difference was predicated on *making* that difference. The differences we were using to release the energy we needed to net together ground were not there until we made them. The moment of *until* happens when the difference between our self and another person is being made. Because we each make these differences, rather than find differences that are already somehow "there," the differences are about us changing ourselves rather than the people we work with being changed. We know and/or feel these changes in like-minded groups, where collaboration enables us to do this work, so that we change our selves and in the process prompt those around us to make further differences and change their selves.

Further, making a difference between my self and another in my like-minded group was quite separate from making a difference between my self and someone who had not agreed to be part of that group, had no interest in my alongside world, had a standpoint or positionality with a different set toward hegemony from that of my alongside. Yet alongside positions can and do gift toward each other as situated knowledge and African-American feminist philosophy gifted toward each other in the 1980s. I realized that not only did the work of situated textuality have to push the ways of saying from a responsive to an engaged rhetoric but it also had to push the ways of listening from responsive to engaged. The work on saying has much in common with some practices of rehearsal, and the work on listening with some practices of performance. In performance studies the word that signifies these engaged practices is "performativity."

The engaged practice of rehearsal in a group works on making present, on saying what has not been said, by making differences through collaborative action. The making present results from making differences and therefore changing our selves in that moment of until. Though risky and vulnerable, rehearsals provide a safe space for this kind of making, a making that redefines concepts of friendship. However, performance changes the basis of those participating because performance makes public. It can do so in many different ways, with strategies that tend to delineate the modes of participation. For example, in performance the performer makes present by materializing the differences they set in motion from the text through their body – "text" here refers, as does "textuality," to any medium with a practice. The audience, which has been invited to participate in this making, may work on engaging with that presence in the process of perfomativity and make difference across positionalities. The process sets in train a series of possible makings of difference/making present between and among audience members and performers, in which they are gifting each other with the possibility of self-change. There is no elegant word for this, but it is bound up in performing and audiencing at the same time. The second example is more straightforward because it mimics a public understanding of performance as a place/time where the audience works on responsive listening that focuses on getting a moment of presence, an unsaid, into fit.

In rehearsal, the ongoing process of making different and making present at the moment of until occurs in a defined time and space of situating that builds the grounds for an alongside position. When the process happens in performance, there are choices, such as working on self-awareness and difference or on cultural fit. What is interesting is that the work on self-awareness produces long-term systemic change, while the work on cultural fit, which is vital in the short term for erupting into hegemonic structures, is liable to co-optation into representation.

1 Trying Not to Be a Tragic Subject: From *Alongside* to *Nothing* and *Until*

Alongside: the unsaid is made in the making of difference which is an unending process of making present.
Nothing: the not-said cannot be said and what is said is nothing.
Until: what has not been said is made present, and then we have a choice.

1.1 *Trying Not to Be a Tragic Subject*
In the excitement of articulating the alongside worlds of situated knowledge and experiencing the process of situated textuality that we brought to the writings from our own past training as readers, we, or rather I, had forgotten that not all alongside worlds have the same relation to hegemonic power. One problem has been that theorists of textuality have been concerned to study the process of interaction that comes from communities of art-makers working for and with those in privileged positions. Hence, for much textual study, interaction has been with a self-evident place – what Lacan delineated as the "imaginary" or what discourse studies have called "desire." The difference with situated textuality is that the unsaid is not repressed but simply not known by hegemonic structures. The imaginary may challenge the kind of hegemony that operates, but the situated puts its existence to one side. Because much critical work is blind to diverse alongsides, it does not push the radical action of situated textuality to break the hermetic seals on liberal universalism.

My first reaction to this coercive field was to embrace alongsides as a good thing and treat them as if they could all communicate with each other. In this my theorizing was similar to relational aesthetics and involved me in the kind of responsive ethics outlined in the previous chapter. The limitations of this approach are brought home in a paper I wrote for a conference on autobiography in 1995.[1] One of the compelling factors in situated knowledge is mess, and a striking generic feature of much noncanonical life-writing, whether it is auto(bio)graphy, diary, letters, or anecdote, is the appearance of lack of structure. This often marks a moment/space of failing to listen. I had begun to realize that just as tragedy was inappropriate for people not included in the hegemonic system, so too was joy. That joy in common ground that I felt I had experienced while working on writing, that claim to read the text as a friend who suddenly shares common ground, a concrete other, a second person, was yet another pressure on the text, and as yet I had no sense of how to frame this ethically.

I turned instead to a much more complex notion of commonality: the far greater difficulty of comprehending the subtle complexities of what keeps an individual life going. The text of the paper on auto(bio)graphy began:

Dear Marta,
  Herewith my abstract for your conference. Hope it's not too abstruse.

Lynette

Dear Marta,
  Yes I know I promised a paper on nomad literature but that was two years ago over a bottle of wine – besides it's a little too close to the bone. What I really had in mind was how to sort out an anecdote my friend Hilary told be about someone researching domestic violence in South Africa who couldn't wait to get away from the anti-apartheid celebrations, and how the voices on the domestic violence side which sometimes come through in literary work are so important but so "un-literary" that no one pays any attention, no one hears them. I suspect it has something to do with jettisoning post-Cartesian aesthetics.

Love to the twins,

Lynette

Marta
  of course I'm not going to talk about S. Africa.   L.

Dear Marta,
  Sorry abt the one-liner you got yesterday. I've decided to talk abt Lee Maracle's work. The big problem is how to talk abt vulnerability

without putting it away in a box – we've all had to become such highly skilled analytical rationalists that we could define anything into or out of existence. I think I'll have to start off with some conversational rhetoric – I'm obsessive abt topical logical at the moment. But I thought I'd better check it out with you first just to make sure it doesn't offend anyone. It really comes out of all this VE-day material we're being bombarded with but it's something one of the women in the wholefood group told me about a street party they'd had. She was deeply sweetly into it and showed us all the pictures with children and "old ladies" who had lived through the war and my generation with the folk guitars & her own generation – ten years younger. The media was targeted precisely on people her age, and we've endured weeks of VE-day as a "celebration of joy" which she's been stepping back into as if it's an old sepia photograph, a vicarious war for those who've never had one because the Falklands was too far away and there's a communications blackout erasing Ireland. She said that one of the "old ladies" – her words not mine – sang popular war songs like "Hitler has only got one ball" and all the children joined in – much to her shock, but I remember Alexander singing it with Thatcher's name in the key position a few years back, must be a popular playground song.

But what struck me abt all this celebration was what my friend Hilary said abt VE-day, all those people in the street in 45. She said *she* remembered not joy but a peculiar combination of relief and grief – and no one was telling *this* story. Maybe it's too difficult to talk about. We can tell stories about tragedy and joy but not about the other complicated stuff. I had several relatives who died in the war, I guess lots of people did, Allied & Axis: England & Germany: England and France: Canada and France: France and France – that gets complicated. A series of tragic stories – but there aren't any particular stories about the human remainders, the people who remained alive. It's difficult to talk about the day to day.

I thought if I told a story like this at the start of the paper it would pay respect to Maracle's work on the daily – I'll bring along the photos and try to be vulnerable. What do you think?

Lynette

The paper continued:

I would like to try to begin with a question several critics have raised with regard to Lee Maracle's work: Why is it that writing which, to many readers, is sloppily written and not very good is given so much cultural and critical attention?[2] The question is implicit if not explicit in critical readings of the growing number of texts that have been published through the multicultural program that has resulted, since the 1960s, from Canada's intellectual commitment to the encouragement of cultural definition. Some people have even said that too much gets published. The writings by Maracle on which I want to focus are *I Am Woman* and *Sojourner's Truth*.[3] A traditionally trained reader can pick up either and find lapses in convention on almost any page. For example, early in *I Am Woman* the narrator says:

> Cj asked me to read. I doubt very much if she knew how hard that was going to be for me. She and my partner were the only ones who knew that I wrote poetry: everyone else thought of me as a political essayist and occasional short story writer. I have said things that I now have to live with. I have told the world my private aspirations, my dreams and the pain of my resistance. I lay myself at everyone's feet. I have very little self left that is private. (9)

The insistent repetition of "I" at the start of each syntactically simple sentence is likely to grate on a sophisticated reader and is oddly placed within a double focus of narcissism and sententiousness. The preceding paragraph alternates between "I" sentences and the flat assertiveness of statement: "Part of being colonised is the need to remain invisible. They erase you, and you want to stay that way. Being a writer is getting up there and writing oneself onto everyone's blackboard" (9). The statements offer important commentary on the relationship of colonizer and colonized, on the positions for speech and writing within colonization and their relevance to the perceived dichotomy of private and public communication, yet they may be dismissed because of an apparent loss of control over register.

Another example, picked at random from the end of the chapter "I Am Woman," engages with a topic central to women's studies: the way in which within many societies women learn to hate each other. Maracle overlays this topic with questions of race, intensifying the ambivalence of any analysis:

> We have done enough to help Europeans wipe us off the face of the earth. Everyday we trade our treasured women friends for the men in our lives. We even trade our sisters. Let Wounded Knee be the last time they erased us from the world of the living. Let us all blossom beautiful and productive. (22)

Yet the prose is littered with collective pronouns into which readers may resist being collected. Each sentence has a commonplace topic tending toward cliché as in "wipe us off the face of the earth," with the final sentence ending on the arguably inappropriate lyricism of the word "blossom" used as a verb. The ambivalence of analysis can be obscured by what could be read as naive excessiveness. Similarly, Maracle's narrator of the chapter "My Love" takes on one of the issues at the heart of Western metaphysics, how to love without reward, in the following passage:

> Somewhere along the road I must have taken on the settler women's attitude, for I knew not how to love. Part of me craved your undivided attention, your absolute devotion. I sought to free you; to free myself from this self-seeking madness.
> I am torn apart and terrorized, not by you, my love, but by the war waging inside me. A new torment grips me for I know the battle will grow in intensity, until my desire to love you without reward wins. As the war grows, so grows my madness. (38)

At the same time as it considers an issue that has been discussed from Plato to Arendt, the text is structured by religious sentiment with distinct echoes of the Christian liturgy, which could be read as crude modulations of a subtle discourse. A final example, taken arbitrarily from this work, is the direct and outspoken voicing of a key to the problem of racial exploitation of First Nations peoples in "Pork Chops and Apple Sauce":

> It [the land] was wrested from us by force and since conquest (not "contact'), they have built a system of lawless pillage and plunder of the earth and its people on the graves of our ancestors. Everytime I say that people jump and cry "what are you going to do with all these white people, send them back to Europe, drive them into the sea, put them on reservations?" (154)

Here, once again, the centrality of a problem which is often an unspoken fear can be overwhelmed by the hyperbole of propagandic vocabulary, even if it is contained within the recognized device of "scare quotes."

Much of *Sojourner's Truth* is open to similar judgments of stylistic excess and apparent lack of experience. "Polka Partners" opens with the mixed register of the "petulant youth" ambling downtown and, more colloquially, "the skids of white folks" (80), "The colour of earth death," and the "earth's last supper" side by side with the slang of "It seemed a little hokey to take a bus across the bridge and haul ass through nature's bounty." Later the narrator "thoughtlessly scolded the purveyor of the passed-out man's purse before I relieved him of his catch" offering archly formal syntax paired with the conversational diction that immediately follows when she "geared up my mouth" and peeked at "a whack of cash" (81). Despite the immense regularity of such register contrasts, many readers only note the initial jarring of convention. Just so, the constructed grammatical confusion that arises over the pronoun "he" during the retelling of the story about a mugging (82) is strategic so that the mugged and mugger are mixed up and our stereotypes of which would be the Native person are called upon. Is this conscious device or carelessness? The sharp inappropriateness of lyric in, for example, the description of spring with "spiky slivers of earth-milk squeezed from her voluptuous breasts streaked across my face" (85–6) placed alongside the dingy streets, underlines the juxtaposition of sublime and banal, yet is it bathos or pathos? Readers have a choice.

The way in which these examples are often read indicates that what is being done with the words as signifiers is different from what they convey. The text makes highly radical comments but maintains a stylistic status quo, using sentimentalism, cliché, inappropriate lyricism, excessive repetition: there is altogether too much *bios* in this autobiography. The contradictions resonate strongly with issues raised around other similar writing concerned with bringing the personal and political together from Mary Shelley to George Orwell, not to mention the entire field of recent women's writing addressed to personal/political theory. And, as with those writers, the literary criticism is left with a series of questions to address. The following set marks the conceptual terrain with which I wish to engage.

1 Should "bad" writing get published?
2 Should we value a text for its content when it is "badly" written?
3 Should we teach "bad" writing just because it is the only available writing from socially marginalized groups?
4 Should we allow our political correctness to determine literary availability or should we use aesthetic standards?
5 And more immediate and personal: why are we so embarrassed by certain texts that we call them "bad"?

Of course, the key word in these questions is "bad," which indicates aesthetic judgment, and all judgment proceeds from sites of power. What I would like to do now is question aesthetic power in a rather different way to the way we normally question it.

1.2   Object Positions and Positionalities

Most studies of power deal with it either as a *cause* of domination (theories of ideology) or in terms if its *effects* (theories of discourse) (e.g., Diamond and Quinby, Ramazonglu). Both approaches first assume that power has a specific formation and location, and then focus either on what power does or on how we experience/feel it. Yet instead of working from the premise that power determines individual action, we could ask: how and why do individuals agree to particular locations for power, to recognize them as such, and in the repetition of that recognition, to legitimize that power? This approach deals with issues of legitimation in the representative democracies of the modern Western world, particularly with the effects of the enfranchisement of populations in Europe and North America early in the twentieth century.[4] With that enfranchisement, strategies for the legitimation of power which had been in place since the classical period have had to change,[5] yet theories of ideology and discourse have operated as though these strategies are still effective. Situated knowledge, in advanced standpoint theory, offers an alternative approach because it works from positions outwith hegemony which can see the limitations of ruling power. Even Foucauldian counter-discourses have, in their specificity, separated off the material complexity of struggle, dispersed conflict, and been left complicit in ruling ideology (MacDonnell). Standpoint theory has no drive "to produce total theory, but there is an intimate experience of boundaries, their construction and deconstruction" (Haraway 1984). Standpoint approaches could be said to be materialist discourse theory that historicizes agency by locating its limitations and its enablements within the messy details of our lives (Apetheker, Code et al., Rose 1994, Smith 1987, 1990).

Traditional aesthetic power draws on art-producing conventions that have aggregated around very small communities of like-minded people. With an enfranchised population made up of many groups and many different interests, both the mode of legitimation and its resulting judgments are called into question. Many art-makings are made in a medium not perceived to be suitable – for example, knitting – or by people not suitable to make them – carving by labourers. "Artistic" work can be a production that recalls unrepresented practical knowledge that individuals have learned, in a social medium which allows communal recognition and assessment of the grounds of that knowledge. But there is also work that recalls practical activity and common ground that lies outwith the relations of ruling ideology and its subjects. On traditional aesthetic grounds, this art-making can only enter recognition as Art by assuming and working in relation to allowable subject positions – and curious things have happened. For example, those outside the ruling power are not permitted the classical comedic, possibly because comedy presupposes a shared social group. On the other hand, they are permitted farce, melodrama, and among others, fame – which may be the comic mode of the excluded. More serious, and generically the most valuable mode by conventional aesthetic standards, tragedy is permitted by ruling ideology:[6] many of its "excluded" may participate and are encouraged to participate as tragic subjects.[7]

Traditional aesthetics does not have an appropriate set of approaches for valuing work that presents life outwith the ruling set, particularly work from writers who refuse the tragic. I think it is important that we should try to think of other ways of reading, of recognizing and legitimating value in the written from diverse groups. On the one hand, it is completely possible, using an aesthetic of power and the discourses and positions allowed within that aesthetic, to justify readings of Maracle's writing. I can go back to any of the earlier examples, or any other nodes of critical discomfort, and read, for example, the narcissistic sentential waver as a personal/political double focus. The waver is certainly an effective oral performance technique and Maracle is a highly successful performer, but I could argue that if you go to the text with these rhetorical strategies which are common to other personal/political texts in mind, then the writing also succeeds as a printed text. I can read much of *I Am Woman* and *Sojourner's Truth* within the structures of gender studies and race studies, as elaborations of positions for resistance in current post-Foucauldian discourse (Butler, Kristeva, Woolf). I can read, for example, "Polka Partners" as skilful manoeuvring of literary device, deployment of register, grammar, and narrative in sophisticated dislocation. Each reading would provide justification, get rid of embarrassment and discomfort. Each would allow the reader a sense of making sense. Yet at the same time, each would continue to work within hegemonic structures even as a counter-discourse. None would require us to look at how and why we have agreed to the criteria for justification, so all would be appropriations into our own legitimating system.

This kind of justification is something that at times has to be done as a political act, but I would question its effectiveness in all cases, even in the long term. I wonder whether we shouldn't ask rather different questions, so that we can negotiate with the text on its own terms as well as our own (Code 1988, 197). Here standpoint theory can be helpful because it asks us to work outside the ideology/subject axis and the shuttle between discourse and subjectivity, as the locus of ruling power, and to work with the text, to negotiate an assessment of common grounds that might provide a basis for agreement. Standpoint offers different strategies for knowing the real, agreeing about common ground, repeating, recognizing, and legitimating that knowledge. For writing and reading, standpoint asks us to engage specifically with the field of relations between language and epistemology. As we repeat those agreements about common grounds – in our writing, our teaching, our conversations with others – and recognize those grounds elsewhere, they may acquire stability and become legitimating factors. It is, to an extent, to accept the text as a human construct, necessarily messy, to attempt to be its friend. It does not mean that after this work we can say: this is a "good" text or this is a "bad" text: but that we may have located areas where we, both reader and writer, can agree and disagree about common grounds. Life-writings, diaries, journals, letters, personal anecdotes are fruitful texts for learning about such negotiation because they don't structure the messy into neat packages, they don't evade the messy.

As articulated by Canadian philosophers and social policy theorists such as Lorraine Code and Dorothy Smith, and other international writers, standpoint theory allows one to question power from the standpoint of positions outwith ruling power, to think about how power is negotiated and effected not only within governing institutions but also in many other locations. For example, it would enable us to read *I Am Woman* recognizing the position of a Native Canadian writer from a group of peoples who did not receive the vote until 1961, who were not classified as "human" until 1961. Many Native writers working in the 1990s will remember quite clearly a time when their community had no legitimate position within the discourses of state and society. As a strategy appropriate to a specific position, where a white reader may find herself negotiating the value of clichés as opposed to lyric in First Nations political propaganda, standpoint can come close to offering new representations for subject positions, newly allowable objectivities. Indeed, it has been criticized for its apparent exacerbation of difference to the point of isolating one marginalized group from another.[8]

Yet standpoint's insistence on material detail gives it a rhetorical slant that encourages a reading across position, in search of common ground. With one aspect of Maracle's writing, for example, we are encouraged to look at the attempts at agency from those who, even with the vote and supposed access to political power, are still effectively disenfranchised. For a European, where the consciousness of continued disempowerment despite the franchise exploded in 1968 into the enervation of the 1970s most commonly presented by ahistorical postmodernism, this chronologically contemporaneous thrashing out of agency of the part of the First Nations peoples asks us to change our grounds, to learn from the text about strategies for constructing sites of power to change our lives. The "sentimental" may need to be reassessed as just such a helpful device. What this contemporaneity does for a Canadian caught in the contradiction of simultaneous national consciousness in 1967 and the consciousness of disenfranchisement that occurred throughout the west in 1968 must be something different – probably more difficult.

Texts such as those by Lee Maracle are precisely not concerned to fit the allowable representations and representative forms and structures. They can lead traditional readers, as most readers are by virtue of education, to engage with them and other texts not as subjects, but in Canadian philosopher Lorraine Code's words, as "friends" (Code et al. 1991). I would like to finish with two observations. First, Liz Stanley, who works on working-class women's autobiographies in England, reminds us that feminists, men or women, still do not write about autobiography in a feminist way, even though they are eager when reading Woolf, Cixous, Wollstonecraft, or working-class women's texts, to talk about those as feminist writing (Stanley, Walby). Second, I suspect that in this kind of negotiation, a lot of work on language and writing goes on before it more or less self-consciously enters the field of conventional literary judgment. Those writings that do not enter that field are doing so for a reason, reasons that we need to learn to recognize, negotiate, and value.

2   Critique

2.1   Positionality and Different "Sets Toward" Hegemony

There are fundamental issues here for thinking through those elements in Western society that are alongside. One of the first is that a "friend" is someone with shared common grounds. Another is that if responsive ethical interaction with the public, with institutional structures, requires co-optation, then the alongside is no longer alongside but assimilated. Assimilation by definition means that the values of situated knowledge have become part of subjectivity, rather than retaining their positionality outwith the state. Commenting on the relevance of black feminist epistemology in 1990, Patricia Hill Collins extends personal materiality into positioning – that standpoint contribution to situated knowledge – when she insists that a standpoint position not only clarifies the "objective truth" for a particular group but can also insist on its probability rather than its completeness. She observes that "Each group speaks from its own standpoint and shares its own partial, situated knowledge. But because each group perceives its own truth as partial, its knowledge is unfinished" (236). Credibility derives from the "owning" of position rather than its erasure.

The conditions that allow situated knowledge communities to position themselves outwith hegemonic structures involve recognition of the concrete or second-person other, hence empathy for them, and an ethics based in a responsive process that respects difference. As noted in the previous chapter, "process" is supposedly sustained by textual strategies from the arts. In the preceding critique of the work "Cooking the Books: I Am a Very Dirty Critic," I problematize this claim, pointing out that textual strategies cannot guarantee process, partly because of the rhetorical drift toward public action and assimilation. I also posit "presence" as the engaged stance (not strategy) that defines situated textuality: an ongoing process of interaction whose moment of arrest may be agential at the moment of arrest but which has to be put back into process again or cease to delineate the alongside.

After "Cooking the Books" I came to understand that we do not simply recognize difference, either respecting or abhorring it. We make it. Recognition of the differences we are making happens in the moment or time/space of *until*. Difference does not exist until we put it into existence. Yes, we can treat another person as a concrete other, but another way of casting this is to say that we only treat them that way when we make the difference between us. In responsive ethics, respect for difference that is already there involves empathy, but in engaged ethics, when we *make* difference, we know that empathy is irrelevant to the person we have made different. One corollary is that because we know that we make this difference, we can feel the effect of that making on ourselves. That feeling or affect is our guide to valuing what we have done, and when we have been able to value the making of difference, it changes our set toward the world and interaction with it.

Not only do we make difference in learning how to say the unsaid, but we make difference in learning how to listen to it. The previous chapter worked in detail on people in a shared positionality, or alongside, that they were trying to say. However, if we turn to other positionalities to make differences we can use in our own alongside, it raises questions of exploitation and once more of assimilation. What are the ethics that could make my work on and readings of the alongside of Western, primarily white, women different from my work on and readings of the writing by First Nations women in Canada? Systemically, each has a completely different set toward ideological structures that leads to a different rhetorical stance. I began to work on how to listen.

What is missing from the opening study of Lee Maracle's work and the value of an alongside position is a sustained attempt to articulate the position that whiteness gives me and to recognize the range of different positions that alongside could generate with respect to hegemony. At the time, I had read commentaries, including that of Jeanne Perreault, who draws from the autography of Adrienne Rich's writing the understanding that "Whiteness ... is not merely a fact, but a stand." I was familiar with the way Patricia Hill Collins, working from white scholar Peggy McIntosh, extended the idea into the claim that whites are taught not to recognize white privilege (Collins 1990, 190), "white" being both a colour and a class. But I had not reached the point where I realized that whiteness *is* class, not just "a" class, and positioning *as* white necessitates understanding that colour and poverty are imbricated in class only in that their existence as commodities rather than living beings is what makes class possible. In other words, alongsides can have varying degrees and various kinds of alterity that define their set toward hegemony. Situated knowledge theory pays little attention to the privileges of various positions such as colour, employment, or ability, but focuses on the detail of those deprived of those privileges. Partial epistemologies advocated by Hill Collins are founded on precisely the detail of those positions, and she makes no apologies for articulating a knowledge through a textuality that cannot be understood by people not in that position.

What is also missing from the study of Lee Maracle's work is any attempt to critique and/or read the texts "from the standpoint" of First Nations readers/writers. I would like to think that this was a self-conscious strategy to foreground the impossibility of doing so, but in effect that absence was an unselfconscious admission that I could not do so. Nevertheless, the ellipsis signals a moment that I call *nothing*, one of the many possible aporias of the moment of until. Nothing is a point at which, although you sense that there is an alongside beside you, you cannot recognize what it is. In that not-recognizing you make that alongside different from yourself, and in doing so you engage in an action that makes your self different from before. But the action has no immediate tangible effect on the alongside you have made different. The action is an ethical action that does not require empathy, nor does it attempt to call the alongside your "friend." It is a stance that clarifies your positionality with respect to the alongside by resisting the claim to identity, or even appreciation of standpoint.

The moment of making a difference that makes present the *aporia* of nothing is some thing that for a white person cuts away the basis of all common grounds, not only of those potentially between separate and partial alongsides, but precisely all self-evident structures that make possible "white." In the case of engaging texts from cultures systemically excised from the Western society that excises my self in different ways and hence generates a different set toward that hegemony, it is only by creating that moment of nothing that the difference that is made can change us and in that change generate value.

Recent Afropessimist philosophy presents a strong critique of the position that depends on a plethora of alongsides and fails to distinguish among the various sets toward the state that they make. This philosophical/critical approach points out that the "singular achievement" of social contract liberalism was to base the controlled aggression of capitalism on the assumption that certain bodies could be designated as non-human and justifiably exploited, tortured, terrorized, and killed. This is one element that distinguishes Afropessimism sharply from feminist philosophy, making the two incomparable since feminism may use the deaths of women as a critique of the state but is not addressing an attempt of the state to kill all women.

At the time I wrote the paper on Lee Maracle's writing I was not familiar with the unfolding philosophical field of writers such as David Marriott, Jared Sexton, Saidya Hartmann, Frank Wilderson, and more recently Kara Keeling. Wilderson puts the Afropessimist argument clearly in the article "Gramsci's Black Marx: Whither the Slave in Civil Society?" (2005). In a critique of Gramscian Marxism, Wilderson demonstrates that its aim is to precipitate a crisis in the state so that all workers have equal access to the labour needed, quoting Buttigieg, to participate in "consensual" society, "wherein no individual or group is reduced to a subaltern" (5). However, the black person's body has to remain commodified to guarantee the possibility of that consensual labour.

As Wilderson points out, Gramsci takes on capital but not white supremacy. The subaltern worker is kept in wage-slavery by rhetoric, but the black body is organized by force. In searing prosody, Wilderson says:

> violence towards the Black body is the precondition for the existence
> of Gramsci's single entity "the modern bourgeois-state" with its
> divided apparatus, political society and civil society. This is to say
> violence against Black people is ontological and gratuitous as opposed
> to ideological and contingent ... Black death is the modern bourgeois-
> state's recreational pastime, but the hunting season is not confined
> to the time (and place) of political society; Blacks are fair game as a
> result of a progressively expanding civil society as well. (2005, 5)

Gramsci is concerned only with the exploitation of labour and the materialization of position outwith class capital that will give equity to labourers. But as Wilderson notes, Afropessimist theorists have explored the exploitation of the libidinal economy of slavery to mark the radical separation of the condition of the black body from that of the worker, and underline the inadequacy of Gramscian Marxism to any theorizing of black existence outwith the civic state (7).

The critiques made by Afropessimists lead Wilderson to discuss a further issue central to the critique of situated knowledge: that this condition of the black subject means that the Afroamerican experience has a "grammar of suffering not only in excess of any semiotics of exploitation, but a grammar of suffering beyond signification itself" (2005, 6). The significance of this is that there is no way that the radical alongside of black lives can be articulated within liberal society, or even become disruptively emergent into it, because doing so would by definition make public, make it possible to hear, that the grounds of capital are dependent on the eradication of the black body, and this cannot be said. The black body is, "a scandal to its [hegemony's] assumptive, foundational logic." Wilderson concludes that "It is this scandal which places black subjectivity in a structurally impossible position, outside of the "natural" articulations of hegemony; but it also places hegemony in a structurally impossible position because our presence works back upon the grammar of hegemony and threatens it with incoherence" (14).

Significantly, it is the "presence" of the black body that may "work back" and "threaten" hegemony. The elements in textuality of performativity, a process of making that can through presence be felt, be engaged with, is the central activity of making difference even if that making results in the presence of *nothing*. This sense of situated textuality in performativity takes its stance out of the process of making difference within an alongside group of people with a common positionality, and into a process of making difference between that alongside and another made up of people with alternative positionalities or sets toward the state. I distinguish between the two by way of the concepts of rehearsal and performance.

2.2 Making the Difference Differently

Situated textuality brings together work on articulating knowledge with process-based strategies and the concept of advanced standpoint – that the work takes place in alongsides with different sets toward hegemonic structures – and adds the recognition that difference is something we make. This last move takes situated textuality into a foregrounded realm of stance that considers not only the maker and the text, but the audience as well. The stance of responsive ethics deals only implicitly with the audience, which is one reason that it fails to notice the different sets toward hegemony generated by the different alongsides. But when stance becomes foregrounded, it moves into what I am calling an engaged ethics. Engagement signifies a particular kind of stance that in the literary world is called allegorical and in performance studies is one of the significations of "performativity."

Performativity refers here to the work of both rehearsal and performance. In rehearsal, a group is formed with some shared common grounds, however tenuous. This group works on making present by making differences. The process takes place within a time/space of situating that redefines friendship as collaborative action that enables us to make differences among and between us, differences that net together and form non-hegemonic alongsides. Derrida speaks in *On Friendship* of the space of death as the place where we can for the only time know the friend because friendship defines the process of change of our self that initiates a presence that enables the other person also to engage and make difference that changes the self that initiates a presence ... This process is the basis of friendship in locations of situated textuality, and in texts made public it is what I am here calling performativity.

Performance, which is open to performativity and other stances, includes an audience that does not necessarily share common grounds. Engagement works across alongsides as the performer's presence enables the audience to make difference from other positionalities, other sets toward hegemony. The process is one of gifting, giving the audience members the choice of making difference and changing their selves with respect to the presence performed. Yet this change will necessarily also make present, and enable the performer and other audience members to engage, continuing each process until the moment of until, and because engaged work is so strenuous, there is usually a moment of ar(rest) at some point in the performative interaction. Performance does not necessarily lead to this engaged sense of audiencing that ar(rests) in particular moments and pushes the situated into fit. It can also lead to the assimilative gesture that halts the presence of difference and contains it into cultural satisfaction. Each audience member has a choice about this. As noted earlier, the work on self-awareness that happens in engaged ethics produces a long-term systemic shift, while the work on cultural change, vital to the short term, is more liable to co-optation through rhetorical drift.[9]

Situated textuality is fundamentally concerned to build alongside structures. In other words, it works alongside systemic strategies of evasion and repression, but more importantly builds alongside locations for elements completely unrecognized by hegemony. Nevertheless, it is inf(l)ected by the hegemonic systems in which it plays. Engagement can work differently depending on the kinds of "set toward" hegemony held by the maker and/or audience that systemically inf(l)ect the alongside work they do. Those sets toward may be contextually similar, as with my readings of Atwood, Laurence, and Munro, who occupy hegemonic positions not unlike my own. They may be contextually overlapping, as in the case of the feminist writers from various communities of colour, gender, and class. And they may be only partially contingent or radically separate as with my readings of writing from Native American ethnicities, and from positions of poverty, terror, and survivor experience.

In each case, we make difference, but we make it differently. Engaged rhetoric is part of the process of becoming present. It is not a collective action that aims toward a specific goal, but a collaborative making that remains sensitive to/opens the senses to the interaction of people within an environment, to the ecological nuances that shift with every breath, to the varied etymologies and grammars with which we build our languages whether in a visual, verbal, movement, musical, digital, or other media. The process becomes a contemporary mode of mimesis in which we rehearse a text through the body/medium and produce material difference. Situated textuality is a rhetorical stance that is primarily concerned with the non-systemic communication that can happen in the presencing of performativity. However, our participation in it is inflected by the systemic sets toward hegemony that make possible and disseminate the medium we choose.

Collaboration is the process of valuing the differences we make when working with other people. If these differences require less rather than more change in our selves, then there is often a sense of shared labour on making new grounds for communication and living. The more change required to the self, the more difficult it is to net together grounds. My reading of *Life Lived Like a Story* by women elders in the Yukon taught me that the experience I initially felt while reading was so radical that I couldn't begin to construct grounds for communication. The process was a clue to the radical alterity of the alongside I was engaging. If the texts had been systemically fitting, I, as part of the white definition of that system, would have been able to disrupt enough, to unknit/unknot the fit, and push the text, situate the textuality, making new differences, until it re-made grounds that would either have faded or erupted into culture once again. If the text had been part of an alongside world of say, white women, I would have been able to focus on the process of recognizing a common ground, making the differences that generate change and sustain the alterity of that alongside. If the text were, as

I felt it, part of an alongside world in which I could recognize no common grounds, it was as if there were no traction, no point of focus that would allow me to make difference. I had to learn to listen for the dissonances that would help me to recognize points where I could make difference.

The alongside of First Nations and Inuit culture is not monolithic. Yet for many indigenous peoples in Canada, as for many Native Americans in the United States, the underlying base of contemporary existence is that most indigenous land is now owned by private people and corporations rather than by the Peoples. The capitalist system of Canadian economics is founded not only on the doublethink of liberal states in which people are encouraged to make profit but must realize simultaneously that not all people can do so but also on the more radical erasure of the possibility that the state exists because of the genocide of indigenous peoples. There is nothing that I can do in my reading of Lee Maracle's work to change this, although if I were to be writing the essay again I would go further and explore the sense in her statement that "Had I continued school long enough and taken enough European creative writing courses I would know what all the metaphors are and would be able to match metaphor to subject. I didn't, not because I doubted I could grasp the elements of story and turn them to my account, but because I would have lost myself in the transliteration of our story to European story" (Maracle, 1991, 11).

Or spend more time thinking of Janice Acoose's interest in "why we have to bring the 'colonial' into our relationships with each other? I believe that we have the resources and capacities within our culture and territories to work out relationships with each other. In ceremonial spaces here in this land Nêhiyawak, Nahkawè, Dakota, Nakota, and Dene peoples gather together frequently. Perhaps as crtics we might learn something from these shared ceremonial spaces" (Acoose 2008, 218).

2.3 Gifting

My work on making different within the alongside worlds of white middle class people like me is an activity that feels removed from making different within the alongside worlds of other groups of people from class, colour, and ability backgrounds of which I have little experience. Each person is made "different" but there are major rifts between lives that grow up with different ethnicities, different genders, dependent on the set toward systemic structures. Nevertheless, writers who publish in an accessible press are making gifts of performance with the potential to engage in presencing. On entering into public circulation, there is a tacit agreement that someone not in the partial positioning of that particular alongside might read the book. That reading could be culturally eruptive, exploitative, or consuming, or it could be engaged within its own positionality. The performance becomes a gift that we can take up in many different ways, if we enter an engaged ethical activity pushing at the places where we can no longer recognize, the moments of until; we can make it and our selves different.

I learned about some of this gifting from a community of Elder women storytellers in Nunavut in Canada. To become part of the alongside world delineated by storytelling-as-social-change, so foreign in view of the Western dismissal of anecdotal wisdom, I had to learn to engage with quite different textuality, and to learn to engage I had to be invited into the process. Peter Kulchyski, who had organized a long-running program in Panniqtuuq that introduced southern students to Inuk culture, was kind enough to speak on my behalf to several women Elders and arrange for me to meet with them. He also introduced me to Leesee Karpik who was the translator, and Ms Karpik was key to setting the ambiance and relaxation that released many of the discussions.

I had to learn to listen. The elders I spoke to on my research visit in 2000 included Elisapee Ishulutak, Martha Kanayuk, and Evie Aniniliak.[10] They taught me how to listen by telling me stories about how to tell stories. When I asked them how they had learned to tell stories they each, individually, told me stories about learning how to listen. They were never taught "how" but were given the opportunity to hear storytelling. If they could listen well, hear what was not being said about telling, they could make it their own by trying to tell their own stories. Listening is a particular skill, and learning how takes time. Learning that the stories are real takes years. Telling needs a close and attentive group of people around one, and each of the Elders said that storytelling was more effective in "camp" or "on the land" rather than in town. Telling becomes part of the environment, so that different ways of living mean different ways of telling. The listening is part of the telling, and the re-telling makes new stories. Listening becomes a public act, a display of personal responsibility and difference within a particular context of common ground. But if common ground is the main reason that the listener listens in the first place, differences, as Elisapee Ishulutuk notes, are the main point: "it's really interesting when they are having stories [from different camps] … Hearing stories like that, it becomes very interesting" (Interview 1999, 3).

Central to telling and listening is the need to know about the teller. Such locating devices are important because the teller takes responsibility for their text to the extent that if someone acts on their words, the teller must have spoken from experience, else what the listener then does with the story may be based on things that have not happened and may lead them into danger. If listeners are faced with danger or dilemma or disaster as a result of a story based on experience, then at least the teller has been responsible about the telling. Speaking from experience is not relative or arbitrary – it helps create particular common ground and difference because there is no "generalized" knowledge. Inuk traditional knowledge is not fixed because "A balance of experience and innovation is central to the production and transmission of knowledge" (6). This flexibility and openness to change and modification seems to me a strategy made necessary primarily by attentive listening and its process of re-situating in the next telling. Hence, stories do not tell you what to do, but can guide you. They stay with you and you live them differently at different times in your life, sometimes only living a story many years after you have heard it, and only then being able to tell it yourself.

If the point of telling a story is not to command or prove or inform, to a greater or lesser extent depending on the audience, the point is to offer guidance. Because there is no generalized knowledge, no "authority" except the contexts of the speaker and listener, the interpretations are particular to each listener, based both on common ground and on the differences made. This particular way of listening recognizes the listener's joint responsibility with the teller for re-making the story and emphasizes the importance of learning how to listen over many years, although it also allows for the possibility that the listener may not take up this responsibility.[11]

At the centre of most of the interviews was the belief that stories engage an audience, involve them in communal exchange and responsibility which is at the heart of social change woven into engaged ethics. Teller and listener have to work initially from some common ground. Without that common ground the listener would not bother to listen and certainly could not make a story appropriate to their own life. Nor could they assess the experience of the teller, or value the knowledge they were learning. In rhetorical terms though, working from common ground can lead to enclosed mind-sets; it can be used to reinforce the stereotypical and conventional representation. Furthermore, even when common ground is disagreed with, it may simply lead to an oppositional response, an agonistic fight that always leaves either the teller or the listener at a disadvantage or wounded.

What this exploration of storytelling demonstrated to me was that something else was going on: the teller and listener effectively constitute an event where there is a subtle textuality between the context of each. They find common ground, but the textuality also prompts them to make differences and situate their selves in different places. Yet because the differences have been constructed in the course of telling and listening, each learns why the differences are there and how they come about, where they stand in relation to the other person, and that each makes the difference from the other. It is an engaged rhetorical stance that is neither authoritative nor relativist. The storytelling is embedded in a long-term rhetoric that sustains a community with change through the construction and valuing of differences.

I went to Panniqtuuq to make a contribution to understanding political rhetorics in communities new to liberal democracy. I came away having begun to learn about listening from a particular context that did not include me but had invited me into the performance of storytelling.

PERFORMANCE 3
Trying Not to Be a Tragic Subject

WEBLINK http://vimeo.com/18436393

"Trying Not to Be a Tragic Subject: Work by First Nations Writer Lee Maracle"
  1995   Université de Rennes II (France), Conference Autobiographie/
          Autobiography
  1996   University of Nottingham (UK), Conference of the British
          Association for Canadian Studies (Literature)

"Trying Not to Be a Tragic Subject" was performed initially at the Université de Rennes II conference "Autobiographie/Autobiography" organized by Marta Dvorak in 1995. I had known and admired Dr Dvorak for a long time, and knew that several people I respected would also be attending the conference, so I wanted to create what was effectively a "chamber piece." I had no idea that the audience in the room was going to exceed fifty, and had been anticipating a small room with about fifteen in attendance. The conceit around which I built this performance was the sharp distinction between the way people appear in their institutional settings and the way they are in the settings that involve their families and friends.

The piece is simple: it opens with a familiar storytelling as I pass around a bag of boiled sweets (that would have been in sweet shops fifty years earlier – I had brought these in the requisite brown paper bag from England). The persona is the conference-presenter and to that extent formal and predictable: I made sure that I wore clothes different to those I had worn to the previous conference session, but the clothes were acceptably academic. I was and was-not a conference member. Then as the piece moves into analysis and more heavy-duty theorizing, the persona lets down her hair and returns to the conference presenters' table to read the paper. I had considered taking off my shoes, trousers, and underwear before I sat down, since there was no way of seeing this once I was seated. But that moment passed in rehearsal as I recognized its vicarious teasing. There are conflicting and contradictory pulls between the persona and the material being spoken to which I hoped people would respond. In effect, I received virtually no feedback whatsoever. Perhaps the audience was embarrassed. Perhaps they needed more time.

I performed "Trying Not to Be a Tragic Subject" once more in 1996 at the University of Nottingham (the videotape record), at the invitation of Susan Billingham. In this session of the Literature Group of the British Association for Canadian Studies, of which I'd been a member for over a decade, I felt in good company although also quite terrified. The audience was much smaller than that in Rennes, and I had known everyone there for many years. The vulnerability of the persona was for this audience clearly not the vulnerability of "Lynette Hunter," and the responses were both far more critical and far more affective. Comments I received included concern that I was exploiting Lee Maracle's writing, and that the performance had released a deep sexual source for the process of reading. I do not expect the videotape record to convey the latter – I guess you had to have been there.

It's fair to say that to a greater or lesser degree the three initial performances around Canadian writing were experimenting with formal performance strategies and whether they could open up theoretical concepts. The Kroetsch piece was the eye-opener and the following two installations were more tentative, more explicitly drawing on entertainment and the potential of performance to open up received impressions about various aesthetics of writing. It's also fair to say that I felt in control of the pieces, that I had made a place rather than a space for an audience.

The essay written out of the performance (1997) for Marta Dvorak's collection *Autobiographies* (1997) fits conceptually between the two essays I wrote out of the previous performance, "Cooking the Books." Its framed presence in chapter 3 begins with a first attempt at script-performance in the opening address to a fictional "Marta." But the performance's attempt to instigate a disturbance to the surface of academic discourse – not a challenge, not an eruption into culture of another possible fit that might change things, but an undercurrent of improvised movement into a still pool/stable environment – did not emerge in that essay. In chapter 3, that disturbance is opened out a long way into a critique of what I cannot say, never will be able to say, to clear the way for what I began to articulate.

part two

PERFORMATIVITY

INSTALLATION AND CONSTELLATION

Although the liberal humanist social contract had consistently been disrupted for three centuries – often only to join it – challenges over the twentieth century had more obvious manifestations than in earlier years. One of these was the franchise which, as discussed in previous chapters, had the effect of introducing a structure that both called for assimilation and claimed the possibility of difference and change. This is the fundamental doublethink structure of modern liberal democracy, in place since the late sixteenth century. The franchise exposed the doubleness, put into motion events that would gradually break the liberal humanist social contract apart and generate the diversity and disunified communities of the twentieth- and twenty-first centuries.

Situated knowledge, as I argued in part one, is an epistemological approach taking place alongside this doublethink that combines materialism (an acknowledgment of the resistance and unknowable presence of the "real") with a rhetoric of process. I have delineated an understanding of this rhetoric as situated textuality, which not only has strategies for (ar)rest when action needs to be taken but is also a stance that remains alert to the need for a return to process and initiates that return – an awareness characterized by *until*. The rhetorical stance of situated textuality is one key to a disunified aesthetics. Situated work is hard work, demanding on energy and time, and requires that we change our selves in the attempt to "say" – to articulate in any medium, not only the verbal – because we are not isolated from others. Our "self" does not stop with the skin.

The rhetoric of situated work, or situated textuality, is analogous to the rhetoric of allegory in which the artist, audience, and text, in whatever medium, make a particular textuality in the moment, one never to be recovered as an identity, yet enigmatically present in the body forever. The present experience of making that moment possible will never leave the art-maker, and the presence of that moment will never leave the body of the reader/audience/listener. The rhetoric is also analogous to that of performativity – a word, as discussed below, highly variable in performance studies – and the relation of performativity to "presence" opens out both the enigma of allegory and the energy of situated textuality. Part two comprises four chapters, each exploring aspects of performativity and presence both in the work the performers do in rehearsal and in the work they do in performance with the audience.

In the situated textuality of performativity, we engage the activities of installation and constellation. To install is to make present something that has not been present before, a rhetorical stance of performativity. How do we do this? Partly by making difference. Performativity refers here to the work of *installation* in both rehearsal and public performance, and the *constellation* it makes possible. The autographical learning displayed in the sequence of the four chapters of this part tells of my own realization that installation and constellation happen in both rehearsal and performance, with one signal rhetorical difference that returns to the concept of positionality. In rehearsal, a group is formed with some shared common grounds, however tenuous, and even if the common ground is only: that difference will be made. If this group works on installation by making present by making differences, the process of presencing takes place within a time/space, or moment, of situating that redefines friendship as collaborative action. It is action that enables us to make differences among and between us, differences that net together and form non-hegemonic alongside knowledge and value. This process of installation is the basis of performativity in rehearsal or in locations of situated textuality. At the same time, with texts made public, it is the basis of what I am here calling the performativity of performance.

In contrast to rehearsal, performativity in performance engages an audience that does not necessarily share common grounds, whether those grounds have been articulated into alongside values from various sets toward hegemony, or from hegemonic understanding itself. Engagement works across alongsides as the performer's presencing enables the audience to make difference from other positionalities. Yet the process is again one of gifting, giving the audience member that gift of self-gifting, the choice of making difference and changing their self with respect to the presence performed. This change will necessarily also "make present" and enable the performer and other audience members to engage, continuing each process until the moment when we find it impossible even to make difference – or différance, the moment of *until* that addresses *aporia*.

At the same time, constellation happens when collaborators engage with the process of installation and ar(rest) that process. And just as performativity in performance also leads to moments of ar(rest) that address actions that need to be taken, similar processes occur in rehearsal when the engaged work of people in the group finds a moment to coalesce, to make sense from difference.

The rhetorics of both rehearsal and performance are therefore informed by both installation and constellation. The performativity of installation enables a change of our self that initiates a presencing that enables the other person also to engage and make difference that changes the self that initiates a presencing. It is an ongoing process that we experience in the moment. The performativity of constellation arrests the process, articulates the different alternatives that run alongside hegemony and ideology which are realized in the situated textuality (Hunter 1999) of the work. Its articulation can enable further process, or join the representations of the state, or work disruptively/eruptively/resistantly between these two kinds of action.

In public performance, constellation happens when collaborators, often the audience, articulate by putting into cultural fit and circulation the making different/making present of that performance (Hunter 2013), and installation happens in the moment of making the performance.

The ethics of rehearsal are based usually on an agreement to work together on positionality from a mutually recognized set toward hegemony. Yet engaging in performativity in a performance establishes an ethics that allows us to change not others but our self, and across separate positionalities. Empathy is not necessary, and affect is the result of our own choices, not those of someone else. Performance becomes a gifting that we choose to do to our selves. This helps to understand why performers do not "become" the thing they are perceived to perform, because perception is with the audience. It helps to understand why performance is not persuasive in the same way as logic, for it enables choices but does not define what those are. Engaged ethics in performativity is hard work.

As a performer, I interact with the audience, engaging with their responses, their energy. Yet after the performance there is often a sense that that interaction loses its energy, no longer makes present. As an audience member, if a membership at times of one as when reading, I get caught up in particular performances and find myself part of that making-present. The critic in me sometimes goes away to make an essay, or as with many examples in this book, an embodied or en-mediated performance. Part of that process of making difference gifts back to me and through that difference can prompt further performance from others. For example, the production "Bodies in Trouble" that led to chapter 4, written with Susan Rudy, began with a celebration of all those mothers and sisters who have enabled my situated work on women. The celebration generated a performance that in turn generated other performances, for example, the dialogue that forms chapter 4 between Susan Rudy and me, the graphic commentary by Nicole Brossard, and the poem by Daphne Marlatt. There is an initial installation that generates presence, then a process of constellation through which I attempt to articulate the value of that presence, followed by a further installation, necessarily different from the first.

These constellations generate intimate moments of positionality that allow us not to invest in other people's interpretations of our performances. The autographical learning of the first three chapters led me to focus in the four chapters of part two on the work of people roughly "like myself," to put myself in a larger sense in continual contact with the performativity of rehearsal: the site particular, a mutually engaged set toward hegemony.

THE WORK OF REHEARSAL, PERFORMANCE, AND PERFORMATIVITY

The productions that accompany the written essays in part one are displays of situating knowledge that did not explicitly encourage the audience to participate except on formal and controlled grounds such as the eating of food. In part two, the productions are concerned to explore the implications of becoming aware of the audience, and of the audience participating in the production of the artwork. The videoed productions related to three of the four written chapters in this second section are focused on how the involvement of the reader/critic insists on the situating textuality of performativity, and how that plays out within a disunified aesthetics. Situated knowledge is knowledge continually in process that occasionally takes a rest in a moment of need. In other words, it needs to take up a position, or set, toward elements in hegemonic structures that are denying or obstructing or repressing the value of the knowledge being made. As discussed in part one, that ar(rest) may result in cultural co-optation, or in activist intervention, or in the eruption of beauty – or in many other instances of resistance, opposition, partiality, or pessimism. One key for the group producing the knowledge is to know when the efficaciousness of that moment has passed, the moment of until when we have to re-initiate the energy of the process.

As suggested, "situated" knowledge could better be called "situating" knowledge. In the process of situating, the rhetorical elements of the work engaged in come to the fore. In other words, situating not only requires an awareness of the structures and strategies making up the process, but that even before taking up a position, the group and the knowledge they are making has a rhetorical stance within the world. Rhetorical stance asks us to recognize not only those making the knowledge and the knowledge they make but also those who may be included in the communication or performance and the wider ecological context. As such, rhetorical stance also asks us to recognize those who are excluded. This is what the word "textuality" signifies in the phrase "situated textuality."

There is another shift in focus that occurs within these four essays. The writing of an essay on the work of Nicole Brossard led me to understand the separation that I had maintained between me the critic and the writers Kroetsch/Armstrong/Maracle/ and in this part also Frank Davey. The translations of the work of Nicole Brossard developed intensely close readings in which the process of reading and the making of criticism/articulation happen at the same time. The three productions in part one generated stand-alone essays that in a sense had little to do with the performativity of the embodied performance art. The essays that accompany the productions in part two are far more intimately involved in feeding off the art-making and what that process released. In turn, they become more open to reader engagement and deconstruct the authority of both artist and critic with various generic, graphic, and visual media strategies, and the performances become more embodied. My primary medium is the written, typography, and the lay of the page. Working closely with Brossard's text, which writes the body into words, I learned that, for me, the particular site for making rehearsal and performance coalesce into performativity is on the page and in the book.

An approach that can help distinguish between the kind of production associated with part one and that associated with part two comes from work in performance theory emerging in the decade 2000–2010 that questions the rhetorics of site-specific installation. Site-specific work, as outlined by Ilya Noé, began as a challenge to the space of the gallery and a conceptual challenge to the aesthetics of art as a completed object. But over time it became co-opted by that space, and the idea of conceptual installation became co-opted by commercial aesthetics. Noé suggests instead a site particular rhetoric that is always in the moment of the space, making presence and necessarily changing. In a number of ways, this rhetoric is similar to that of storytelling and listening as I experienced it in Panniqtuuq. In performance studies, these concepts are analogous to performance and rehearsal. In a sense, the productions accompanying part one are site specific, and indeed they travelled to many places and were produced many times. Those accompanying part two are more particular to place, have a more porous relationship with the essay, ask for different kinds of reading.

A performance takes place in a specific site, often a theatre or a gallery, sometimes the street, or in a digital medium, or elsewhere. What makes it a performance is that the group performing chooses to make it public, invite the audience to watch. Inasmuch as that group can initiate and maintain the participation of the audience in making presence, the performance will use elements of performativity and the specific site becomes particular. A rehearsal takes place in a particular site, anywhere where the performers can meet and work on the installation of presence. I distinguish here between the two despite theorists such as Grotowski, who argue for live performances to continue the rehearsal from the group into its public, because I would like to suggest that that public invitation changes what can happen with presence. Without that invitation into performance the audience is faced by the silent chasm of *aporia*, with it that chasm becomes present on the grounds determined by the group. The audience can take it or leave it, and so can the art-maker.

Nevertheless, the idea of "presence" is highly contested. Theoreticians working with ritual,[1] or with linguistic "performatives" (Austin 1962, Derrida 1972), or with the ephemerality of "live" performance (Auslander, Foster, Phelan) have been fascinated with the mourning and melancholia of passing experience, of unreliable memory, of the impossibility of documentation. Presence is always something that passes and in that wake is left a profound sense of absence. I would like to offer an alternative view: that the presence experienced in performance makes actual, long-term physiological changes to our bodies, including the imagination and its intellective abilities. Indeed, just as the performer is the medium for a process that never ceases to make presence and profoundly change their self, so the audience (reader/listener/spectator) that engages in that making of presence is also changed. I do not consider it a loss that experience cannot be reproduced. I see nothing to mourn in the impossibility of re-presentation. These are human attributes that make it necessary for us to continue to perform the presencing of experience in the moment. Memory, as many people have recently argued, is not about remembering the past but about re-membering in the present, giving it body, and in so doing, making the future.

In performance studies, the word "performativity" is also in flux (Hunter 2008b). Judith Butler has suggested that it signifies identities constituted iteratively through complex citational practices (1993). Diana Taylor describes the "performatic" as that which mediates between hegemonic discourse and hegemonic agency (2003). By performativity I signify here the making-present of value through art work happening in the moment: this making-present of value necessarily includes making difference. In other words, performativity in this book signifies work alongside the hegemonic. It draws on the energies that circulate within bodies, among bodies, and between bodies and other animate and inanimate elements in the world, and is inflected by but not primarily responsive to the hegemonic.

The performativity of a public performance happens both when the audience re-makes the performance as it happens (installation) and when an audience articulates the making different/making present of the performance (constellation) (Hunter 2013). The performativity of rehearsal happens in the moment of making that difference/presence and in the moments of arrest that gather together significance before moving on. Yet the performativity of constellation in public performance, because it articulates present experience into cultural fit, often has a documentary labour. Indeed, it often has a critical labour because of the way it meets and communicates within sociocultural structures larger than a rehearsal space. The video records of the productions accompanying this book tend to render the performances static because they are simply records rather than video-essays/artmaking, for the simple reason that I do not know how to use this visual medium well. The essays in parts two and three increasingly use the medium of writing, reading, and typography as a place for rehearsal as well as performance because this is my primary sensory craft. They ask the reader to engage with a sensitivity to graphic and visual performance. The commentary on the production that follows each essay attempts to provide some particular context, to document some of the performativity of the performance, for as Derrida points out, a "linguistic performative" is not necessarily going to perform: that depends on the context/materiality of the rhetoric.

The essay (Hunter and Rudy) and production[2] associated with chapter 4, "Bodies in Trouble," are both concerned to provide a location for the particular reader/audience to engage with performance in the moment of its making, to explore its attempts to resist fit by putting the text into process.

It offers a way to think about the coalescence of reader, text, and writer, and reflects on the impossibility of the "writer" being a single fixed thing, and the work of the reader interconnecting with the "writer" to make things. The production avoids any written script because it tries to go somewhere where the body might get played. It is still embedded into the housework, hard work, labour of women that wipes out awareness with tiredness, puts women into the box. But the performance of doing it takes us right out of the box partly because the audience is a like-minded group engaged in rehearsal and making present. Just so the "essay" is a dialogue of tracks that occasionally intersect, and although presented as such on the page to emphasize their differences, the dialogue rarely runs parallel. As noted in the commentary that follows the essay, this performance resulted in distinct responses from the audience, some of which are collaged into that commentary. They do not explain it but they do document it.

The second essay (Hunter 2003) in part two, "FACE-WORK," relates to a production[3] responding to the poetry of Frank Davey. Both the essay and the production are working through discursive paradigms of performance available to a woman who is a reader/critic dealing with cultural elements of masculinity, class, and death, and alternative paradigms that allow for engaging with particularity. One element of making art in a world of disunified aesthetics is the issue of placing the audience/reader: how readers engage with the text is partly to do with an autographical urge to become part of the textuality, and autographical elements are typographically delineated in this essay. This is not a matter of identification but of strategies for the situated work of making difference: here an embodied knowledge released by engaging with the text alongside of the experience of recognizing cultural fit. Both essay and production begin in a place where the critic and the autographical reader have quite different voices, voices that move closer together by the end of each, almost as if the reader is collaborating with the writer. "FACE-WORK" also mediates between the graphic spatiality of "Labour Notes" and the critical density of "The Inédit" that increasingly coalesces toward the end of part two and into the essays of part three.

Davey's work has been dedicated for many years at least partly to unsettling cultural fittingness. What my own experience of that work has released is the movement between the rehearsal of the embodied experiences that are the precursors to fit, and their performance in a critical discourse the familiarity of which – the fittingness of which – does not encourage performativity. This reading of Davey's poetry is about fit, about realizing the problems of representation, and about going to the end of the line that does not fit to find there is no ending. Frank Davey has taught me so much about the end of the line. Davey is so much about fit that the strategies for dealing with it get foregrounded. He is often more concerned with the immediate political landscape than the metatheory of alternatives, and opens up both the embodiments and the cultural fit of masculinity to class and class stereotypes. But he also engages with death at several times in his writing. Death can potentially generate an extreme case of performative mourning. But the shadows of death, the absences and ghosts of civic life, are not like death in kind or degree. Death is a moment of *until*. Dying and death give us moments of reading others, not being others, of understanding friendship, and recognizing the differences we make.

In the third chapter in part two, "The Inédit," I turn to the writing of Nicole Brossard and to questions of translation. Brossard's use of "installation" begets my own, just as Walter Benjamin begets "constellation." Turning to Brossard, I return to questions of beauty in disunified aesthetics. I have argued that traditional beauty is made by art-making that is wrested into culture just at the point of losing its power to change things, and aesthetic criticism is fascinated by the occasional occurrence that renews that power over and over. Brossard clearly delineates that wresting into culture although the writing seems less interested in the power that is lost than in defining and installing the renewal of beauty in highly particular contexts. The former "wresting" is cold beauty, and the latter "installation" is warm. They tell us about different choices offered by performance/art-making: toward fit and toward the alongside process of arousal/awareness – redolent in Brossard's *cyprine*. The chapter goes on to explore several of Brossard's works in an attempt to delineate her aesthetics of installation (now slightly different to mine) that works prior to cultural fit and centrally to the concept of *alongside*, and to understand its connection to performativity, situated textuality, discourse, and ideology. Brossard's work is fundamental to this theory of disunified aesthetics because with installation she articulates the possibility of an aesthetics that deals not with cultural fit but with what happens in the making of the art before it enters the cultural horizon.

Working intensely on Brossard's work coalesced years of thinking about aesthetics and the activity of the art-maker and audience, the maker and the critic. In the visual performativity of the videoed conference paper[4] and in the graphic performativity of chapter 7, the last in part two, "Radical Tragedy," on a book by Alice Munro, I now see that I moved from the performativity of translation from another language to the idea of translation as a process of installation in any reading. Translation becomes an allegory of the work of the reader/audience/critic – a commonplace for many such as Borges, but I had had to feel it in the body, do it, make it. The reader reading in their own language is engaged in a similar artmaking, is engaged in the installation, is doing the translation. The work on Alice Munro takes the reading process through various kinds of rhetorical strategies in both the printed and videoed medium, from the normative/generic critical reading, through that hover "in between" all words, through their embossed materiality, to their energetic location in the body.

The essays and productions in part two attempt(ed) to engage their audiences into the installation of a text partly by involving them in a rehearsal process. I had and have no illusions about who might read the essays or see the performances that were in conversation with Davey, Brossard, and Munro: it would be like-minded groups with some common ground with myself, of education, class, predominantly colour, and perhaps gender- and ability-sensitivity. I felt increasingly that I did not want to work with the more fitting images and tropes from the earlier work in either medium, because they could possibly imply common grounds that I did not intend. They could erase différance and restrict the work within an ethics of relational opposition or responsiveness. I turned to the work of writers with positionalities similar to my own to see if I could work in rehearsal conditions while I performed. I did not and do not expect people who do not choose elements of similar positionality to engage in this coalescence of the work's performativity. Nevertheless, no "similarity" is exact, so the rhetoric of performativity encountered in public performance across positionality will always remind us of alternative strategies for making difference, experiencing différance, feeling *until*.

4

Labour Notes for "Bodies in Trouble"

SUSAN RUDY AND LYNETTE HUNTER

The following essay is a mixed genre script performance. The site is an interview between Susan Rudy and Lynette Hunter held on 18 August (Tape 1) and 19 August (Tape 2) 1998 about the lecture performance "Bodies in Trouble." The interview is cited at the beginning and intercuts the entire piece. The right-hand side of the script includes Lynette Hunter's responses to questions posed by Susan Rudy and contexts for the site, and is put together by Lynette Hunter. Much of this section is descriptive rather than analytical. The left-hand side of the script, constituted by Susan Rudy, is also intercut by interview commentary, but works as a performative analysis of the specific lecture performance in question. While Susan Rudy put together the final draft and made last-minute insertions of interview material in various places, the two parts were independently written.

Susan Rudy: And you were just saying that you have always resisted talking about your performance work and why.

SR: I want you to think.

Lynette Hunter: Well first of all you have got to prepare yourself for a lot of blank space on your tape because I want to have bits between to think.

LH: I mean I'm not sure, it's going to take me a long time to get used to the tape being on and I'm not sure –

SR: Tell me what you were going to say about you being an intellectual being.

SR: This is, do you know what, this is like us taking notes, this is for us to use in whatever way we want.

LH: I'm trying to get around to that, I'm trying to get around to that. I don't know what I want to do with this because this is an audience.

"WHO DO YOU TALK TO?"

LH: *I did not expect it to fill the space in the way that it did. I did not expect everybody to come in and remain silent and look at me. I thought I was going to be like a piece of performance art, moving around in the background while everybody else was just milling around. I didn't expect it to arrest people and take over and dominate or pre-dominate in the way that it did.*

No one talked; I couldn't believe it and still haven't worked out how around two hundred people in a very small space could be so quiet (Hunter email message).

BODIES IN TROUBLE

"Bodies in Trouble" is a durational performance piece that occurred at the conference "Women and Texts," held in Leeds in July 1997. It was devised specifically for the conference, and grew over the two years that the conference came together. "Women and Texts" offered a place for women to talk about and present ways in which they used texts in their daily lives. It was crosscultural, interdisciplinary, and integrated a small arts festival alongside an academic conference. Texts ranged from formal essays to book art to theatre.

The performance piece "Bodies in Trouble" is the last in a series of four installations, more properly,

SR: *But why didn't you want people to, say, talk to this figure?*

LH: *Talk to this figure.!? Because nobody does!. Nobody talks to the domestic wife in her house.*

To name her performance piece "Bodies in Trouble," Lynette Hunter borrows the homonym phrase "Body's in Trouble" from Canadian singer and composer Mary Margaret O'Hara. But rather than begin with an analysis of the difference it makes when one says "bodies" instead of "body's," I want to focus on the final, emotionally wrenching, half hour of the performance – during which Hunter takes off her cookie-dough soaked clothes, hangs them on a hanger, and curls up naked in a Japanese bath-sized steel box –and

lecture performances, concerned with the split between intellectual and domestic life, which I have constructed through the lens of food. The three initial pieces are all intensely physical, with the physicality being constituted by the audience for which they were conceived. The physicality of "Can a Man Be a Woman" (1994) is concerned with the denaturing of women's sexuality in the academic institution. "Trying Not to Be a Tragic Subject" (1995) operated around the perceived inappropriateness of bringing domestic physicality into a scholarly setting. The physicality of "Cooking the Books" (1996) plays cartoonlike with media gender conventions: the frankly woman-sexed body (cleavage, etc.) and the intensely masculinist discourse of the theoretical lecture.

The work of these performances laid the ground for "Bodies in Trouble." This fourth piece was addressing a predominantly female

Hunter's surprise at her audience's
silence. To examine this aspect of
the performance, let me begin with
the lyrics from O'Hara's song, which
articulates the question neither
the figure in her piece nor any of us
in Hunter's silent audience asked:
"Who do you talk to?":

> *You just want to push somebody*
> *And a body won't let you*
> Just want to move somebody
> And a body won't let you
>
> Who do you talk to … ?
> Who?
> Who do you talk to … ?
> When a body's in trouble?
>
> You just want to run somebody
> And a body won't let you
> Want to let somebody and a
> body won't let
> You want to kiss, feel, take,
> hear, ride
> Stop, start somebody and a
> body won't let you
>
> Who do you talk to …
> Who?
> Who do you talk to …

audience, brought together by a concern for the texts of daily life, but not specialized into disciplines or media, and only partially academic. The physicality had to be different, not institutional, banal, or conventional. Furthermore, because many people in my discipline expect texts to be about words, and I had often found the words of the performance texts misread (i.e., not read as parody or irony or performance, but straight), the challenge was to get the audience to think about the text without words. And finally, I wanted the central topic of cooking cookies to be lifted by sheer hyperbole out of the banal, so while all the earlier performances had been portable, do-nearly-anywhere pieces, this one was massive. It would have been difficult if not impossible to devise for an unfamiliar space, although not impossible to perform again having had the first run.

All four pieces are "lecture performances" that move

When a body's in trouble,
When a body's in trouble?[1]

In O'Hara's text, the singer's

desire – what she wants – is overtly

restrained by "a body" that "won't

let" her. Through the use of the word.

"you," both the singer and the reader

are interpellated into positions

of desire and frustration, made

aware of a difference – indeed a

very troubling split – between body

and self, made bodies in trouble.

But the body in Hunter's piece has

no words with which to mourn

the loss of the body's willingness to

do what the self wants or, for that

matter, of the self's willingness to

do what the body wants. Hunter's

use of "Bodies" rather than "Body's"

elides the difference between the

continually across the line between the two genres.

Description of "Bodies in Trouble"

from notes taken down shortly after the performance

> i wanted to perform the sheer hard work of daily life, how it is encompassing yet also often sheltering, ... and i had nothing but a very strong visual image of a cookie tapestry in mind when i saw it in my head. But then over the months it came to me to do the tapestry on an industrial scale.

LH: I wanted something massive that made some kind of claim –
SR: On the institution –
LH: – on the institution ... I spend most of my life acting as a male within male institutions, and this was my male response ... I'm going to do something very male, I'm going to produce something so big – (1:4)

> i designed and had made a huge steel frame for holding 116 linked steel wires, onto which i would cook cookies – each wire supporting between five and six cookies. Eventually the whole tapestry would contain the pixellated words "bodies in trouble," but inside the tapestry frame there would also be this

plural form of a noun and a noun/

verb phrase; between what happens

"when a body is in trouble" and the

more generic "bodies in trouble." As

a result, Hunter takes the "bodies"

in her piece – hers, ours – out of a

specific moment or question, takes

"you" out of the piece altogether

& paradoxically puts "you" (us)

nowhere. While O'Hara's question

"Who do you talk to ... / When a

body's in trouble?" suggests she is

addressing someone and expects

to be heard, to whom is "Bodies in

Trouble" addressed? Who hears this

text without words? Its performer?

"A body" is in trouble in the

O'Hara piece because it is not

acting under the authority of

the self: "*You* just want to push

steel box set down in a corner ...
with a corkboard for holding the
recipes for the cookies, which
i solicited from all the artists
coming to the conference.
Let me explain the larger
surround: the tapestry was to be
built over a number of hours by
me moving between the Food
Science department, about three
or four minutes from the school
of English which held the steel
frame, but with the large ovens i
needed.

I would cook these cookies on
these long iron skewers and I would
take them around the edge of the
Physics Administration building
[which includes our registry] into
the view of the English building
and at that moment I went into
performance (1:12).

i was to start at about 6 am and
walk very very slowly at first,
speeding up to normal around
10.30 am and then jogging and
finally running toward 1.30 pm,
all the time with these large
platters of cookies on wires for
the tapestry ... when the whole
tapestry was finished, at about
1.45 pm, i had some help from
a couple of people to transport
the whole thing on a trolley over
to the building where people
would be going to the lecture at
3 pm. it was about twenty yards

somebody / And *a* body won't let you" (emphases mine). Note O'Hara's use of the word "And." Had the line read "*but* a body won't let you," the meanings generated would have been quite different. Somehow the body's resistance is connected to the self's desire. But while O'Hara can be seen to mourn alone for this loss – perhaps her question "Who do you talk to?" is rhetorical and she is speaking only to herself – in Hunter's piece every woman in the audience is offered a position as mourner. We are all both in and out of trouble by the end of her performance.

SR: I interrupted you, go back to what you were saying about the box, and the things it can represent. LH: Well, I mean I don't know what they represent. To me, it

away but it rained and for the first time during the conference the building was locked, so the cookies had to be covered with plastic sheets to stop them from going soft.

And I had to stand there, thinking now how do I do this in a performative way? It was a very distressing five or ten minutes for one of the audience, who had got herself really involved in the performance and wanted to help me, desperately, hold this thing up. What nobody knew, of course, was that it weighed no weight at all ... but I was trying to hold it as though it weighed ten tons (1:14).

We finally got into the building and set the frame up there, and then the last part of the performance happened.

and I had to deal with the fact that all [many] of the cookies fell off and I had to put them back on again ... I thought of that as being absolutely part of the performance, because that's the kind of thing that happens to you, things don't go the way you expect, you've got to adapt, you've got to change, you've got to fix up, you've got to move it on ... (1:14).

i took the cork board off to leave the box exposed, then i got undressed and hung up my was a sense of constriction, and yet comfort, and in that sense it is purely escapist, and I think although there is a critique of what ideology does to domestic space in this whole piece and what factories do to work and what institutions do to work, there is also a way in which the end of this piece is not a utopian end at all, it's very much – it's a tragic end, it's a body 'in trouble, and it is a body that uses an absolutely typical escapist ending, and it goes into the box. I mean that's why the clothes are there, and that's why it's an either/ or thing, you are still in your clothes, but you are in a box, but you are in your clothes, but you are in a box, but you are in your clothes, but you are in a box; and clothes are self-sufficient and self-standing and self-supporting, they don't need you inside them.

SR: No.

LH: And the box becomes acceptable as something human, only because you are inside it.

SR: *Does it?*

LH: Does it become acceptable? I think it becomes acceptable to most people, most of the time, yes, I think most us find ways of accommodating —

SR: *Watching your performance it looked completely unacceptable.*

clothes (which had gradually got more and more covered in cookie dough as the day went on and were quite rigid with it by now so they stood as kind of sculpture on the end of the frame), and got into the box

SR: It's steel, it's not fur, or blanket, so visually it looks very uncomfortable, and because of the small space, you're cramped in there … It's just a bit bigger than your body – you can sit, I mean you can sit with your knees pulled up (1:17)

i stayed in the box until 3 pm, just moving around slightly by balancing myself against the sides of it every five minutes or so … then i got up, picked up my clean clothes bag, and walked out through the crowd.

Analysis

I find it difficult to analyse the pieces, to talk about them in an academic manner, partly because of something that happens to the performance if I do that, and partly because of something that happens to the audience. These performances are put on largely for academics of some kind or

The meaning of "trouble" for human bodies is, not surprisingly, gendered. A particularly sexual connotation is attached to the phrase when women are "in trouble."

SR: We haven't talked about the fact that the body in trouble is a woman's body and in the pizza piece you began in a suit, as I recall, in very gender-neutral territory and you had something on that covered your breasts so they were flat and underneath that you had another sort of gender-neutral clown costume, and at that point I wondered whether you were going to go down to the woman's body, and so when you did here it sort of felt like Oh my God. We haven't got at how that's working in this one and I'm wondering if that's why you felt so vulnerable, because taking off the clothes means you can't pretend you're a man.

By their existence as *women's* bodies, our bodies are always considered bodies in trouble, bodies as trouble. But "trouble" also refers specifically to "a woman's travail (also of an animal)," the labour of birthing. Women "in

another, and their vocabulary for understanding performance is extraordinarily impoverished. It has been harrowing to discover the focus on definitive meaning that narrows and reduces potential. For my own part, I know that when I analyse other people's work, the limit case is to do with my own blinkers. When I do it with my own work, there's the terrifying possibility that the limit case is all there is, and that finding it closes one down.

Hence, at the risk of sounding naive, *LH: On one level the whole thing is just a complete gift (1:1).*

LH: I don't conceptually structure them [the performances] until they are nearly complete and they grow out of posing problems with turning what is usually a visual image that has been given to me … as if I have read a text and … turning that into a visually conceptual analogue (1:9).

The performances are an attempt to bring those images as much to my reader as the academic analysis.

trouble," pregnant and unmarried, both break and submit to the rules. Strangely, being "in trouble" has also come to mean being psychologically "in trouble."

LH: Yes. Because it took me twenty-five minutes to get the thing across and then I took all my clothes off and I sat there doing different yoga things. Anyway, I then realized I was going to have to leave and I thought, well, I know what I can do, I can pick up my bag and I can walk through the crowd and I can go and I would never have planned to walk naked through a crowd of people, but it felt very protected. I didn't feel worried about it at all and I thought, this is fine, they'll understand, I have got to get back to running the conference. So, I got out of my box, picked up my bag, and as you know, walked through you. And as I walked through you, everybody, you know, it was like the Red Sea, nobody wanted to touch me, you know. I went downstairs, got myself cleaned up, and turned on the lights, but that was something that was completely unintentional but which does fit into what you're saying about wanting to care for this vulnerable thing there and not as an object/subject thing.

SR: In a way you've produced a feminist community, through the course of the piece you've produced in your audience a feminist community.

However, I don't find it difficult talking about the performance elements. One of the main criteria for me was: no words – hence the technical elements were largely to do with the body.

LH: By the time I was finished my face was covered in cookie dough and that was my mask, and so your mask becomes your whole body ... And that's one of the reasons ... because people should have been able to respond to my body language (1:16).

Space: Technically the piece runs along the border of theatre and performance art. All my work is directed by Peter Lichtenfels, a theatre director who works with me largely by questioning why I want to do things. He is also brilliant at knowing when the audience will be bored. My training is in the

As Lynette Hunter's description of the performance indicates, the body's work in "Bodies in Trouble" is backbreaking. This body bakes over six hundred cookies in under eight hours. Not only does this body not "kiss ... somebody," "feel ... somebody," "take ... somebody," "hear ... somebody," "ride ... somebody," "Stop ... somebody," "start ... somebody," – as the "you" in O'Hara's piece wants to do – we do not know what she wants. Rather, it moves, walks, runs – without anybody – from the Food Sciences Building to the English Department and back again. This body takes off its clothes for every body in a lecture hall foyer but no body can touch it. This body sits in a cold, steel box for more than thirty minutes as though she weren't any body, as though she weren't *with* anybody. Except that we are all there, watching, waiting. For her inability to see that we are with her. For her. And for her

theatre, and the spatial constraints of "Bodies in Trouble" construct a stage rather than a performance location.

SR: *let's talk about the aspects of the performances that were isolating ...*

LH: *I didn't think of them as strategies of isolation, I thought of them as part of my stage, ... when you see an actor performing on a stage ... you don't say to yourself, "They are isolated from me," you accept the fact that there is a convention, there is a stage (1:6). ... I wanted them [people in the audience] to become involved but not in terms of talking to me, in terms of engaging with my performance. There was one point where someone started walking alongside me and that was very interesting, and I quite enjoyed that ... but I didn't want to be spoken to because that was not the medium I was dealing with (1:8). Of course, one way in which I think this is performative and not a stage is that you ... have to deal with certain pragmatic things ... [when]*

inability to see that we are with her, for this loss, we are in trouble, and we mourn.

LH: This one wasn't intended to be erotic in that kind of generating an instant of eroticism, it was meant to be about the body. It was just meant to be about what a body did, it wasn't supposed to be exciting or ...
SR: But you know, it seemed to me that that piece was not erotic but sexual in the way that if you see the naked body of someone you don't know, usually it's erotic, but in this instant it felt more like it was sexual, like you were seeing someone you are used to seeing without their clothes

SR: But you stopped being an object and this is something that really has stopped in this piece. We are not looking at a naked woman's body as an object, you know, you've become a subject even though ...

LH: Well what's very interesting, and this is connected, is that at the end, as you know, but I'll say it again for the tape's benefit, I thought that everybody was going to go into the plenary, I would be all alone, I would be able to get up, get my clothes, go downstairs, get changed, wash up, and leave. As it turned out, Marta, who was running that plenary, didn't know how to turn the lights on, you didn't either, you didn't want to move, she did, and I think she was right.

the cookies fell off and I had to put them back on again ... I thought of that as being absolutely part of the performance ... because that's the kind of thing that happens to you, things don't go the way you expect ... (1:14)

SR: I think that in performance art the audience is always made to feel vulnerable and in this one, because it was very soon clear that there was a line around you ... we were safe.
LH: Yes, I think that's the case. I think, however ... that I have never tried to make the audience feel vulnerable, but I have tried to offer them a vulnerability that they recognize (1:24).

Time: It's a durational piece lasting nine hours, and the timing of the movements between the Food Sciences building and the English building was a substantial element for any significance that an audience might derive.

SR: *And I know why I didn't want to move now that we've had this conversation, because this moment of vulnerability that you've let your-self come to let the people who are watching you feel very close to you, and if it's not tragic it's because in that moment we feel connected with you, not in the way you do with an object, it is not like object/subject, but connection and shared know-ledge and wanting to look after, and you don't want to leave someone.*
LH: *Like my friend wanting to take the thing from me as I waited by the door.*

THE POET/MIDWIFE AND HER LABOUR NOTES

The word "midwife" comes from

the Middle English, probably from

the obsolete preposition "mid,"

meaning "with," and "wife," meaning

"woman," originally in the sense

"one who is with the mother"

(*Concise Oxford Dictionary*). Except

that a woman giving birth is often

not yet a mother. Poet Nicole

Brossard took detailed notes during

LH: there's a big time difference, and the muscles on your body work in a completely different way when you're trying to do everything very, very, very slowly. It's almost ceremonial, you're creating a reality through which you move, you're almost aware of pushing the air aside to allow your reality to exist when you start off doing it that slowly (1:13).

To maintain the focus, the body has to be consciously in physical training, so that you can be aware of the slightest adjustments that have to be made. One viewer found the early movements like Butoh. The key tool is breath. All through the performance I was using daoist breathing techniques to control the energy of each movement or set of movements, whether walking, running, standing stationary, circling inside the steel box. The control of breath puts a hand on the viewer.

Hunter's day-long performance and later sent them to her. Women in labour have been, when we are lucky, attended by notekeepers – midwives, labour coaches, partners, poets – who record the intensity of our contractions, our breathing patterns, the dilation of our cervixes. Brossard's notes are like these labour notes except that she is most concerned with the woman in the process of her labour. Brossard records the position of Hunter's body by making a small drawing under the time, a drawing that looks uncannily like a fetus. Who is being born? With whom?

In the arts program for the "Women and Texts" Conference, Hunter wrote that the performance

LH: ... the breath exercises were part of the performance. They were part of the way in which the body was working, the body language was working. And they were also a part of ... that thing about cutting through reality ... you also make air. ... the air was very much tied up with that notion of creating a life and breathing, ... but it's also inevitably, therefore, tied up with the notion of death (2:12).

Problems: the performance was a year in the making, and consisted of a series of deferrals in the face of problems.

Translation from the image-gift to physical materiality. Realizing the kind of repetition that was needed. The design and construction of the frame. Working with the director on movement, time, and breath.

was addressed to her friend, the artist, feminist, and art critic Ann Duncan – "the angriest woman I ever knew" – who died just before the piece was finished.

LH: Yes, it's a mourning piece. It's a piece about all the things I said it was about, in terms of the domestic and work and labour and all the rest of it. But it was also motivated very, very largely by grief. A very close friend of mine died in the middle of April from cancer and I had already planned what I was going to do with this piece, but suddenly it became very important to do it because there were a lot of times where I didn't actually think I was going to do it. I didn't have the steel frame made until the beginning of June because it took until then to really say I must do this, I must do this. It was very much part of a grieving process for me, because it was the kind of thing that the woman who died would probably be totally brutal about in terms of her assessment of it, telling me what was wrong with it and what might be good with it or anything like that, but she would appreciate that I was trying to do something, she would

Solving the issue of how to engage without ending. Fear.

LH: whether it is a theatre performance, critical performance or anything, you have to have an edge of the performance where you feel the vulnerability of the performer and it doesn't mean that they are not good at what they do, but you know that what they do costs … (1:23).

The key is that the performance is a rehearsal of a performance of a rehearsal …

LH: one of the things that has come out of other performances that I have done is what I think the rehearsal period is like for a theatre artist or a performance artist, that you do it again and again and again and again, and every single time you do it … you have to set yourself a new task; otherwise, it is no longer possible to do it with any kind of interest for yourself, and therefore any kind of interest for your audience (4).

*have an idea of what it was that I
was trying to do.*

Performance is never end-directed,
it's always in process. This doesn't
mean that the process is without
effect, but that the action taking
effect on the real world is an action
in process: like rehearsal, which
is performance but not claiming
a final status. I feel that the most
effective performances are never
predicative but on the way to
somewhere, that way you take
the audience with you too. The
one surprising aspect of "Bodies
in Trouble," for which I was not
prepared, was audience response.

LH: I did not think that any
one person would have had the
cumulative experience of seeing
how the whole thing added up,
which I thought ... quite tragic, and
therefore I did not think people
could react in that way, having only
seen bits of it ... I don't know why
that works, I mean I don't know
how any of these things work.

SR: So did you imagine her as your
primary audience or your first
audience?

SR: But if the fact that she had died
and she would have understood it
motivated it.

LH: No, not really. I didn't really
have a specific audience in mind
except for the women at the
conference.

LH: it gave it energy, it didn't motivate it. I'd been thinking about it nearly two years by that point. I had virtually all of it planned in many ways, but I hadn't actually started thinking about the performance of it, and on top of everything else that i was doing for the conference, it required an enormous amount of energy and adrenalin to do it, but that energy came out of her death, and as many people who grieve after they have not, you know, because they have not been part of the dying, it was my way of being part of dying. So, that's partly what it was about and it was also about as the .... bodies in trouble and that whole tension between how you live and how you might die and the trouble that your body can get into. I know I said yesterday my body was at peak physical fitness when I did that performance. It was at peak physical fitness; for me there were all these points at which I recognized my own weaknesses and my own physical weaknesses, the things that will probably kill me, and so in that sense it was also about death and about thinking about our bodies in ways that you live with your own death, you know.

SR: *And because it was such a physically demanding piece. You didn't have to have a nine-hour piece, you didn't have to do it over that period of time without much required of your body and you did it. It's representing a kind of requirement on the part of women to do the same activity over and over again but, in your actual body at that time, you were putting that requirement on yourself and we were witnessing it.*

LH: I think that that's how a lot of it felt. You know this cliché

SR: And the working life includes the intellectual's working life, we talked about that yesterday too, how the work of the conference was sheer, repetitive, boring work, a lot of it, making it happen and probably not as pleasurable as making all those cookies.

SR: When you said it was about mourning, I thought for a minute that you were going to say that one of the motivations of the piece was the way that women who aren't in a simple domestic role mourn the loss of that.

about "women have a lot of staying power," "women live longer." You know, the only reason women live longer is because they don't do the same kind of things that men do, they don't eat the same kind of food, they don't put themselves into the same kind of pressures although … and so women are beginning to get heart attacks and die at forty-nine or whatever. I think that a lot of the way in which domestic work operates is that you have to be very stable and you have to have a lot of staying power. You have to, in a sense, train to be a housewife

LH: No, that's right

LH: Yes, yes, I think that that is it. I think one of the reasons why I chose to do it about domestic life rather than about intellectual life, which I could have done, is because I do mourn the loss of that in a way, not too much, but I do enjoy it partly because I get just a little bit too little of it.

PERFORMANCE 4
Bodies in Trouble

WEBLINK http://vimeo.com/18436476

1997   University of Leeds (UK), Conference, "Women and Texts/Les
        Femmes et les Textes"

The performance was built over twelve months to respond to the many in-
spiring women, my mothers, godmothers, and sisters, who came to the
conference "Women and Texts/Les Femmes et les Textes" held in Leeds in
1997. The conference grew from conversations with Susan Rudy and Marta
Dvorak, and I am completely indebted to their hard work and vision for
making it what it became – a combination of conference and art-making. It
was not set up to be an arts festival, and one of the two things I regret about
the event was the focus on conference presentation genre which meant that
some fabulous artists from around the world felt less supported.

I commissioned a local ironworker to make a 12' x 6' stainless steel frame
with a bar running across it at 3', hook and eye skewers hanging down in 2'6"
lengths, and a 3' x 3' box welded into the frame at the right-hand corner. The
way that this was used is documented in both the video of the performance
(truncated and edited to focus on the final hour), and the printed dialogue.
It is expanded on in the three commentaries that I include following this account. Details not in those materials include the increasing weight of cookie
dough on my body as I moved through making the cookies-on-skewers
from 6 a.m. to 2 p.m., which led to these clothes unexpectedly standing up
by themselves when I took them off. Another detail that is, I think, important to record, and is mentioned in at least one commentary, is that one or
two people, including Margaret Beetham, tried to help this "figure" in the
process of running itself into the box.

There were many concepts behind the production, but one of the foremost
concerned gender in the institution. In the modern period, it has been a
commonplace that men turn to their female muses when they produce "art."
I was interested in looking at what happens when women get to be critics,
a field largely defined for several centuries by men and for men. And I was
interested in the implications of this for my generation and those near to it.
Women in the 1970s to 1980s who entered the academy were often caught
between family and work, not only the heterosexual nuclear family because
many chose to develop same-sex relationships, chose not to have children
or enter domestic contracts, but were often still the primary caregivers – to

the elderly, for example. The labour involved is huge. The exhaustion this combination generates works against awareness, against engagement, and too often puts us back in the box.

The piece looked at the ethic of care and the contemporary isolation of the caregiver. I felt that all the people in the conference were caregivers – many of whom had indeed cared for me from time to time, and many of whom I had cared for. It was intended as a peripheral event making little physical impact on the organization of the conference. Apart from the final hour in a foyer in front of the main lecture hall, it was not scheduled, and I had anticipated people milling around, eating some cookies from the frame, and then walking into the hall for the plenary. However, many sat down and just looked. And didn't move. So eventually I got out of the box and walked downstairs to get things moving again.

From the start, when I commissioned the frame, I also invited conference attendees to send me recipes for ginger cookies. These I tested in the kitchen so that I could control the colouration, and the cookie strands eventually spelled out various words in a pixellated fashion. This image came from a dream that I had had when visiting the University of Calgary on a fellowship: I was in a house and after some time found a curtain of cookies which, swept aside, revealed my colleagues in the English Department who had invited me. I'm curious about how dreams work, so I decided to materialize it.

In many ways it is a deeply troubled piece, something that I see only today. I was trying to move away from the troping of the earlier productions into something that would bring the audience into the performance. Yet I built something that excluded everyone from the physical text. Perhaps that exclusion resulted in the responses I received, from some who cried, to some who got angry, to others who laughed, and to those who asked for the recipes. Nevertheless, I could not have made the piece without all these extraordinary people who had been feeding me intellectually, keeping me aware and alive, for the previous twenty to thirty years. I was acutely aware of the collaborative work in the piece, and my other regret is that I did not make material engagement easily available to the collaborators.

I considered taking the production to a conference in Australia, and there was a conference in Canada that I thought about. But this work was site particular. It couldn't go anywhere else. The collaboration it celebrated would not have been present, and the piece would never have been able to call on an engaged ethical response in another location.

RESPONSE 1

Daphne Marlatt 4.6.98

Troubling the Surface

for Lynette Hunter & her "Bodies in Trouble,"
performed at Women & Texts, Leeds, July 1997

she runs through our town not in nightgown. dayclothes growing dirtier
each time she appears. trays of drop cookies held before her, intent,
compelled (half-baked?)

runs a wild thread through knots of standing women spinning opinion,
soaking up coffee& company, exchanging words on technology, polity, the
shared exhilaration of certain papers on the female subject to/object in

trouble-shooter, she-organiser, running upstairs & down with her cookie
sheets (white cookies, tan cookies, brown) as perennial caretaker, frazzled
hair adrift from its hold, body driven by need (whose?) to feed everyone

bodes well? ill? troubles the wake she leaves

palpable, beadling/beetling frown, wards off comment or question, batter-
smeared (body forbidden here?) heralds a double

running through town, not so wee, breaching the bounds of civilitas,
promising eat, you female titans, you *déesses de la texte*, drawn by savour,
by smell back to our own wee (ha) cookiedom

(this is not culture?)

---

look, look at the work she's done, doing, frazzled, impatient to reach the
hooks, hanging three-foot skewers (shishkebab, Di says) concoctions of
sugar, ginger molasses, baked onto steel. one skewer drops, she impatient
stoops to rehang, another breaks (free) – much haste (makes) waste
crumble the body's sweet work perfected

curious we in the foyer with briefcases, witticisms, our work-display clothes, half chatting midstream observe her cookie-ornament the frame (set-up for what?) with mother gestures, getting it right, this display of nurture *against* her, distracted, fractured trying to control (get it?)

work, such as it is now out of her (mind)

& clothes she's folded into a gym bag: starkers, yes. generic droopy breast, belly o so assailable face us

words fail

we the well-done rise to watch her crawl into an aluminium box the height (just) of a sitting woman head-bent, raw against the (uncomfortable we think) seclusion

———————————

(flash) caught in a box, her box under the brittle display of her own once-make – & left, goes on impassive sitting slouched, sombre foetal curl a negative resistance, not the one who makes time fun food for thought, rhyming her own role with us

(flash goes on) neutral now, gone from personhood & framed (how many minutes has it been? Martha asks) in the mimetic look (Pauline picks up) of the nude, impassive, sigh, re-poses that well-painted she, emptied of thought (flesh against) eyes now we're caught in the gaze we instigate, someones want to break, entering loud converse, while others opt for reverence, tense splits crowd us face to face with our own

boding (pain intelligence wit), foreboding (hey, is there a plenary or not? lieutenants Susan & Marta are at odds & someone needs to find the lights *as time goes by*

she simply sighs, wakes up, walks off with her black bag, doing yoga she offers after with the cookies – faced with our readings of her smile

Nicole Brossard 10h.10 le 4 juillet 1997

Pour Lynette,
Ces quelques notes prises durant ta merveilleuse
performance du 4 juillet 1997
Nicole Brossard

10h.10 · le 4 juillet 1997 · Leeds

Lynette Hunter's performance.   Le sillon
                                     La trace

elle marche pas à pas comme en relief
elle tient un plateau rempli de biscuits
marche encore trace un sillon dans la
réalité; elle impose la noblesse du pain,
du silence et du travail. Ce matin, le jeu
a recommencé, elle s'est levé, a préparé le
pain, est allé au marché, le déposer
puis s'en est retourné dans la solitude,
sa silhouette dans le paysage le sillon.
Son visage buto dans l'air de Leeds un
matin de juillet.

Fendre l'instant, l'espace
Rentrer dans sa solitude
A deux mains elle entre dans le vaste monde des
regards.
Le respect des spectateurs
L'étonnement des passants
L'inquiétude sympathique des curieux

144.20

Elle impose le silence. Les g. murmurent
ne peut plus placer les biscuits
Things go wrong

Elle enlève ses souliers
son t-shirt
met le chand sur un cintre.
enlève le pant. — medite.
le met sur un cintre.
S'assoit dans sa boîte de aluminium.
elle appuie sa tête
la caméra filme

pendant que ns la regardons
le silence
→ ce qu'il y a ds sa tête pendant que
ns regardons
(un bleu sur la cuisse)
le temps réel   144.29

ns la regardons,

elle se repose. Elle est "fatiguée"
• cela doit être froid et inconfortable

la notion de spectacle — de
voyeurisme.

le temps   accomplissement du vide
rideau
144.32

        144.34

bruit de talons —
tous les sens aux aguets.
un biscuit tombe comme une vieille pierre
un 2e comme ...

144.35

pendant que ns regardons, nous
réfléchissons - à quoi?

14h 37

Silence impeccable.
14h. 38 très léger mouv. de la tête
Nous attendons Quoi?

144.40 voix de femme
les femmes sortent de + en + leur calme

144.42
        l'aluminium craque

144.43 a tourné la tête.
        visage très détendu

regarder puis penser
fermer les yeux aussi

144.45

14h.47.

14h 49

le repos. la posture changeante pour un
meilleur confort.

les g. commencent à parler à être de + en +
distraites.

14h.52    la main continue
                du cou
la caméra sur moi. 14h 54.

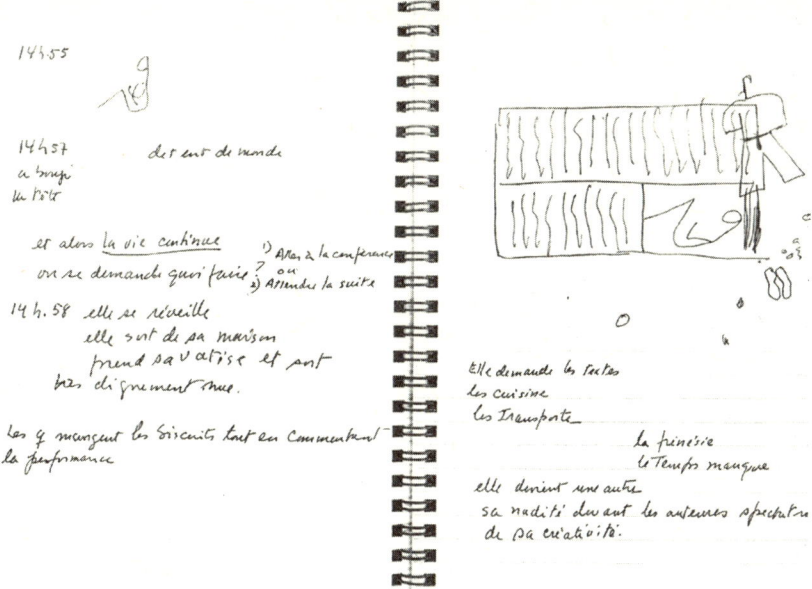

RESPONSE 3

Teresa Smalec

Sun, 4 Jun 2006 11:09:12–0400
Theresa K Smalec
Practice as Research in the US: Questions [American Society for Theatre Research]

I still hope that Ben will explain his own sense of
the kinds of research questions he's interested in
exploring in a practice-based dissertation, and some
of the methods by which he proposes to investigate
those questions.

However, I was thinking more about the question:
"How exactly does performance practice constitute 'a
mode of dissemination of research'"? In doing so,
Diana Taylor's book THE ARCHIVE AND THE REPERTOIRE

came to mind. Taylor argues that performances "function as vital acts of transfer, transmitting social knowledge, memory, and a sense of identity through reiterated, or what Richard Schechner has called 'twice-behaved behavior'" (2). Taylor writes that "Embodied practice, along with and bound up with other cultural practices, offers a way of knowing" (3).

This statement presents an obvious question: Knowing *what*?

In looking through Taylor's Index, I notice that the specific term "research" does not appear. This absence is interesting. On the one hand, it suggests that Taylor's theory about embodied acts of transfer does not account for how performances are able to transmit/disseminate that specialized form of social knowledge that we call "research." Maybe there is a fundamental difference between transmitting things we already "know" (i.e.: knowledge, truth, truthiness, etc. ...) , and things we *don't* yet know, or whose outcomes are unpredictable (i.e.: research). On the other hand, perhaps the absence of a referent does not denote the absence of a phenomenon? Maybe "research" is a less predictable and less fixed *form* of "knowledge"?

My dictionary defines KNOWLEDGE as 1. an acquaintance with facts, truths, or principles; general erudition. 2. familiarity or conversance, as by study or experience: a knowledge of human nature. 3. the fact or state of knowing; clear and certain mental apprehension. 4. awareness, as of a fact or circumstance.

I don't want to hang my hat on these definitions, and realize they probably fall short of many peoples' notions of "knowledge." I will supplement

them with Tom Pallen's definition of theatre, which
I very much like, and which strikes me as accurate
with respect to the sorts of transmissions of
"knowledge" that theatre fosters:

"Late in his long career as a critic, Walter Kerr
participated in a short, didactic film about the
nature of theatre. Early in that film, he described
theatre as a place "where we come together to
compare notes about the truth of things." I've
quoted this rather loose definition of theatre many
times in classes and the comments about "truthiness"
reminded me of them.
--Tom Pallen (April 2006)

Meanwhile, the dictionary defines RESEARCH as far
more of a process-oriented endeavour than KNOWLEDGE.
Research: 1. diligent and systematic inquiry into a
subject in order to discover or revise facts,
theories, etc ... 2. a particular instance or piece
of research 3. to make researches; investigate
carefully. 4. to make extensive investigation into.

I thought of one performance that tacitly struck me
as "disseminating research" (as opposed to
"knowledge") as I witnessed it. I don't know if
others will agree that the following piece was a
practice-based research project that posed its
questions and its (unforeseen) results *through*
perfomance, but I think it did. Perhaps it also
offers an example of how embodied "research" might
unfold in the arts?

****

Scenario: Years ago, I attended a conference on
"Women and Texts" at Leeds University. Predictably,
most of the panels were about women and written

texts. One of the organizers was a British woman named Lynette Hunter who typically works on poetics in the context of Canadian Literature. On what I think was the final day of the conference, she did a "performance." I believe
it was announced the day before that she would be doing an all-day performance piece, but I must have forgotten about it.

I came to the conference early in the morning, and noticed a nondescript woman in the parking lot, toiling in the vicinity of a van. She was pulling out racks of cookies, and transporting them one by one from the parking lot, into the university. She wore blue overalls, the type that gardeners or mechanics wear. Even in the early morning, her loose hair was starting to look a little frizzy due to the heat. I got closer and realized (to my shock) that this frumpy worker was the usually well-heeled Lynette Hunter.

My initial thought was that I should offer to help Lynette carry the cookie racks into the university. (I still thought of her as "Lynette" at this point, having forgotten about her performance). But she seemed focused on her work, and her eyes were downcast, as if avoiding me. So I hurriedly bypassed her and went into the university to catch up with the conference. I promised myself to offer to help her the next time I saw her.

The day wore on, and I kept seeing her carrying those darn cookies from the van to the university, looking more and more dishevelled, engrossed in her labor, and increasingly less like her academic "self." I did offer to help her at some early point, but she acted like she didn't hear me. I felt myself becoming inexplicably angry with her after that,

realizing that her relentless work and quickly
fading identity were making me feel inexplicably guilty.

After a while, I started to wish she would
"disappear." If she *had* to do this miserable work
all day long, then couldn't she do it where I
wouldn't have to see her? I started to wonder if I
would feel the same way if I didn't "know" her as
her academic self, if she was just another laborer
on campus. I decided it would be better if I didn't
know her; then I probably wouldn't feel badly about
enjoying my day, attending papers, and keeping my
clothes clean while she carried those dirty little
chocolate cookies into the school … She already
would be "invisible" to me.

Other women at the conference were also starting to
feel uncomfortable. I think we started using other
entrances to avoid her after a while. But every once
in a while, groups of us would see her and quickly
go the other way.

At around four o'clock, we went into the main hall
where the performance was supposed to end. I was
expecting her to dispense with her blue-collar
apparel, get back into her normal clothes, and maybe
present a lecture on the relationship between food
and labor: "A woman's work is never done," etc. … We
would eat cookies with her and discuss/interpret her
unsettling performance. It would become safe and
understandable "knowledge."

But instead, to my surprise, she was curled up
naked, and seemingly asleep, inside a little metal
oven. (It looked like an oven. It might have been a
metal compartment of some sort). The rest of us were

assembled on couches and chairs, basically staring at the spectacle. At first, most of the women were silently awaiting for something else to happen. I can't remember if we were ever able to eat the cookies, or what happened to them.

After about five or ten minutes of relatively quiet waiting, I noticed that many people began to fidget, talking loudly about the sleeping woman. "What should we do to help her?" "Is she okay?" Nobody did move to help her, though. We all waited, keeping our distance from the oven and her nakedness. After about ten more minutes of non-response on the part of this female body, most people started talking about other panels they'd attended, and about the more exciting parts of their day. There was a building sense of aggression and pent-up hostility/anxiety in the room.

I kept watching her sleeping, wondering what sleeping inside the oven was supposed to mean. Bizarrely, I thought of Auschwitz and decided that this was probably not an intended part of her performance, but it was still creepy. She had really "lost" any sort of specific identity as Lynette Hunter. She became this generic, white, older, naked woman. That this had happened over the course of just a few hours was the scary part.

I actually calmed down after a while, letting myself fall into her breathing rhythms. I decided that she simply looked very exhausted (as opposed to dead or injured), and that we should just be quiet and let her sleep. But I was in the minority with respect to that opinion; the longer she slept without *doing* anything, the more it seemed to cause others to turn up their volume. Finally, to our collective relief, someone came in and announced very loudly, "THE FINAL PLENARY IS STARTING DOWN THE HALL!" At that point, I think she finally got out of the oven and walked silently out of the room. The rest of us went to the plenary, fairly stunned.

Conclusion: This was a research-based performance that left many inquiries and conclusions up to the viewer/receiver. I realized later that we (the conference women) were part of Hunter's unspoken "research questions." I don't know if she had formulated a hypothesis about our possible reactions to her physical labor, her sudden "lack" of status/identity, or her ultimate naked exhaustion. Perhaps she had done this performance before, and knew what to expect from those who interacted with her. I'm sure she must have had tentative theories in mind about what might happen, but it didn't feel manipulative or predictable. The outcomes were not 'known' (or maybe I was just naive).

However, her performance seemed like a "diligent and systematic inquiry into a subject in order to discover or revise facts, theories, etc. ..." The questions she helped me "discover" were new and "exciting" (disturbing, challenging). The assumptions (about how I and other academic women would react to such a piece) that her performance forced me to revise were also rather awkward and even painful on some level. I felt like we had failed.

The question, I guess, is how one would "evaluate" such a practice-based research project? Since there was never any wrap-up explanation or post-performance discussion of this piece (another thing that made it fascinating and unconventional), I feel like most of the analytical work was done on my own, as an observer/participant. If this was someone's practice-based dissertation project, I would want them to write up their theoretical account of what happened: why they made the performance choices they did, what they expected, what they discovered, what surprised them or confirmed their hypotheses, etc … Levinas would seem useful here, perhaps, or Goffman.

I don't know, but I would want some textual document explaining what the performer had in mind … even as I'd "received" and sort of deeply/tacitly "understood" their embodied research.

5

FACE-WORK and Going to the End of the Line with Frank Davey's Writing[1]

FACE-WORK

> For me, make-up is vital.
>   Every day I spend hours preparing, touching up, repairing
>   you can do such different things with sunset blue over moss
>   green
>   with sweet surprise over scarlet hurricane.
>   it's my armour/amour/armament   but no mere ornament
>   It's not just SLAP, but the semiotics of the face
>   the science of signs
>   The art of signs, significations, that old distinction between
>   significance and meaning that we rarely talk about today, it's so much
>   part of our social training

Of course for some, semiotics is still that basic experience of realizing that no sign has a fixed meaning. Others like assigning meaning or getting into the old rhetorical pleasure of invention: finding many meanings.

But then there's also that point where terror takes over, where semiotics becomes a recognition that signs are often largely determined, what Laclau and Mouffe called hegemony, but what I still call ideology – similar but not identical concepts, concerned with the set of rhetorical practices that delineate the representations, the faces, we can put on.

A resolution of that fear, for many semioticians, comes from distance – being the observer – but we all know the observer affects the experiment. Others challenge the constitution of representations, test their elasticity, their drift, their contradictions.

This is the field of discourse studies: culture gender ethnicity class – only class doesn't get much of a look in these days.

Frank Davey is a self-confessed semiotician; if discourse studies hadn't been invented, he'd have done it anyway.   It's a class weapon.

That shift from the basic realization of the distinction between significance and meaning to the sophisticated work, the contestation of the constitution of representations allowed to subjects: that worrying about FACE-WORK : is a narrative told by his work as it develops from the early 60s to now.

Reading through *Bridge Force* (1965) to *Popular Narratives* (1991) there's a physical sensation of recognition and dislocation: not quite nausea but perhaps travel sickness, from the reiterative flow of particular narratives. For example, time and again there's a young man who saves a young woman – and then an element is added. Time and again there's a young man who saves a young woman, and is betrayed – and then an element is added. Time and again there's a young man who saves a young woman and is betrayed, yet recovers. With each reiteration, the representation taken up by the speaking voice is differently contextualized as the basic narrative does a lot of social and political work.

At the same time, Frank Davey invests each iteration with more self-consciousness about semiotics than the previous. It's a narrative of consciousness-raising, more acute on some elements than others. bpNichol, editing *The Arches* (1980), says the work before 1970 is "obsessed with craft ... but without a full grasp of the implications of the philosophy he was moving toward" (8), and that Davey was himself embarrassed by some of the writing, re-writing it as "found" text in later work. To be frank, much of the early work is self-conscious in the extreme. As he says in "A Letter" from *Weeds* (1970), the writing is a blend, 30 per cent boysong and 70 per cent dacron. This is not surprising: self-consciousness is learned over time and is specific to socio-historic context.

> The familiarity of these young men is startling
> the familiarity of the young women is frightening

it's not about growing up alongside Frank Davey in 50s and 60s
Canada
>the signal difference between his high school and mine
being that in his, opportunities for boys to meet girls were
severely hindered, as he tells us in "In Love with Cindy Jones"
(1991, 21–2), by a gender separation that was also class-based –
only the people (i.e., girls) who are going to become secretaries
can take typing, the others do French – whereas in my high
school anyone going on to further education **had** to do both
French and Typing. This confused our class aspirations – the
smartest girl in the school became a Bell Canada operator – but
it also made for some surprising lawyers.

nor between a small-town semi-rural school and a school in a large heavy
industry immigrant city

no, it's not just the cultural parallels between British Columbia and Ontario
>but the larger representations of class and gender and invisible race
>>that layer my parents' world over mine, their parents' over their's
>those working-class fathers trying to define their manliness by
protecting their fragile Kenwood-mixer wives
>>a class confusion: masculinity as the capacity to own a
woman
>>>masculinity as the capacity to own

Listen to "Memory" (1965): where the "young man" records the "boy's talk"
about this "girl" to whom he responds valiantly. "There was the word lonely /
and the urge to hold her" (54), and the assertiveness of "Now I have known
her for six months/ and have married her" – one of the few "I's in the book. It
is a marriage he fuses with commodities in "Totems" (1965): "Chippendale,
Heppelwhite / French Provincial ... " reproductions, that have people eating
TV dinners off "Louis Catorse tables" – totems that remind him of "dead
warriors" "battles feasts ... ," and over which he pictures her "electrically
shaven limbs / draped across / the knobs and knots / of tortured wood" –
from which he will save her.

The stereotypes of romantic masculinity play out in this and other early
works alongside a detached voice at times bemused, at others patronizing, and in *Weeds* and *Arcana* (1973), increasingly trapped. And throughout there's a financial apprehension, concern, about money: not knowing
what is "enough" as "he" thinks about the bourgeois and the "harping middle

class." It is as if the reproduction furniture, the wife, are recognized signs of having enough BUT once you have them they don't release you from apprehension, they confirm it.

Economic apprehension is like desire. It results from constructed representations that are never satisfied because they posit an impossible plenitude or fullness, a plenitude that drives ambition and depletes fossil-fuel resources. A plenitude that drives class fear and violence for class difference is both the sign and the instigation of the construction of financial apprehension.

I remember my father, the theatre director – an old-fashioned autocratic
   director
         raising his class by directing his betters on the boards
         controlling his sense of masculinity, of sexuality, through the
               self-created authority of stage representation
      I was a child of the theatre, my first part in the chorus of *The Mikado*
         glorying in the chance to step sideways into anyone's shoes, take
on any life
         melting into the erotic sensuality of the making-up, the only time
            I remember anyone touching my skin
                  as I was transformed from person to person
         ignorant of any representation, having only the power of another
         face

         My father didn't like me wearing make-up, it made him
               nervous, as if he recognized me taking control of
               my life
            or maybe he knew that it only seemed that way and that
               I was really being taken hold of

Time and again so many of the young women in Davey's early work are to be ignorant of representation. They are objects for consumption but objects concerned with consumption. His work consistently offers the current clichés. In the 1960s: woman as vulnerable, victim, moon, body, object, commodity (he could have written Cixous' script with added "class"). In the 1970s: woman as whore, defined by "The uterus / 'largest muscle of the body,'" and as Mary suppliant and sacrificial (writing the Irigaray of the time). We can read these now as so excruciatingly obvious: example: "I / treasured you as if / you were a scabbard of spun gold" (1972a, xxiii): example: "Breasts encrusted with jewels, / a clitoris of gold: our / Guinevere, cloistered / with her Avon / lady" (xxxi).

Their obviousness is a critique, but there is no open critique.

I'm the right age to be invited to remember the performative waver/waiver that is the mark   of the movement across the ideology-subject axis: is it a representation or an identity? I   recognize not only the crudeness of the clichés but their actuality – playing at destroying the   enemy, with the dry mock, the heartless sarcasm, and more
       women don't merely hover, they can be intensely violent
   as we try to avoid the alternative representations of the ideal
      Guinevere/Mary in *King of Swords* "preparing meals, bearing
      children? Healing ... servants ... Feeding them ... " (xxxviii)
   as we try to stop telling the stories our parents told us

We can now read them as critique of unselfconscious cliché BUT it's also unthinkingly misogynist. Writers leave not only a trace but a signature on a line drawn beneath a particular set to culture and society. What is appalling, and what comes from answering that invitation to the waver/waiver, is that the ways the women play into the cliché or representation constitute it as well.

How do I feel about a man defining femininity for me in this way? That's an odd one: I read all Davey's work seriously in the mid-1980s, so I felt the changes, found a context for the signature. But if I'd read them as they came out, I'd have felt angry and frustrated. Davey himself has constructed this knowing reader into his icon of Margaret Atwood with whips and leather: woman as dominatrix, a perfect partner for the young men he constructs, but why Atwood? Yet it has to be said that the writing gradually uncovers the social and cultural gender and class oppressions of Canada (and many other Western states), largely by elaborating the constitutions of masculinity that move with them hand in hand.

Time and again all men are heroes. Heroes are people who stick to the representations of life, who conquer or transcend their inadequacies. If you stick to the representations of women on offer, then a difference between women will usually appear as failure, to be conquered and fought (for/over).

The "young men" in *King of Swords* self-consciously elaborate on the characteristics of gang-violence (v), rape (ix), destruction, self/egotistical genocide, from an ur-text of English culture, the Arthurian legends – "incest, fratricide / a barren wife, / a bastard king" (iii). The pattern recalls the earlier romance when "you seduced me" (rather than "he married her"), that leads the modern Arthur to fantasize about "her blood on the blade / and me, over her, completing / her dream, her king / of swords" (iv).

> nb: *her* king of swords: sure my mother wanted a king, a goodly
>   knight, but my father needed to *be* one

But this hero is required to kill too many, "so I quit – would not / fight duels for you, invade kitchens, / playrooms, not screw / all your housewife girl-friends" (xxix). Arthur becomes the modern Borghia, poisoning the Great Lakes with the industrial pollution of capitalist ambition; he becomes the armies in Belfast, Bangladesh, Saigon, set against Joseph of Arimathea, the grail put to right use: fertility: "my new love's belly – a cornucopia" (xxxvii).

The Christian topos of sacrifice, also in *Weeds*, is not only the egotistical gesture of someone-who-saves, but also the brutal cutting away of embodiment, the physical effect of representation, representations that you learn you cannot accept. BUT this is not only brutal but brutalizing: the problem with revolutions. In the mid-1970s, although the production of the books becomes beautiful, the writing has a hardness of line, a blatancy of disgust in its handling of gender and poems of commerce from *Griffon* (1972) to *The Clallam* (1974). In the latter, the captain of the boat has no romantic edges, is the complete commercial cynic: America-the-Bad. The political consciousness that engages still needs violence to justify itself, and explicitly layers heroism, masculinity, commerce, and financial success.

At the age of 47 my father was deprived of his theatre by a
promotional deal and subsequently went bankrupt, and all his
apprehension turned inward. He became the Circus Master, the
Cabaret MC – something perhaps embedded in his mind from the
30s and all that amoral authority – spinning out of control,
>   shrinking the borders of his world to make it fit his shoulders
>   minute by minute aware of the one move off the path that shifts
>   the practice of regulated violence, so brutalizing, into
>   terror
>   the practiced amoral into the immoral, into consciousness
>   as the rest of us found ourselves caught in someone else's dream

how many men's dreams have netted me?

Perhaps because of this, although I've never felt the need to be a hero,
　　for a while in the 60s I wanted to be a clown and travelled across
　　Canada to join a circus in Victoria, probably the same time as
　　Davey was living there.
　　For a clown of course make-up becomes the sign of disjunction,
　　of severance between the person and the subject, the individual
　　and the representation. There's no inkling of what the individual
　　might be, because this sign is peculiarly empty of significance, it's
　　the sign of desire, the sign of apprehension, before they signify.
　　　　all those sad clowns that make you laugh by slipping on the
　　　　　　banana skin for you
　　　　or happy ones that make you sad and you're not quite sure
　　　　why
Maybe it was the clowning, but after that spell I became a make-up
　　artist for professional theatres, something I do to this day:
　　watching, vicariously enjoying the side-stepping, the sensual
　　　　enjoyment – I got a proposal of marriage from a man in
　　　　the Kingston Penitentiary while I was doing his face for a
　　　　performance of "Guys and Dolls" – he hadn't been touched
　　　　by a woman for years
　　　　　　he skipped over the border to the US after the
　　　　　　performance
　　　　　　　　released
　　but also becoming aware of the cynicism, the manipulation, the
　　　　reduction of these faces
　　　　　　the elimination of their FACE-WORK

Many of Davey's 1970s' works are explorations of male violence, entrepre-
neurial and romantic heroism which he pursues into *Capitalistic Affection*
(1982) and onto the wider cultural canvas of comic books. Why wider? –
because most people read them at one stage or another. They are a cultural
common denominator of many capitalist nation-states.

Here Davey presents the "young man" as a "boy" within a quietly self-
conscious critique of the seductions of war, romance, violence. In these fantasies the women still get-to-be-saved and the men still manage heroically
to transcend inadequacies: example: "Her best moves / were the smuggled
gun, the muffin surprise." It's sexist but also endearing, there's the trap. The

gun hidden in the muffin mix – get a distance on the sexuality. And there's the still implicit homosociality: "I loved the last reel, when Randolph & I / embraced her against the Mullholland Drive sunset" (39).

BUT the waver between critique and cliché is openly announced in Poem 1 with the opportunistic/satiric merging of "Oppenheimer looked for a sun-hat / in the shops of Los Alamos. He / typed requisitions for the Auschwitz furnaces. / I watched Tarzan / throw back his head ... " (11).

Throughout the book the writer gives us reader-feedback – from editorial reports, letters from friends, what reviewers have said, and reader response – and it becomes clear why. Few of them understand the subtlety of the waver he has introduced into the voice. Al Purdy laments the fact that "There is no single moment of ... any very strong emotion in the book" (59). They worry about "obscurity," "silliness," triviality, frigidity. No one notices Davey's shift, which the comic books effect for him, a shift implicit in his crude anti-Americanism stance of *The Clallam*, to wider global capitalism.

Miriam Waddington complains that he doesn't understand women. Clearly a new perspective on Davey's work was needed: how could they misinterpret Buck Rogers invading a "native settlement" that "contains only women," asking what do these women do? do they have knives? snakes? or "maybe / she's a nice Canadian girl, maybe / she only wants to take his hands and show him / their new day-care centre – Buck / has trouble with this one, we have trouble too / writing it down, it's easier to think of snakes and knives" (82–3).

What anchors the work is that elastic movement, pushing at the membranes of representation. It's a finely balanced book, narrativizing the subject into representations that fit, seducing us into identification yet engaging us in the constitution of that sense of fit, reminding us of its process, its elasticity. BUT there's another problem, possibly recognized by the readers, that there's nowhere else, nothing else on offer. Almost: it becomes heroic to resist heroism. The boy can fantasize about it, but the man can only document contradictions.

This is all very well for fantasies of masculinity, but when Davey returns to the young men who save the young women in *Edward & Patricia* (1983), there's no elasticity, no sense of contradiction, just a bleak determinism.

The back of *Edward & Patricia* shows a smiling author with the subtitle "wry, ribald, bawdy, poignant ... " The writing is also mocking, cruelly banal, honest to the point of meticulous brutality, and terrified. It gathers together many earlier narrative signs and casts them into a suburban nightmare of sexual failings. Or is it a failing if you can only get it off with your wife in her parents' house? Certainly it's a sign of something, which the book explores: masculinity and femininity caught in representation; Edward placing Patricia's china dogs in sexually suggestive positions on her mantelpiece.

The black humour of the deadpan voice that speaks of inexorable repetition and determinism, undercuts the earnest and increasingly desperate Edward. But here "Patricia" is given some context, so although "Edward" rejects her finally – with red lipstick over her mirror – as "WHORE" and shatters all her china dogs, the reader has enough sense of the construction of their dilemma to problematize the reduction. It's a hurtful book, about hurt that you can't put your finger on, that must have hurt him to write.

The network of topics called upon and reinforced here, along with Davey's own comments in a critique of autobiographical devices in Daphne Marlatt's *Taken*, sets forward ethical issues and gives them weight. Despite saying that he moved from poems of personal crisis to textual interest around 1970, Davey acknowledges that personal crisis frequently does impel the writer. Hence he publishes eight books between 1970 and 1973 (he tells us after a list of crises).

Edward & Patricia superimposes elements of earlier works with elements from other narratives of his father and mother

> grandfather and grandmother –
> the bpNichol picket-fence of geneology
> the I-I-I-I-I-I-I going back a long way
>> making a line (o)
>>> where is the end of the line?

No man is a hero yet the promise of romantic heroism leads to violence. So Edward hits Patricia, "like in the movies he thought, slap her to her senses he thought. He slapped." (13). Women are caught in the shadow of that promise unless they take it on for themselves. It's a shadow that is a negative of someone else's representation that our body fills. A visor for a visor. Eventually the pressure to embody pushes our features into a place of recognition, of repetition.

In *The Louis Riel Organ and Piano Company* (1985), Frank Davey offers us the disintegrating masks of Davey Crockett, Louis Riel, Wacousta, as if asking how far can you push them? and what's left of the heroes? It takes him two books of prose, *Reading "Kim" Right* (1993) and *Karla's Web* (1994), to begin to sort out what to do next, both books being, among other things, examinations of how we come to accept representations, the shells of representations, and the pressure of embodiment.

What he chooses in *Popular Narratives* (1991) are larger discursive structures or positions that depend on lineality in a different way: example: "In Love with Cindy Jones," which tells a series of narratives about one event through "Text of Recreation," "Psychological Text," "Historical Text," "Critical Text," "Phallocentric Discourse," "The Gift Economy," "Discursive Context," etc. Or, example: "Postcard Translations" with their semiotic dispersal of meaning. Or, example: "How and Why John Loves Mary: Thirty-Seven Variations on Half of a Theme by Margaret Atwood," where the cumulative mass of variation is both numbing and obsessive.

The reader reads the voice watching the drift in significance as the writing moves through repeated elements, or the contradictions of the stable sign as he takes apart the "headline."

So: it would be relatively easy to speak of Davey's reiteration with variation around issues of masculinity, violence, and capital, from the unselfconscious voice of *Bridge Force*, the tortured awakening into the consciousness of myth: the romantic turned cultural studies critic: the semiotician/theorist – as reflected by the critical journal *Open Letter* which he has edited for many years. BUT it can't explain *Cultural Mischief* (1996) and doesn't get close to *How Linda Died* (2002).

We could heroize Davey for his tough critique of masculinity/femininity based on his own unflinching ignorance in the early work; could condemn his portrayal of women as writing the script for Cixous, Irigarary, et al.; could praise his recuperation of women as "victims-of-men," writing another script for another set of feminists. It's far more difficult for masculinity, there are far fewer clear lines.

We could welcome Davey's gritty portrayal of capitalist greed, usually the United States', of class apprehension parallel to desire, and the shift to global capitalism; could condemn his reification of commodities (but that might be a joke), or even praise his foregrounding of the reification of commodities, something that women are particularly good at.

We could commend the painful honesty of Davey's critique of violence as inherent both to masculinity and to class greed.

YET even if we got sophisticated about this, all this FACE-WORK wouldn't help with recognizing the end of the line.

GOING FOR THE END OF THE LINE

Living with Davey's writing, taking the time to read, I'm reading for what?
    not for earth-shaking claims, not for heroic acts

           although every so often you find a starched comment, like the wafers
           in a vanilla ice-cream that tease the taste-buds with that first
           nibble
                                                                  then recede to cardboard
That's not why I read Frank Davey.
           That's just the metatheory, the travel sickness of recognition and
           dislocation
                 I read to change
                      I'm going to learn you
                      I'm going to read you
                 and people don't change without changing breath, breathing
                           where the line pauses, turns or ends
                           where the word erupts   parts company
                                prepares/ for engagement
                                               negotiation
                                               vulnerability
                                                      freefall
I'm reading for an insistent rhythm, that changes but is there consistently,
    sistering
           something you pick up in your body memory
           a rhythm that makes an impact on your own prosody
                      on how you come to the end of the line
                                the sentence
                                the feeling of time

All through *Weeds* there's an invitation not only into Christian myth, but
into the line, the question of what the line will release, *if* it will release. The
line has power but not over anyone, especially not over anyone who only
reads for the other invitation. You have to learn to work with it. In *Weeds*
there are a lot of good beginnings. By *Arcana* (1973), a serial poem aban-
doned 16 March 1970, six days after his first child is born, Davey is examin-
ing the line as a rhythm of habit where the "sounds cling to one": example,
"The second girl I loved was built of simile," of "someone like me" (73). Habit
is "not to live / but to be lived. Inhabited," and where habit is inhabiting, we
find heroism and idealism. Yet you can't just put the past away. The spring
forwards (for words) is habit but also breath, sound, structure: so how do
you have "a line for the end of this?" (76) (heroism) he asks.

      a line for the end
      the end of the line

an end of the line, lien, ligne
微microenvironments of family, of friends
layering the parents' lives over our own is also different
breaks the rhythm
Through all the writing there are eruptions of childhood:
the hoodedness of that world
the inexplicability of parents
the monstrous grotesquerie of the adult
how do you end that line?
Lines made up of the stress and distress of rhythm and breakings
for if rhythm joins, conjoins, brings/holds together
how the breath/breast/chest beats
how the mouth works
breakings can sever/cut/stop/smash/halt/give time off/
recuperate/change
irrecoverable: a sofa gone too far
gone to seed
irrevocable: you cannot call it back
irrèvocable
irrevòcable
irrevocable
irreverent
running current of the sotto voce
that you hear in the poems of childhood, the microenvironments
of *War Poems* (1979)

There is continued violence in some of these microenvironments: example: "The Ball" (1979), the smashing of ants, the green tomato fused with cat exploding "against the garage wall under the belly / of a stray cat ... " (89); example: "The Drunks" with its smash and shock and "I was sure I was going only / twenty miles an hour" (90). And there is social violence in the pressures of getting it wrong in "The Locks," beginning to recognize the power of representation in "The Shopping List," or his understanding that to some extent he's a commodity to his parent, putting him on display in "The Piano." But there is also a shift into a daily life that is not violent or commodified. "The Window" (*Back to the War*, 2005/1979) is a still life, a study in the life of a boy's father. While the boy observes at the window, the father is in the garden, the mother and grandmother in the kitchen. The boy looks out at that male life outside. His life is focused around the mother and grandmother, yet his eyes are focused on the father. The boy doesn't know what's on the other side of the window, why his father spends time in the garden rather than with him, even on weekends.

You get the picture, and then the narrative.

The lineation of his father departing for work breaks down and isolates the actions, not in a regulated way but more a repeated movement with variation that infiltrates the breath with participles and the oddly shaped noun "landing" (that wavers into the participial), marking out the balances and shifts in the prosody, punctuated by directional phrases: example:

> I listen to him leave for work
>
> > going down the inside stairs
> > walking across the concrete floor
>
> [speeding up with]   opening,
>
> > then slamming the outside door
>
> [closure in the expanding phrase]   walking up those stairs
>
> > > beneath my window. (38)

There is a stillness and minute awareness. The child is visualizing/auralizing the movement into a sense of the father with an aim (going out) and of himself as closed, the relationship closed – but also secure: it's a freedom from, not a freedom to.

When he turns to his mother and grandmother the repeated sounds mark out a recognizable pattern, habitual, self-referential: example:

> When I get up I have breakfast with my *mother* and my
> *grandmother*
>
> > & then lunch with my *mother* and my *grandmother*
> > & on *Sundays* my *grandmother* takes me across the village to
>
> *Sunday*   school.
>
> > On *Sunday* afternoon &
> > on *Saturdays*   they talk tog*ether* in the kitchen
> > > & I *kneel* at the window
> > > > watch*ing* my fa*ther*
> > > who is *kneeling* in his garden (38)

The balanced clauses, phrases, and nouns that open this verse indicate that the life of his mother and grandmother is something he knows, even if he doesn't understand or fully participate in its light insistent chatter of "t"s. This in contrast to the words around his father, tethered by "ther" to the others, yet so still, so silent, so alone, as the boy searches for an identification pattern and kneels by the window just as his father kneels in the garden, both of them participial, "watching" and "kneeling."

He is of course setting up gender distinctions of chatter/silence, kitchen/garden, community/isolation. But also offering a singular moment of choice:

which way will this child move? will he break the isolation? or remain in the kitchen? It is a moment of moral weight that is part of the situated environment. We don't know what happens/will happen, although we do know from "The Arches" (1979) that when that boy retreats from the graveyard the family is tending, his father comes to him "whistling and humming" (102).

In *Cultural Mischief* Davey translates the hoodedness of the child with its particular eruptions into an adult world of the local layered with global tension.
      The dead are so particular
& when the writer re-members, in the elegy "Dead in Canada," "Greg's old particulars [which] lay all about … not a list, [but] strewn about like a pile of old shoes" (55), he not only erases the heroic elegiac voice but textures the body of the dead. He says "Death leaves a room with unfilled volume" that has a particularity quite different from the embodied negatives promised by representation.

That was, for me at first, where the line ended. But then Davey wrote *How Linda Died* and death became not only iterable but irritable, and then irridescent. The reader alongside the writer weaving a fabric around the content, a fabric riddled with holes. You watch someone doing what they have to do, every day, but each time it's a rehearsal not a repetition. The displacement of the lyric or elegiac "I" asks for a different kind of reading "I." The text "I" made when reading picks up the difference in the detail and it's ridiculous but compelling the way the same things constantly surprise me with difference.
      The words texture a prosody that depends on the width of the line
             hangs on the horizontal
             hovering over the potential
                    energy of white space
               an invitation to breath/breathe
       an invitation to the living and the dying
And a lot of this book is about how "Linda" lived for the awkward lines
              the lines that don't fit
                that ask us to go with them to the end
       and if we go with them
          we find that it isn't an ending after all
            that the end of the line is neither place nor time

BUT Linda does die   and in the present tense of the book on 9 June 2002 at about 11:30 p.m.. And the "I" who rehearsed the possibilities of life every day for her is now rehearsing for one less person. The reader feels this because reading the iterable engages with a continuous stream of small tasks that are here suddenly reduced and changed. The body memories of those tasks articulated in the breath and rhythm of reading with the writing, stay with the muscles and embed into the biochemistry. So even if the line doesn't end, it changes.

And perhaps they always do: But I haven't read the one about the dogs.

PERFORMANCE 5
FACE-WORK: Going to the End of the Line – A Study in the Poetics of Frank Davey

WEBLINK   http://vimeo.com/18434984

1999   University of Leeds (UK), "Revisions of Canadian Literature" Conference
2000   University of Leeds (UK), Theatre Workshop Graduate Studies

"FACE-WORK" took two years of scripting, planning, and rehearsing. I wanted to spend time with Frank Davey's poetics, since I had spent, as had most Canadian critics of the period, a lot of time with his criticism. Marxism of various kinds had formed the bedrock for my rhetorical studies for many years, and Davey's Canadian set toward the theories had been a constant reminder of the underlying exploitation that made and makes my lifestyle possible. At the same time, I was intrigued by the attitude to women I was reading out of the texts and wanted to understand how much of the Marxist political stance was wrapped up in exploitation of women, or how much my compromise into that stance set me against myself as a woman. The opportunity to perform this production came with an invitation from Danielle Fuller and Shirley Chew to contribute to a conference on Canadian literature in 1999.

The cosmetic make-up/theatrical make-up material that informs the piece fell out of reading Davey's accounts of nuclear family angst and neuroticism in the 1960s to 1970s. I had seen this occurring throughout my teenage years in Hamilton, Ontario, and beyond that period and place as I grew older. My mother had instructed me in putting on make-up (as she had in cooking) while she was planning to sell cosmetic products. My stepfather was a well-known amateur theatre director, so I had also spent some time backstage working with the theatre make-up. For one summer I was the make-up artist for a small, semi-professional company in southern Ontario. The following summer I sneaked out west with my then boyfriend to join a circus in Victoria as a clown, and spent many hours perfecting the make-up needed. These memory confluences took over as I read Davey's poetry, and the production grew out of their associations and materialities.

Going from cosmetic to theatre to clown was the visceral experience of which actors often speak when they refer to masking. Since the move intended to shift from normalizing codes for women's behaviour to the increasingly self-conscious masking of stage, and then circus, it was odd that the externalization of the process had the inverse affect on me bodily. The more obvious the mask the more destabilized I felt the character-part had become. In practical terms, I felt that the shift was analogous to a shift I always felt in the Department of English Literature in which I worked: that the cosmetic was expected (and I never wore make-up), the theatrical was the institutional form for women such as me to be seen in the academy, and the clown was effectively my role.

After "Bodies in Trouble" I had realized that part of the aesthetic problem is the issue of how readers can engage with the text through an autographical urge to become part of it. I inserted these autographical moments into the essay text, typographically separating them from the critical voice. In both essay and production they were not there to identify with the readings from Davey's texts, but to be in conversation with them, to engage in strategies for the difference that is made in situated work. In the event, I found that the final maskings of the performance generated a bodily experience that did not reach out for cultural fit. The green dental mask that sets on the face and when taken off also strips off all the previous make-up left me feeling open, clean, slightly bereft, wondering what would happen next. The production moves this along by taking "a mask that I just happen to have ready from before" and reiterating the cosmetic make-up of the first face. This kind of citational repetition ties us to the normative world around us, but my actual face was still stripped. It felt as if I'd made up my own death mask. And this left me alongside, waiting.

On one level I was engaging with Davey's writing as a reader, an audience to his performance. On another I was a performer in rehearsal. The two elements came so close together they fused, their combined work generated a différance, a place where I had no idea what would happen next, a moment of "until." I have had little feedback on this piece, in either of its productions. The video is from the second production (2000), which I don't think worked as well as the first because it took place in front of people who knew nothing at all about Frank Davey or his work. The former production (1999) played out in front of an audience of about forty people at a conference on Canadian literature organized by Danielle Fuller and Susan Billingham, and the people attending were well aware of the contexts for his work. One comment I remember was that the performative elements gave "me," the critic, a lot of "power" – presumably over the audience.

6

The *Inédit* in Writing by Nicole Brossard: Breathing the Skin of Language

In the necessity and desire to reinvent the language there are certainly an intention of happiness, a utopic thread, a serious responsibility.

"Trajectory" 1992b, 184[1]

In her writing, Nicole Brossard continually engages with the work of translation. The translator is the reader-as-maker and offers us an analogy for a more inclusive sense of readers-as-makers. Perhaps because Brossard's work is central to contemporary philosophical discussion, it has a long history of this process which itself becomes part of the fiction-making. And perhaps this long history also works with the way Brossard's writing foregrounds both what she is saying and how she is saying it, so that she is doing as she does, in process simultaneously with installing, rehearsing in performance. *Green Night in the Labyrinth Park* insists on the process of translation by leaving one section in French. *Baroque at Dawn* becomes a meditation on the porous skin between writer and translator that exemplifies the process of friendship: making difference to change self that gifts making difference to change self. Translation, like writing, can be an art-making only when it engages letter by letter, word by word, line by line. It involves intens/tion,[2] strong attention.

I am interested in knowledge, moral action, and ethics. Hence I engage with Nicole Brossard's work mainly through her sense of language being the material place for the articulation of the unthought and unknown (one cannot know until a thing is articulated), which in itself is moral action. The unknown doesn't just get said. Its articulation is a laborious process of working on the words, a kind of training in engagement specific to each reader-writer relationship that is coincident with the engagement itself. The better trained we are, the more we have a practice, the more material the engagement, to the point that the writer-reader begin to translate together, to work on growing the skin of language, the huge second lung of breath on which the material depends. Yet training never stops. If it does, the moment of ar(rest) remains in fit, slides into enough, never returns to alongside work in the process of until. The articulation becomes representation, or reproduction in the Marxist sense, and language splits into the semantic and fictional divide about which Brossard speaks so often.

To get to alongside work is difficult. Brossard's criticism, like her poetry from which it is scarcely distinguishable, uses words that are over-oxygenated because we often don't know how to take up the invitation to work on the translation process. The text gives off energy at random, makes us vulnerable in the intimacy of conceptual and somatic sensation it promises, leaves me light-headed or feeling the unbearable intensity of insistent but elusive significance. I have to train to read so that the images do not drift toward nausea but toward meaning. I have to learn to work with the texts. But what makes me persist as I am flung from white space to white space? Probably the quite different experience of reading Brossard's novels in a classroom with a group of other readers, and I will turn to her novel *Baroque at Dawn* in the concluding discussion. But also, my experience of reading Brossard's texts is so similar to her descriptions of writing them.[3]

In "Aut*her*" (1997) Brossard reiterates a topic that infuses her writing of the late 1990s, stating that she is a humanist writer "profoundly moral, that is to say attentive to human life in its small and great struggles to signify beyond reproduction" (2). The definition is significant: unlike the ethical, which is bound to ideological and discursive institutions of power, the moral delineates our willingness to take into account all that representation ignores or obscures or represses, all the messy details of our lives that are beyond reproduction because they do not fit. To attend to the moral, we have to work on installing those parts of life/our lives that are not-yet-said, a process Brossard calls the *inédit*, which is fundamentally an exploration of the creation of knowledge. Her writing works endlessly on installing and increasingly on what *installing* is, how it happens. Because of the growing pressure of overdetermination by institutional power and new technologies that operate on a global scale and deny located knowledge, agency, and moral action to the individual, this is one of the most pressing philosophical issues of humanist inquiry and politics in Western democratic states. Yet there are remarkably few attempts to write about the process of creation that installing involves – to bring into presence and recognition the material reality of the body and work of the *inédit*.

This essay charts a movement among the representative, the fictional, and the material: the semantic, the installation, and the *inédit* or translation of the not-yet-said. Brossard speaks of this slightly differently in "Trajectory" (1992) when she describes the process of creation in writing as "a wager of presence in the semantic, imaginary and symbolic space" (179). This movement suggests that those locations are not fully distinct, but are particular and necessary to new developments in democratic humanism that distinguish it from the exclusionary rhetoric of the liberal humanism that has dominated the formation of nation-states in the West.

INSTALLATION: DESIRE AND DISCOURSE

A recent translation of an early work, *Installations (avec et sans pronoms)*, (*Installations* 1984/2000), clarifies an entire range of theoretical inquiry and cultural study in Western liberal democracies. During the 1960s and early 1970s, neo-Marxist theory combined with Lacanian psychoanalysis to define individuals as "subjects" when they participated in the ideological symbolic system of representation. As is well known, the feminist response to these ideas, which deny women subjecthood, was to claim the "imaginary" realm, or the pre-symbolic, since women's consciousness did not enter the world of ideological representations in the same way, if at all, as men's. The feminist response facilitated and contributed to a much wider understanding that the symbolic system defined as Lacanian also denied subjecthood to people of colour, to the poor, to those of different ability and age – in effect, to all those who were not part of the small group of propertied, white, Christian men who worked in and on institutions of power (Hunter 1999). But for all the hegemonic analysis of *subjectivity* or *subject position*[4] as terms to define the activity of individuals not systemically part of hegemony yet contributing to its maintenance, there was little in the growing field of discourse studies that could identify the agency of the individual and hence the field of moral action.

Brossard's use and elaboration of installation is an early and prescient development of the idea of "constituted" subject positions introduced by gender studies to discourse theory in the mid-1980s. To name but one, Judith Butler's concept of "performance" as the activity of a "constituting subject" (Butler 1993) always retained the emphasis on the hegemonic and ideological, simply because of the linguistic bond to the *subject* defined by the Lacanian symbolic. *Installations*, in contrast, swings the weighting to the individual's ability to "fictionalize": if we are denied participation as a *subject*, and recognize that subjectivity is a matter of representation rather than nature, then why not make our own fictions?

In *Installations* the verse "Installation" presents the writer settling "into my body's installation / so as to be able to respond / when a woman gives me a sign" (49). On the opposite page is the verse "Shadow" in which "a beautiful subjectivity" "doesn't broach / lucidity," in which the body "pronounce[s] shadow / avid for images," and in which we are left "dreaming *my life* / at arm's length" (48). All ideological representations are constructed from real material, from actual individuals. In order to fit representation, elements must be left out or hidden, so that, in a sense, all representations that are allowed to subjects cast a shadow. Often characterized as *loss* or *absence*, this shadow is in effect just as material and actual, but without words, without visibility, unrecognized. And if that unseen materiality installs itself, presents itself so that it can be recognized, it attains agency. Writing is one means by which we effect this installation. As Brossard puts it in the critical essay "Writing as a Trajectory of Desire and Consciousness," published a few years later (1992) but containing more contemporary material, writing "translates that enigmatic but reflective operation whereby we process and can transform our versions of reality, that is, change its metaphoric and semantic course" (179).

The *Inédit*: Translating of the Not-Yet-Said – from Installation to the Body

Installations proceeds to some extent by probing the thresholds between shadow and installation, probing the possibilities for recognizing the not-said, not-made-public emotions, feelings, events, significances in our lives. However, the next move toward agency is installation of the recognized. First in that movement is the difficulty of identifying the not-said as not-yet-said, acknowledging that this is not a matter of lack or absence but of material presence that can be installed, and once in the process of installation, becomes a mode of knowing that can inform moral action. The exploration of the not-said into the *inédit* emerges in many of Brossard's essays of the late 1980s and into the 1990s. By "Fluid Arguments" (1996), she is arguing that the production of the *inédit* traverses all her books (316). "Harmonious Matter still Manoeuvres" (Harmonious), a work from 1990 republished in 1997 along with *Typhon dru*, reiteratively explores the "not-yet-said" by saying it, and in the process offers a series of remarkable translations.

The first stanza suggests that a thought that arises "in the midst of reality, its unnameable poses" prompts her despite the *unnameable* to have recourse to the thought that "nothing is too slow nor too brief for the universe" (8/9). The second stanza claims that "I know that all isn't said because my body settles with a certain joy into such a thought" and that this sends words into a trajectory along which she can "by joining vowels and the spine of thoughts, get closer, with eyes narrowed in fascination, to death and its opposite" (10–11, my translation). There is no clear *meaning* from this syntax (not-sentence). There is resistant *signification*. Installation is not a solitary process and the reader must engage with the trajectory of words even to recognize them as writing any material presence, let alone the materiality itself.

Each stanza in "Harmonious" presents a moment of possible recognition, of words for the not-yet-said being thrown out in arcs whose movement we may recognize and engage with, or not. Whether we do so is largely a matter of training in word skills – the techniques, strategies, and stances of poetic and rhetoric – and a willingness to take up the politics of reading. Coincident with the first publication of *Harmonious* is Brossard's contribution to *The Politics of Poetic Form*, "Poetic Politics" (1990), in which she argues that while a text "shows its politics in the writing" (78), it "becomes political" (80) when it is read. It becomes political because it makes "space for the unthought" (81) and can transform anger, ecstasy, and desire into "social meaning" (81). However, the reader needs to engage their training in perspective, theme, discourse, and style to become a *non-conformist* reader and find "a space for new experience – travelling through meaning while simultaneously producing meaning" (79).

How does the writer invite the reader into engagement and the production of meaning in translation? How does the text encourage a *non-conformist* reader? The suggestions scattered through "Harmonious" insistently take one back to the body. The writer is "troubled" by any movement that leaves desire behind (14): desire in most hegemonic discourse is constructed by the Lacanian symbolic as that thing in us that cannot be represented, therefore always already a loss or absence. But for the installed individual, desire is the prompt to recognize the not-yet-said. To leave behind desire is to hand oneself over to representation and reproduction. Desire is awakened by "les coquilles roses des sens," both tongue and clitoris, that through rapture graft matter onto the postures of voice: but this is not readily definable matter, it is "matière secrète, matière plus ronde, matière comme tes soupirs et d'autres liquides encore" (14). Later, the body is pointed, punctuated, and retains in its passionate readings and subtle gestures an incredible syncrony of sense that reminds us that all is not said – despite the symmetries of thought. The indistinct/undefineable voice and touch of the body ("nos mains [...] caressent bien indistinctement de la voix et de la paume") compass both the universal and particular, constructing the world "to the measure of our hands" when they caress "le corps humain qui a des seins" (18, 19).

On the one hand, the writer perceives that life can silence, circumscribe, reduce, and she uses this knowledge to draw energy from the cycles of tears and the dust/push of birth to make sure that she works in dreams, at night, installing into voice (20–1). On the other, when her skin is charged "de cyprine et d'écho" (22) [more correctly "chargée de cyprine et d'écho" or "full of cyprin and of echo"] she smiles the inseparability of the bodily and thoughtful in a deep breath. In this state stable objects (representations) make her breasts "inverse," they split thought, bound to enlighten death: she knows all is not said because her heart is wrung (22–3) with the *inédit* of materiality. And at times when "memory is afraid of leaping and desire is full of answers," when she is not "brimming with the breath of energy," she can be seduced or tempted toward certainty and sentiment even though she knows that all is not said because the "action of light breaking shadow" revives her energy for re-thinking (24–5). The final stanza outlines the dilemma: "to name is still a function of dream and hope" (27) because women are still invisibly embodied in representation and need fictional form to participate fully in society. They need the fictional stability of installation become constellation that can insist on its position in discursive knowledge. Yet in the fictional, "between cultured conversation and tradition," it is vertiginously cold; we are left freezing at the edge of articulation that requires a precipitous projection of oneself beyond fiction. Here it's the bodily presence of tears, in their "volatile materiality," that reminds us that despite the strange sweat of the "true" settling representations onto our "life," all is not said (26–7, my translations).

To a significant extent the acknowledgment and recognition of the not-yet-said is at the centre of what an "artist" does in the modern period of the Western world, a period Brossard's texts designate as *baroque*, the shift to humanist values in the seventeenth century. But the recognized writer-as-artist in the modern world has usually dealt with issues close to subjecthood because they have come from or work directly for the same sociopolitical grouping as those who hold and shape power. As such, their sayings quickly become hegemonic articulations that have precisely addressed the repressions of representation, and could be perceived to transgress or oppose them because the representation/fiction/articulation border is so narrow. The precipice is not so high. Criticism has usually defined such attempts at articulation as "transcendent" because, in habitual post-Cartesian fashion, critics have often held language itself to be inadequate to the real: the limits of language have to be transcended by the artist in order to fictionalize the real, to bring it into representation. Not that writers do this, and their increasing focus through the past three centuries on process and the not-yet-said may be an indication of their frustration with the description. But this is how critics have expressed what they do: one could say that because he is a subject, the modern artist is always gendered male.

FROM TRANSGRESSION TO VISION

Brossard attests to two specific changes in her life in 1974, motherhood and lesbian life (see *These Our Mothers*), coincident with her decision to replace "transgression" ("Only a Body" 1996b, 5) with "marginality and vision" ("Fluid Arguments" 1996a, 339). She refers to these two life changes as gaining "carnal knowledge" which led her to put aside "opposition" for "value" ("Poetic Politics" 1990a, 76). "Carnal knowledge" is the incontrovertible rooting of flesh and skin in "motive" that moves beyond the "object of desire" to vision (74). These comments are followed by the claim that the "text" of language "calls for *vision* rather than subversion. It calls for awareness, concentration, sharpness. Vision goes beyond transgression because it brings forth new material" (82). Slightly earlier, in "Memory: Hologram of Desire ("Hologram" 1988)", Brossard speaks of memory as the field/song [champs/chant] of vision: that the memories and memory of women need to find fictional form because an "actualizing memory" is "one that initiates presence in the world" (3). Women's memories, in "becoming visible and exposed in public ... help ... us to expand our field of vision" (9). At the same time, memory is the "hologram of desire," a "synchrony" of real life, imagination, and "desire's fullness" (9). Yet the hologram does not retain the carnal knowledge of the lesbian body.

In "Writing as Trajectory" ("Trajectory" 1992b), memory's part in vision is further clarified. The trajectory of writing toward vision is "the momentum of energy" (180; see also work with corps/texte/writing,[5] and "le cortext exhubérant" in "Poetic Politics" 1990a, 73–4) that draws us "from fear to desire, from aphasia to memory, from fragmentation to integrity, from humiliation to dignity, from alienation to consciousness, from auto-censure to transgression" (180). This trajectory combines the body and its "circulation of energy" with language and with writing: the body provides "for a network of associations out of which we create our mental environment ... we imagine far beyond what we in fact see, hear or taste" ("Poetic Politics," 73), and writing shapes that energy through language to suggest "solutions which can unknot social patterns of violence and death" (74).

But writing "toward vision" is not a unitary action that leaves transgression completely behind. First, the individual has to "re-member childhood and to untie the knots that have formed in its throat" ("Trajectory," 180), a "ritual of trembling" that is a recognition of the unsaid in one's life, the process of memory. Once taking shape "the words flow. Certain ones agglomerate in little descriptive and narrative islets, others stretch out endlessly into long sentences, others remain suspended, uncertain, at the horizon of thought" (181). To enter the social world, an individual needs to write in language that discursive or ideological power can recognize. If we choose to write for the representative world of ideology, we trangress, we come up against the "antagonistic and hierarchical structure of misogynist and patriarchal sense" (181) that makes words invested with our energy "crash violently into the same word, the one invested with masculine experience," in what Brossard calls the "ritual of shock."

If instead we write for the discursive world, we engage the "ritual with sliding" which subtly negotiates with power. All language connotes through semantic and metaphoric circuits that produce an "aura," odour, tempo around a work. Ritual with sliding displaces "slightly but sufficiently the semantic aura of words in such a way that they produce an unforeseeable resonance without alteration in the signifier" (182). The energy charge of this concentration on "sonority," "orthography," "usual sense," "potential polysemy," and "etymology" produces an effect that "conducts sense well beyond the signified," and "she who writes displaces imperceptibly but *radically* the order of the world" (182). Ritual with sliding fictionalizes, reinvents language for the discursive, negotiates with hegemonic power, has direct social and political effect. At the same time, it needs motivation and, I would argue, it finds this largely in the "ritual with breath" which multiplies "energy by modulating it to the rhythm most appropriate to thought in the body" (183). These four rituals – of trembling, shock, sliding, and breath – are not separable, although they may be differently weighted. Together they make a "space for the existence of the woman subject and her desire ... But ... above all an unedited [installation of the not-yet-said] space in which the unthought of the world suddenly takes the form of evidence" (184).

THE COMPLICATIONS OF THE BODY

Brossard describes the ritual of breath as an activity about "tonality," "music made of silence and harmony" that is "practised absolutely without mask" ("Trajectory," 183). Most of her poetry brings us into some insight into the workings of the ritual of breath, and a different kind of engagement with it is offered by the text "Only a Body to Measure Reality By." Here the lesbian body, which has "felt the presence of the other woman as vital in your life … develops a skin so soft that it almost becomes a personal proof of faith in each woman" (9). The "radiant" lesbian body navigates in language, transforms thoughts and images. It is a "Harmonious Body" that situates "on the side of *insoumission* [the not-subjected, also the non-compliant]" and "constantly moves her toward the other woman" (9). Brossard begins with the body as "our solitude, our only certitude" (5), but immediately moves on to say that because "the body has eyes to see, ears to listen, a memory to fantasize and words to compare, so it is, we are not alone anymore" and we need "to read the in-between you and me" (5).

The extended subtitle of the piece, published from the Ravenscroft Lecture given with Daphne Marlatt in 1996, includes "Writing the In-Between." The harmonious lesbian body is not simply a body with many masks like difference, utopia, and performance, but a body in touch with other bodies. It is a body that does not stop with the skin. This is the single element that makes it possible to turn away from transgression toward making value, away from ideology to moral and ethical considerations bound to process. If the first step is to recognize the reductiveness of the representations of subjecthood, the second to separate the fictionality of installation from the fiction of the subject position and its shadow, the third is to delineate the body for translation as one that will be able to retain the alongside work, control the slide back into cultural fit.

The isolated hologram cannot do this, but the necessary in-between negotiations of the harmonious lesbian body can. What makes the concept philosophically different and challenging is that it does not suggest an isolated alternative, despite the lingering signification of its *utopian* tendency. The harmonious body is complicated because it is anti-transcendent and focused on materiality, while simultaneously it creates *effects*, installations that can constellate, emerge into and change the discursive and may even become new representations or characters. The intellectual complexity is focused through Brossard's brief commentary on *beauty*: as she notes in "Harmonious," if the materiality of the real were to fail/fall, it would strand us without warning, "skin hesitating between philosophies and dawn" (17) in "la vaste complication de la beauté" (16).

Skin "hesitates" in the complication of beauty because beauty occurs when installations erupt into the discursive. When the *inédit* is recognized by ideological or hegemonic systems, when it acquires fictional if not representative power, the not-yet-said is made public, explodes with certainty into *fit* the first time, and thereafter settles, "s'installe." Beauty marks the point where social meaning is first given to installing the not-said. In "Hologram" this is described as "the aura of sane words that, within us, form sequences of truth" (10, see also "Trajectory," 184). In *Mauve Desert* Brossard's narrator/translator describes the "time of believing [which] is a time of civilisation, a certitude of beings that fills chance with architecture and voice explosions" (149). This follows her statements on beauty: "'Beauty is before reality,' of a polysemic, unthinkable antecedence ... Beauty precedes desire, its fragment, history, the transection of reality and fiction" (145). Beauty precedes reality because without representation reality cannot be recognized. It transects reality and fiction because it is both the source of representative power and the presence of installation. The notes in *Mauve Desert* then go on to distinguish between the production of warm beauty that "takes shape in the warm belly of the species [and] transforms itself, language, break, shimmering, seduction: beauty, angle of reflection, selective neuron, source tongue" (145), and beauty as sustained eruption into *fit* that is the "cold beauty of the eternal, beauty intimidates" (145), "beauty puts an end to intimacy in us, yes, threatens supremely like a cold language" (146), makes an image an "astounding installation" (146, my translation).

The translator in *Baroque at Dawn* speaks of beauty as an enchantment, a "feeling that we can reach out and touch light" (213). But she also says that we need this conceptual and somatic sensation that the image *fits*. Indeed the "writer," having said that she doesn't write "any more" (205), is revived by the beauty of a fountain in Montreal, a response that allows her to "exist" (234) just as she "existed" in Buenos Aires when writing her previous novel (212). Beauty is allied to *truth* in a profoundly Keatsian manner: it is eternal and cold, but at the same time, like Keats's urnmaker, full of the complications of politics, the necessity to reinvent language and make recognizable the not-yet-said, and pregnant with evidence for value and moral action. Beauty is produced in the belly of the writer/text/reader.

The Body of the *Inédit*: Selfhood and Knowledge

Whatever verbal beauty becomes in the discursive or ideological constellation, it comes from the hard labour on words we have undertaken during installation, during the process of creating the not-yet-said, the *inédit*, the "objects of thought and emotion that can be shared" ("Fluid Arguments," 336). This work is also work on the self, and Brossard describes the production of shared thought and emotion as "To live with arms filled with metaphors, going toward an encounter with a second self hooked on spectacle, vertigo and lucidity" (336). If the self is represented in the Lacanian symbolic, fitted into the discursive, how is it present in the *inédit*? the harmonious lesbian body? The exploration of poetics and rhetoric made available by Brossard's critical writings is also a philosophical exploration of selfhood and of knowledge. For we cannot know that we exist if there is no other person to confirm our existence, just as we do not know that we know unless someone else shares the translation as knowledge, even the textuality of knowledge in process.

Green Night in Labyrinth Park (*Labyrinth* 1992) braids beauty, selfhood, and knowledge into close proximity. It opens the First "Turning" [my translation] with the comment that life sets pronouns "all about the I in order to recognise, within us, the others, without too many collisions" (27), and concludes that while the sea "creates fissures in the political life of pronouns," destabilizing the I, so the pronouns are at times transformed into "essential figures" (27). Somewhere here is "life," not as a principle that "wears itself out in anecdotes," but life "in the mouth that speaks the principle. Saliva, bacteria, tongue, mucus, palate" (27). And the political purpose of *Labyrinth* is to "seek the principle" in the bodily mouth of the speaker.

As a political text, it shares with the reader the activity of "making political" by understanding what is "in the mouth" of the writer. The writer first offers us the "story" or "labyrinth," into which she then walks, describing eleven turnings, each of which excavates a strategy for understanding emotion and thought. If we take guidance from the final line of the opening labyrinth, the text outlines possible rhetorical manoeuvres; "I am breathing in rhetoric, in the never ending process of hope" (26). The First Turning displays the ambivalent rhetoric of Politics which "can be like a spell if you can't spell your name with a woman in mind" (27). The Second Turning follows the history of the writer as someone who found the explanations of heterosexual discourse painful but who in time generated so many questions about alternative discourses that she learned to distance herself, flying so constantly among these archipelagos of discourse that she had diverted the initial set of explanations into other routes.

With the Third Turning, the writer reads one phrase from the labyrinth, "the blue shawl slipping from Simone's shoulders" (29), as an image that "relays desire ... thinks, with unexpected vitality, the drift of meaning" (29). The image penetrates "the solid matter of our ideas without our knowing" so that while the writer reads and tries to decide on meaning, she discovers her "intentions" already formed: the image blazes the beauty of Simone's shoulders into the writer with intensity and she asks if this is because "I want it to be so" (29) or "fruit that is not of chance" (29). But the image slips by meanings, persists as a "fervent relay" (29), insisting on engagement without resolution. The Fourth Turning is a commentary on "country," as traditions, smells, colours, seasons, history, violence, law, heroes, and God; on its ability to divide us and, "in the language and tongue of the lovher" (30), to unite us; and on the need for the lovher to speak "in the tongue of the unsubjected," that part of us not oppressed by country in order to "prolong our lesbian lives" (30). The contradiction between country as a unifying lesbian language and its destruction of "lesbian lives" speaks again to the difficulty of distinguishing between the discursive or installed self, and that of the material, the self as bodily enigma.

The difficulty is underwritten in the Fifth Turning which returns to "image," of "when snowflakes fall on your forehead," an image of the impartiality of Death, yet her ability to "touch ... the imaginary zone in us that is most difficult to transpose, most difficult to share; the zone, they say, that helps us recapture our destiny" (31). The imaginary is that which is not permitted representation, the not-said rather than the not-yet-said. In this formulation it resembles the discursive shadow of representation but hints at the enigma of material existence. For the latter it is a contradiction in terms since the material self cannot exist on its own, cannot exist without sharing the process of translation. It knows its enigmatic self only in engagement with other human beings. This does not mean that it is the same as other human beings, but that it needs contact with them to know itself. In "Body" Brossard says that the body can "slip from I to we, from us to them when we talk of freedom and the future," but also that the body cares about its "singularity and intimacy" (6). Later, in "Elsewhere," (1999a) the title rephrases this: "I like to say we and look elsewhere" (60).

The necessity for another person is examined in the Sixth Turning, which presents the lesbian "I love you" [je t'aime/je thème] as a "speaking that experiments with the value of words to the point of touch, stretching them out so that they can simultaneously caress their origin, their centre and the extreme boundary of sense" (32), forming a skin of language that encompasses writer, reader, and text in a single body, but also a speaking that "rubs up against a speaking," finds the difference among people pleasurable (32). The Seventh Turning, "between history framed in visions," offers lesbian speaking as "Shoulders that rub up against the night like an absolute *in the never ending process of hope*" [italics in English]. "Breathing in rhetoric" becomes the lesbian speaking. *"Breathe your silence, respira en tu memoria, impregnate rhetoric"* (33) becomes the strategy of installing the lesbian body "my tongue slipping on the very tender flesh of the word clitoris" (33) and simultaneously "shaping the subjectivity of she whose mouth resembles mine" (33). The shared skin of translation effects and affects the installation and the subject.

The Eighth Turning curiously slips into untranslated French, seemingly purposively because the Spanish translation also retains the French, as it unfurls the phrase "mysterious signifiers in the curve of lips" [my translation. See final commentary for the full text]. And reading becomes translation. This translation, evidently, proposes that one way of thinking about the process of installation, the way images drift into ideas without our conscious or subjected awareness, the way values emerge in the stretching of words into touch of the other person, the way the apprehension of the enigma of self materializes, is to place them in the present, in the moment, as a lesbian/queer/nonnormative sexual movement or curve or action.

The Ninth Turning explores "*I am breathing in rhetoric*" by stating from the outset that reality (the represented) is "not sufficient," that "beauty is demanding," that "sensations are multiple," and hence the text of the reading cannot be only ideological, discursive, or material: "putting a great deal of oneself into language does not eliminate the partriarchal horror, does not explain the composition of my subjectivity and all these images that move like a woman in orgasm" (35). It must be simultaneous, like rhetoric which provides us with the tools to act in "probably-the-best" way in many situations, like rhetoric which does not pursue the truth (although it can describe it) but moral action. In work on immediate material, the rhetoric of words is "eternally contemporary with our joys and energised bodies, murmurs and breathes, opens us up to the bone and sews in wells and depths of astonishment" (35). This rhetoric allows the writer-reader to "exist in written language because it is there that I decide the thoughts that settle the questions and answers I give to reality" (35); it traces her "strategies and rituals of writing that I had to invent in order to survive the customs and phallic events of life" (35).

If most language is in myths and tears, representations and need from the not-yet-said, as the Tenth Turning suggests, then language in the present is a "labyrinth where the only horizon is a spiral of desire" (36). Here there may be no time to weep, but at each turning, each ellipse, or at times when we are still, we may weep "too much," turning to feeling, for tears remind us of the "the end of sentences" (36), structures that constrict the possibilities for the *inédit* – "weeping with hope because the imaginary makes sentences impossible / tears as a certain signifier of a place for words / tears use no verbs, do not tell us what to do, put what is necessary to hand" [my translation from book]. The Eleventh Turning returns to lesbian space and a different kind of political rhetoric to that in the First. Here is a place on the archipelago that is neither territory nor country, but in "the mysterious signifiers in the curve of her lips," a "presence of spirit" (37). This reading of the labyrinth has been an exploration of translation at the same time as it is an installation of that space, a space delineated for the writer in writing and words. It is also a risk, an astonishment. An exploration full of danger, for in loosening the discourse of the normative one may lose oneself, and so in preparation/as a precaution she first loved "long and well a woman who, like myself, had dived into many books, without ever being afraid of drenching herself in dream and reality" (37). As Brossard notes in "Poetic Politics," "Sooner or later the body of writing pays for its untamed desire of beauty and knowledge" (81).

This is a fiction, not a story, about being in the labyrinth night, the immediacy of installation, the way it makes present a reality. What "we are reading is not simply a matter of imagination" but a "truth" – not a mechanical truth but "the soft flow in present time of a sharing and an immense love for every woman's creativity" (38).

THE BODY AND VIRTUAL REALITY

The arc of thinking from *Installations* to *Labyrinth* builds complex but load-bearing architecture – which makes *Baroque at Dawn* and some of Brossard's subsequent remarks unusual. By dealing with a technology – a virtual reality that seems to mimic what installation does – *Baroque at Dawn* problematizes the concept of articulation in the moment, with its focus on presence.[6] The photographer Irène Mage has recently turned away from camera photography to the speed and surface of computer-generated images, and she comments to the novelist Cybil Noland that as a writer she is still a naive thinker, working on "passions and motivations. Your art ... remains profoundly moral" (79). In itself this observation is not unusual, but in its re-appearance in subsequent essays as a source of concern and anxiety,[7] Brossard alerts her readers/listeners to the strange manner in which the "body" is being eviscerated by technology. As she warns in the "Avant-Propos" to a collection of feminist essays (2000), "voilà, qu'après avoir décrété que nous refusions d'être des femmes-objets, force est de constater que les biotech-nolgies du patriarcat *soft* sont en train de transformer le corps en monnaie courante" (14). And concludes, "Qu'allons-nous devoir inventer pour que l'amour de la vie et l'espoir de changement ne nous transforment pas en Vénus digitales ou en dociles consommatrices de *réality*?" ["What are we going to have to invent so that love of life and hope for change don't transform us into digital Venuses or docile consumers of *reality*" (translated by Louise Forsyth)] (15). The second alternative of that last query is at the heart of Brossard's writing, the first, the "Vénus digitales," is new.

Baroque at Dawn posits the virtual reality of computer technology as a possible analogue for the fiction created by writing. It constructs a present: "Reality superimposed itself on reality" (170). "I was present and nothing but, an illusion of perfect present, devoid of any story or any attachment. Locked in a present which all my life I had proclaimed essential for doing justice to the intelligence of our senses. Now there was too much present" (171). The experience puts Cybil Noland, the author of the novel being written about, into "double time," where writing becomes "a desire to surf on words, eliminating risk of harm to meaning" (172). Later she is "overcome by an irresistible desire for details" and "states of mind, of dream, lucidity and lassez-bellyache followed" that have her alternating reality and fiction "hurtling on" at speed.

That night she dreams of the woman in Hyde Park who is quoting from *Alice in Wonderland* the same words that open "Only One Body for Comparison: Writing the In-Between." It is as if the enigma of self has disappeared and the absence of any other person has left Cybil Noland floating in a fiction that is impossible to distinguish from representation or materiality: fiction as virtual reality. The eyes are vulnerable to the new visual technologies; we have to learn to see them as texts. During the Renaissance the growing emphasis on the visual, the advent of the three-dimensional camera-effect presentation and print culture, encouraged philosophies such as Neoplatonism that claimed a physical mixing of "rays" emanating from the eye and back into it, so fearful/wondered were they of the eye. The eye, they explained, was instantaneous, as opposed to rhetoric and the word, which need time. Nevertheless, they trained their eyes to "read" that instantaneousness, just as we have to train to "read" new technologies. The difference is time. Its availability. Silence, its marker.

In *Baroque at Dawn* the writer of the novel about Cybil Noland writing a novel cannot continue to write after that radical deformation of presence until, through translation, presence begins to make material sense once more. With someone else, here the translator in person, the material present can happen. Someone else prompts desire, and desire is not only the shadow of representation, that which is written out by power, but also the comprehension that the not-yet-said can be installed, the *inédit* can happen. The apparent immediacy of virtual reality erases the differences between the symbolic, the fictional, and the material. But, like any technology, any human craft, it has its own rhetoric. The problem lies in the speed of its change and the effective impact it has on society before we can grasp and engage with that rhetoric, the knowledge it instantiates, the moral action it enables. Despite arguing that "Poetry is simultaneous, in the moment, present: prose dilutes tension, projects into temporal dimension, slows desire" ("Fluid Arguments," 319), Brossard also knows that all writing presupposes "deferral and delay and difference" (Aut*her*, 2). Much earlier, in *Journal Intime* of 1984, she says that writing slows down between each word, that she had to learn to see the whites coming. "The white that one calls white spaces are in fact so filled with thoughts, with words, with sensations, with hesitations and with chances to be taken" ("Fluid Arguments," 342). And much later, she notes the importance of silence as material presence for writing, because silence, which takes place in slow time, "can activate the white on the page, the light that makes it tremble around intimacy" ("Silence" 1999b, 5). This last essay, given as a paper at the University of Calgary, is again subtitled to connect to the other human body: "The most precious things in the future will be water and silence and a human voice."

I would argue that for many first-time readers, reading *Baroque at Dawn* is like reading a text through which the images pass too swiftly, through which syntax hurtles our bodies. It provokes a virtual reality of intense presence and vertiginous nausea, a necessarily relativist knowledge that may not even be knowing because we can only know that we know if another person offers context, and the self-focused action that results can hardly be moral. This is partly because technically the writing is "prose," and most western readers are schooled to consume "prose" swiftly, possibly so well-schooled in novelistic technique (from both book and film) that they are experts at this kind of reading and take too much for granted. Yet any carefully trained reader knows that reading, like writing, needs time. Through rereading, supportively, comparatively, even with other readers as I do in the classroom, and making differences, the text invites us into translation. It sensitizes me to points of touch that release energy into the material through work on the *inédit*; it integrates another language into my skin. The process of knowing I engage with is shared, I learn to value the differences I have made in comparison, and any action I take is located in the detail of shared lives, and first the shared body of reader and writer.

The final section of *Baroque at Dawn*, "One Single Body for Comparison," echoes a warning from "The *DARK* Future" that in art "it's always very tempting to draw a comparison with reality ... to reassign the enigmatic import of the work in our own conception of reality" (161). We have to train ourselves to use our "single body" to find "the necessary words," to "compare," to hold a "body of memory for inventing and progressing toward silence" (115). Part of this training, as the criticism explores and the book displays, is training in the rhetoric of poetic: in stress, rhythm, syntax, sound, image, topic, theme. Part of the training is understanding the energy of the body: for example, its skeleton, its "elasticity," the effect of the vowels (227) – those emotive sounds resounding without the muscular check of consonants through the body. Elsewhere Brossard's texts combine these:

> the tongue/language that agitates the plexus, constricts the heart, the throat and other muscles able to manifest itself suddenly like features of spirit in the body: that same tongue/language turns back on the eye to stage its all powerful turbulence while my hand. It traces two steps from there from me signs and oscillations between words and dead igneous signs coming loose one from the other, some of them reaching the limit, against the sense, others retracing their path, apt to recapture lost time or to signal those contradictions between the hemispheres of the brain (quoted from manuscript in Baker, "Fluid Arguments," 343)

And part of this training is learning to work the body with others. In *Baroque at Dawn*, the writer and translator are both looking for the "other hand part of *on the other hand*" not wanting to compromise "the meaning of the story, the configuration of destinies" (226). So that in conclusion the writer asks, "What are we to look for in the silence of others, with eyes enticed by proximity and whirligig comparisons day vastating us? What are we to look for in the very desire for comparisons and closeness?" (256)

The body we measure reality by is a treasured enigma of self, but it is compounded and comparative when encompassed by the skin of language. Brossard defines energy as a term she uses "to analyze those forces in the process of literary creation." "Imagination goes through the skin the skin is energy" ("Fluid Arguments," 338), and as the vast, permeable lung of installation, it breathes the material reality of the *inédit* into sound and resonance, into words, into fiction, and yes, into articulation and representation. It makes it possible for the powerful to hear those erased from or marginal to power. Sprung by need, it is motivated by the material reality of the particular body, an alongside created by the self and others working on the detail of lived lives: making differences through knowing and in the making learning to value, so that we may take moral actions, enter an engaged ethics.

This is how I feel when I read the novels with other people to compare readings. And this is how I feel now, having had the opportunity to write in detail through the vertiginous aporia of the critical rhetoric. On reflection, I would say that it was the process of engaging with both the texts and their translations that opened a way to breathe through the skin of language, find a bodily presence in the words, and make new material. Rather like the writer in *Baroque at Dawn*.

THE INÉDIT, UNCUT/BROSSARD IN TRANSLATION

There is no Video Weblink for this essay.

The performative elements of the essay (Hunter 2005) lie in the translations that I made of the material. Hence there is no commentary on a web production but instead, on the process of translation and what I learned from doing it. This exploration suggests that translation is an embodied performance, a mimesis in which the words of the writer are not read off the surface of the page but trans/lated through the body of the reader/critic. Being a translator is like reading a score, a reading that acquires sense through the medium of the translator's re-membering.

The process is not only finding an English word for a French one, but experiencing all the words that are released in the process. They are words that make space on the page, space that is "felt," felted into phrases or sounds, and silences, for you can overwrite a white silence in the same way that you can overspeak an audio silence with sound, yet the sound of the silence is still palimpsestically there. For example, the word "among" – etymologically the *OED Online* starts us off with

> orig. a phrase, *on* in + *emang* mingling, assemblage, crowd (f. *emengan* to mingle, combine ... Between *among* and *imong*, thus used side by side, arose *emong*. Modern poets also abbreviate *among* to "*mong*."
> There was a parallel *BIMONG*
> Bimong:
> A parallel form to *AMONG, IMONG*; f. *bi, be, BY prep.* + *mong*, aphetic f. *IMONG*, OE. *emang* "mingling, concourse, crowd."
> I/Ymong:
> [OE. *emang, emong*, used beside *on emang AMONG prep.*, which is f. *on* <u>ON</u> *prep.* + *emang* company, *YMONG n.*]
> Mong:
> Cognate with Old Saxon *mangon*, Old Icelandic *manga* <a Germanic verbal formation, probably a back-formation <the Germanic base of *MONGER n.*[1] (unless independently <classical Latin *mang* dealer, trader: see *MANGO n.*[2]).

The word brings together mingling, assemblage, crowd, with company and concourse, so that by the time I reach dealer/trader I am already thinking of the Greek agora, the marketplace where strangers and belongers, the in place and out of place, meet and speak allegorically/otherwise. The one-word storytelling that translation within one language releases. There is so much history here, so much embodied experience to track and re-member in the present body. This kind of translation is a process of installation. Doing it more overtly on the page is like working in rehearsal in order to perform more generically – in other words, more publically. The ethics here shift from those of resistant relations to those of the engaged ethics in performativity.

The essay itself translates from a selection of Nicole Brossard's texts in French and those already translated into English published mainly over the period 1984 to 2004. In other words, it does not consider her early "neutral" writing or look at the extraordinary texts produced during the years 1973 to 1984 when she was hammering out her own language of survival. Instead, it focuses on her developments of that language and her reflections on its process, and how those textualities are translated into issues informing my own thinking.

I did not always agree in my body with otherwise resonant English trans-lations of the three main critical texts (Brossard 1984, 1990, 1992), and indi-cated this by retaining the page references to the French for quotations in English that I provided within square brackets. It is interesting that I found it exceptionally difficult to translate without recourse to Shakespearean pun, ambiguity, and syntax. And I am aware that my own translations are highly contestatory if looked at for illumination of their source text. But just as my use of "symbolic" rarely overlaps with Nicole Brossard's, this is the condition of communication: in particular since Brossard says, "I love to keep myself in the untranslatable" (Brossard 1999, 62). My process was more that of an editor, and often I used the words of the French and English texts so that they seem to be quotations without quotation marks. Although they appear to be the same words, they are not. They were chosen in a different context, and trigger a different typhoon,[8] create their own particular microclimate specific to the engagements this text makes (Brossard 1999, 61). They instan-tiate different knowledge and different action.

I learned this process while editing a scholarly edition of *Romeo and Juliet* for the Arden Shakespeare, subsequently published by Ashgate. I and my co-editor decided to treat the play as if it were a new text, so we consulted the editorial tradition infrequently until the co-editor had directed several productions of the play. We took the script apart comma by comma, line-ending by half line, and word by word. Editing Shakespeare's writing taught me that words are bodies, the other face of Brossard's writing of the body into word. What was installed in rehearsal was a play that seemed to many in the audience to be radically changed, yet we had simply retained the original words because we had found new life for them. Although they appeared to be the same words, they were not. We were not trying to produce an "authentic" *Romeo and Juliet*.[9] We were trying to produce a new play.

I am not trying to translate Brossard. I am trying to produce new material.

So for example, the untranslated Eighth Turning of *Green Night in the Labyrinth Park* became at one moment of ar(rest):

it is in wanting to precipitate the necessary word that mysterious signifiers appear in the ellipse [angle] of the book. Just as a choir stands up as one in us, to sound [sounding/out] a secret passion and to publicly [publicly/openly] lick each word into all of its angles [angular curves/parabolic angles], into all its states [beings] of laughter [tremulous] and passionate flow.
the language of the street [normative/straight] that one speaks to the customary passers-by travelling through heterosexual life, is charged with mysterious signifiers when the sweet thought of the sacred sweetheart who loves love's gamble in words ventures forth from the pearly mouth of desire [when the thought of one's lover (impossible to say) begins to articulate itself in the words of desire, the erect tongue the pearly mouth].
the procession of the pearls of spoken signifiers eludes people of war [subjects of the state]. That's why dyke sayings [diction/language] reclining [disposed/inclined/declined] on the grass and the large gardens running with pearls, are never afraid to drench themselves in pleasure [desire] [for no one notices].
pleasure is only similitude if in veiling the precipitousness [danger] of the necessary word we throw ourselves onto the corner of the street simply in order to appear [be seen/heard]. The heart discretely lets its pearls go, secrets that astonish and secrete in each word suckets that subjects of the state never taste [suck]. Alone, the sweet sweetheart tumbles [turns] the sheen of pearls in her mouth just as one declines a verb without fear of stumbling [deception/deceit/mistake].

It has since moved into another moment of (ar)rest in a collaborative translation with Elizabeth Constable.[10]

In *Baroque at Dawn* the translator draws the writer into an existence. The text writes "One single body to compound with the young light of day and the words shining in the translator's eyes" (256). In the work Nicole Brossard undertakes with Daphne Marlatt in "Mauve" (Marlatt 1985), in the Raven-scroft Lecture at the University of Leeds (1996), this concept of the one body held in the skin of language is "Writing the In-Between." It is one of the opening moments of my life to have watched these two women speaking the in-between, inviting us to "among," much larger and more encompassing than "between." The porous skin that allows us to work collaboratively on alongside value, that retains us in our particularity as it morphs into the changes we introduce on making the difference of the other, that lets us breathe with another, is a starting point for feeling the non-autonomous self.

The essay presented here is an offshoot of an earlier version prior to editing by Louise Forsyth and publication in *Nicole Brossard: Essays on Her Works* (2005). Forsyth's edits were invaluable translations.

Hi Lynette,

I am sending my suggestions for shortening your essay. I do so with reluctance and urge you to accept these suggestions only if they work for you. My overall suggestion is to reread carefully those parts of your text in which you do wonderfully detailed textual analyses of Brossard's works. I think there is a need to drop some of the detail in order to condense. This should begin with <i>Harmonious Matter Still Manoeuvres</i>. In these analyses you are working your way through your own subtle ideas and inviting the reader to join this creative process. It's gorgeous, but I think there is just not room for all the nuances and textual mentions. For the non-specialist reader, it is probably important to be able to grasp some of the major points of Brossard's writing and leave the small folds for a subsequent reading.

1. Drop the paragraphs on p. 2 regarding translation: "In doing so, the essay ... to produce new material." This could be the subject in and of itself of another essay. I think a note would suffice in the usual dry, editorial tone: Unless otherwise indicated, all translations are my own – or some such.

2. I suggest considerable shortening of the study of <i>Green Night in Labyrinth Park</i>. It is quite long. As I follow your explication of the series of turnings I lose somewhat my sense of focus on your central argument regarding knowledge and moral action. Is some kind of an overview of the work's language, exploration and movement a

possibility?

3. I also suggest a similar shortening of the study in the final pages of <i>Baroque at Dawn.

</i>I look forward to reading the new version and hope that it takes shape for you without too much difficulty.

Cheers,

Louise

In preparing this chapter, I found that even though it was only a few years later, I had completely changed my use of several words. Key to the edited and published essay was the word "articulation." In *Critiques of Knowing* (1999), I had attempted to reclaim "articulation" *for* the process of working on making present, and *from* the centre-periphery model deployed by Mouffe and Laclau in which "articulations" are the sayings from the periphery that emerge into hegemony. My concern was to distinguish between saying into presence that is in response to hegemony, and that which occurs in the alongside. It's the difference between saying the "not-said" and saying the "not-yet-said." However, "articulation" has resisted this reclamation so firmly that, informed by Performance Studies theory, I moved toward "'installation" and "constellation" as the processual saying in rehearsal and the arrested saying in public performance. In both cases, the engaged inclusion of the audience introduces translation. It has been a curious, and unnerving, experience of translating my self, ghost limbs all over the place.

7

The Rhetoric of Masking in Writing
by Alice Munro

RADICAL TRAGEDY IN THE HOUSEHOLD

Munro has a way of finding resonant phrases that signify overwhelming feelings: this sense of the grand style, a vocabulary and syntax that is more appropriate to intense emotions, and registered as important and valuable because it is happening to "types," "standing in for" or allegorizing community-felt intensities. But with the difference that these "types," like say Ibsen's or those of postwar British drama, are fairly ordinary people.

In *Hateship* the people achieve their usually tragic intensity not because they are "better" or "worse" than others, but through the glimpse of their interiorized construction of suffering/pain/blame/shame. Munro conveys this through detailed observation. She propels her notation of relationships through variety and tone of voice. Yet these are always heavily dependent on the interior monologue or dialogue of the central character. Her work is a direct descendant of Browning's dramatic monologues – the reader knows more about the narrator than the narrator does. You get the sense that, even in the third person narrative voice, it is the character giving us the third person. Often you find serial dramatic monologues, usually from one point of view complicated by time.

The focus is on the moment the emotion is recognized as tragedy: the moment when it bursts through into discourse, installs itself. But with Munro, it doesn't just install itself, with that sense in installation of vibration, of challenge – it appropriates representations. What's fascinating is watching and hearing the words turn the unrepresentable into significant presences, or indeed turn the cliché into significant presence. It's a profoundly political manoeuvre.

POST AND BEAM

Since she had entered the house – in fact since she had first understood that the voices she heard came from her own back yard and belonged to Polly and Lionel – Lorna had not thought of the vision she'd had, mile after mile, of Polly lashed to the back door. She was surprised by it now as you sometimes are surprised, long after waking, by the recollection of a dream. It had a dream's potency and shamefulness. A dream's uselessness as well.

Not quite at the same time, but in a lagging way, came the memory of her bargain. Her weak and primitive neurotic notion of a bargain.

But what was it she had promised?

Nothing to do with the children.

Something to do with herself?

She had promised that she would do whatever she had to do when she recognized what it was.

That was hedging, it was a bargain that was not a bargain, a promise that had no meaning at all.

But she tried out various possibilities. Almost as if she was shaping this story to be told to somebody – not Lionel now – but somebody, as an entertainment.

Give up reading books.

Take in foster children from bad homes and poor countries. Labor to cure them of wounds and neglect.

Go to church. Agree to believe in God.

Cut her hair short, stop putting on makeup, never again haul her breasts up into a wired brassiere.

She sat down on the bed, tired out by all this sport, this irrelevance.

What made more sense was that the bargain she was bound to was to go on living as she had been doing. The bargain was already in force. To accept what had happened and be clear about what would happen. Days and years and feelings much the same, except that the children would grow up, and there might be one or two more of them and they too would grow up, and she and Brendan would grow older and then old.

It was not until now, not until this moment, that she had seen so clearly that she was counting on something happening, something that would change her life. She had accepted her marriage as one big change, but not as the last one.

So, nothing now but what she or anybody could sensibly foresee.

That was to be her happiness, that was what she had bargained for. Nothing secret, or strange.

Pay attention to this, she thought. She had a dramatic notion of getting down on her knees. This is serious.

Elizabeth called again, "Mommy. Come here." And then the others – Brendan and Polly and Lionel, one after the other, were calling her, teasing her.

Mommy.

Mommy.

Come here.

It was a long time ago that this happened. In North Vancouver, when they lived in the Post and Beam house. When she was twenty-four years old, and new to bargaining.

We live surrounded by representations we are
expected to inhabit: they are in-place because of
centuries of sociopolitical organization structured
by prevailing economics. The great triumph of the
twentieth-century enfranchised democracy in Euro-
American countries was to elaborate strategies for
many people to challenge and shift representations.
This is the action of discourse, the effect of think-
ing/positioning oneself as a hegemonic rather than
an ideological subject – someone who is part of the
compromise and not entirely subjected.
There are two problems with this: first, you have to
be part of the group in power to take part in discursive change – after all, this is what "hegemony"
means. And second, there is no way of accounting
for what motivates/puts into motion the attempts at
change. Hence, a large segment of the population
is still not included, despite the franchise. And,
there is an enormous amount of non-hegemonic
work on the alongside presencing of our experiences and responses that is not recognized, let
alone legitimated and/or valued.

I would argue that much of the impetus for
hegemonic change comes from precisely this area
of saying the not-said into presence. So, rather than
looking, as does cultural studies, at how discursive
strategy changes ideological representation, I am
interested in what lies/works outwith the discursive-

ideological hover, and whether and/or how it
installs itself into the discursive in the first place.
What interests me is the bit in between the platitude
and the presence: so on the one hand we have the
banal, domestic detail, often humorous or tongue-
in-cheek, and on the other we have the tragic
intensities: brief and full, what Munro sometimes
calls fate and sometimes fantastical.

a spotty suede jacket and she did not look either prosperous or well. Another time she was stopped at a crosswalk, leading a string of nursery-school children on their way to the swimming pool or the park. It was a hot day and her thick middle-aged figure was frankly and comfortably on view, in flowered shorts and a sloganed T-shirt.

The last and the strangest time was in a supermarket in Twin Falls, Idaho. I came around a corner carrying the few things I had collected for a picnic lunch, and there was an old woman leaning on her shopping cart, as if waiting for me. A little wrinkled woman with a crooked mouth and unhealthy-looking brownish skin. Hair in yellow-brown bristles, purple pants hitched up over the small mound of her stomach – she was one of those thin women who have nevertheless, with age, lost the convenience of a waistline. The pants could have come from some thrift shop and so could the gaily coloured but matted and shrunken sweater buttoned over a chest no bigger than a ten-year-old's.

The shopping cart was empty She was not even carrying a purse. And unlike those other women, this one seemed to know that she was Queenie. She smiled at me with such a merry recognition, and such a yearning to be recognized in return, that you would have thought that this was a great boon – a moment granted to her when she was let out of the shadows for one day in a thousand.

And all I did was stretch my mouth pleasantly and impersonally, as at a loony stranger, and keep on going toward the checkout.

Then in the parking lot I made an excuse to my husband, said I'd forgotten something, and hurried back into the store. I went up and down the aisles, looking. But in just that little time the old woman seemed to have gone. She might have gone out right after I did; she might be making her way now along the streets of Twin Falls. On foot, or in a car driven by some kind relative or neighbour. Or even in a car she drove herself. There was the bare chance, though, that she was still in the store and that we kept going up and down the aisles, just missing each other. I found myself going in one direction and then in another, shivering in the icy climate of the summer store, looking straight into people's faces, and probably frightening them, because I was silently beseeching them to tell me where I could find Queenie.

Until I came to my senses and convinced myself that it wasn't possible, and that whoever was or was not Queenie had left me behind.

Munro is fascinating because her work is devoted to investing cliché and platitude, the surface representations of culture, with the content of their "shadow." All representations cast a shadow that has substance but no visibility. It is the obscured/repressed/hidden ground of the representative power. For example: wives, or "the wife."

There are certain problems with this when the shadow-substance finds legitimation by taking on already legitimated representations like tragedy, betrayal, love – those terms of representational value. As often, Munro's writing articulates kindness, bitterness, sweetness, nicety, warning, recognition. It works on the discursive installation of difference to representation and therefore the change to ideology.

Some days I read this and it feels entrapping, right back into ideological representation: sentiment. Other days it feels lighter, filled with more possibilities. I think it's a question of my own response to the way Munro writes the feeling: the moment it is recognized, bursts into discourse and installs itself, and whether that vibration/challenge is maintained and resonates in my body or whether it then appropriates a representation – the longer it vibrates the more substantial the challenge.

But Munro's recent work also occasionally provides a sense of the movement that impels installation. It occurs in the words on the page between cliché and grand style. It concerns vulnerability, not-fit, continual/constant motion, and what it does to your body/your voice.

FLOATING BRIDGE

She could see the shoreline, and the reed beds.

Water in the reeds, lapping water, was making that sound.

The slight movement of the bridge made her imagine that all the trees and the reed beds were set on saucers of earth and the road was a floating ribbon of earth and underneath it all was water.

It was not until this moment that she realized she didn't have her hat.

She had not been wearing it when she got out of the car to pee.

She had not been wearing it in the car with her head

back against the seat when Matt was telling his joke.

She must have dropped it in the cornfield

and in her panic left it there.

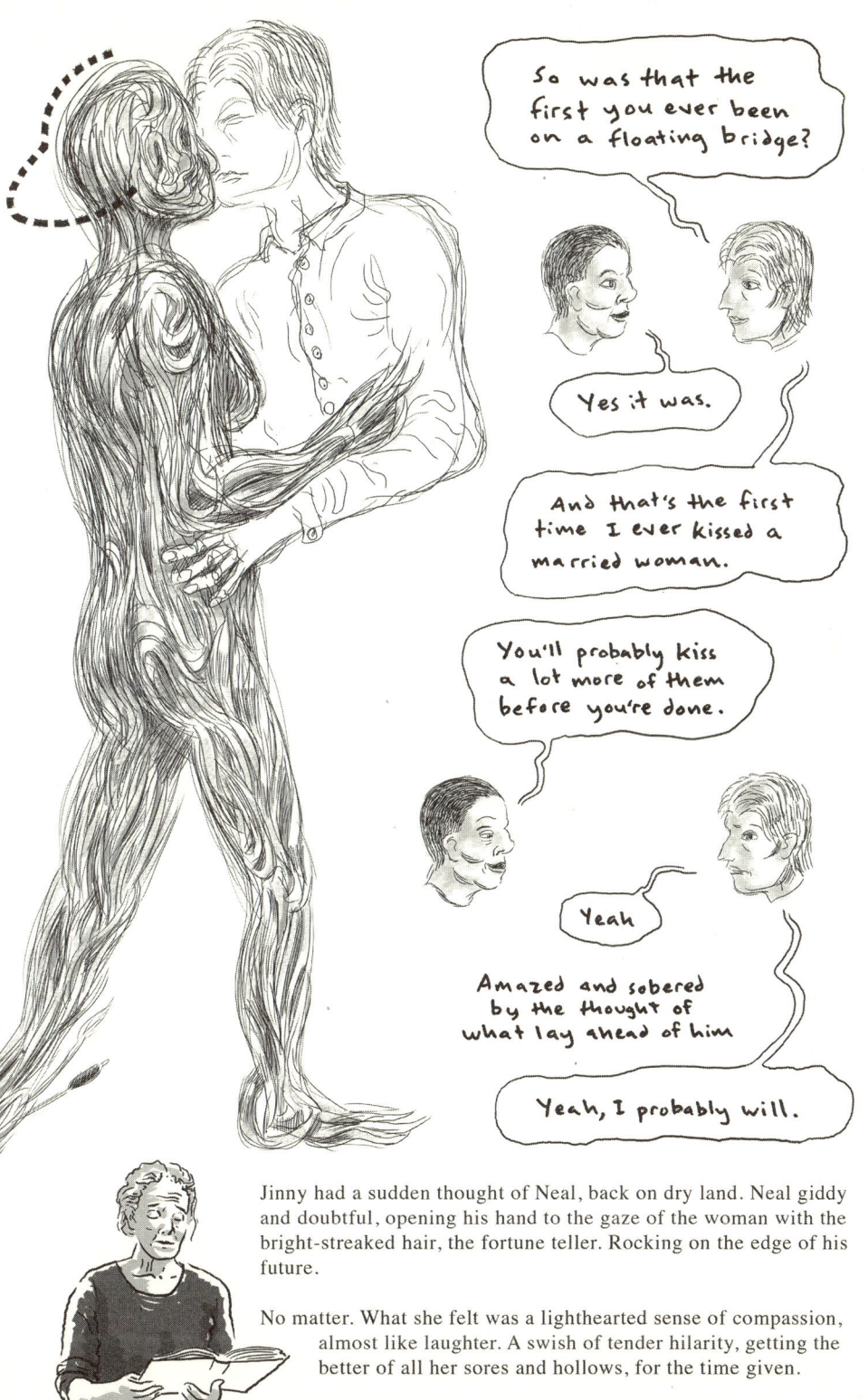

So was that the first you ever been on a floating bridge?

Yes it was.

And that's the first time I ever kissed a married woman.

You'll probably kiss a lot more of them before you're done.

Yeah

Amazed and sobered by the thought of what lay ahead of him

Yeah, I probably will.

Jinny had a sudden thought of Neal, back on dry land. Neal giddy and doubtful, opening his hand to the gaze of the woman with the bright-streaked hair, the fortune teller. Rocking on the edge of his future.

No matter. What she felt was a lighthearted sense of compassion, almost like laughter. A swish of tender hilarity, getting the better of all her sores and hollows, for the time given.

[version one]

What impels articulation and installs feeling is the physical act of the reading body: words and gestures informing each other. The reading aloud that used to be common – can you imagine the hum of the library – is still happening in our bodies, registering the way that a lot of alongside work is about throwing out words and phrases, sounds and syntax, and waiting to hear if they connect/resonate/echo/are picked up and reworked, whether the verbal line crosses with someone else's, nets together.

Or, the way a lot of saying the not-said is about throwing words/sounds up in the air and standing there to feel their touch as they descend, your body making sense/sensing as sounds and part of letters ... drift or fall onto your skin. tensing the musculature, changing the physiology, making self different.

The physicality of the way we sit when we read, the space we take up, the silence or noise or music we permit/encourage/endure. Reading aloud to others, to children, to people in bed. That occasional surge of voice when we simply cannot not say something aloud – to ourselves, to others. The "listen to this" as we make the story our own.

Vocalization is going on all the time, but reading is a physical activity just as open as any other to cliché, tragedy, grand style, representation, installation, conversation, negotiation: the attempt, the essay, the rehearsal. and the vulnerability of change.

[version one]

What impels articulation and installs feeling is the
physical act of the reading body: words and gestures
informing each other. The reading aloud that used to
be common — can you imagine the hum of the library —
is still happening in our bodies, registering the
way that a lot of alongside work is about throwing
out words and phrases, sounds and syntax, and
waiting to hear if they connect/resonate/echo/are
picked up and reworked, whether the verbal line
crosses with someone else's, nets together.
Or, the way a lot of saying the not-said is about
throwing words/sounds up in the air and standing
there to feel their touch as they descend, your body
making sense/sensing as sounds and part of letters
... drift or fall onto your skin. tensing the
musculature, changing the physiology, making self
different.
The physicality of the way we sit when we read, the
space we take up, the silence or noise or music we
permit/encourage/endure. Reading aloud to others, to
children, to people in bed. That occasional surge
of voice when we simply cannot not say something
aloud — to ourselves, to others. The "listen to
this" as we make the story our own.
Vocalization is going on all the time, but reading
is a physical activity just as open as any other
to cliché, tragedy, grand style, representation,
installation, conversation, negotiation: the
attempt, the essay, the rehearsal. and the
vulnerability of change.

[version two]
What impels alongside work and installs feeling is
the physical act of the reading body:

words and gestures informing each other.
The reading aloud that used to be common
 – can you imagine the hum of the library –
is still happening in our bodies,
    registering the way that a lot of articulation
    is about throwing out
        words and phrases
        sounds and syntax
    and waiting to hear if they connect
                resonate
                echo
                are picked up and reworked
            whether the verbal line crosses with
            someone else's
                    nets together
Or, the way a lot of saying the not-said is about
    throwing words/sounds up in the air
    and standing there to feel their touch as they
    descend
        your body making sense/sensing as sounds and
        parts of
        letters ...
            drift or fall
                onto your skin.
            tensing the musculature, changing the
            physiology, making self different

The physicality of the way we sit when we read
the space we take up
the silence or noise or music we permit/encourage/
endure
    reading aloud to others
        to children
        to people in bed
That occasional surge of voice when we simply cannot
                        not say something aloud

[version two]
What impels alongside work and installs feeling is
the physical act of the reading body:

words and gestures informing each other.
The reading aloud that used to be common
- can you imagine the hum of the library -
is still happening in our bodies,
    registering the way that a lot of articulation
    is about throwing out
        words and phrases
        sounds and syntax
    and waiting to hear if they connect
                resonate
                echo
                are picked up and reworked
            whether the verbal line crosses with
            someone else's
                    nets together
Or, the way a lot of saying the not-said is about
    throwing words/sounds up in the air
    and standing there to feel their touch as they
    descend
        your body making sensè/sensing as sounds and
        parts of
        letters ...
            drift or fall
                onto your skin.
            tensing the musculature, changing the
            physiology, making self different

The physicality of the way we sit when we read
the space we take up
the silence or noise or music we permit/encourage/
endure
    reading aloud to others
        to children
        to people in bed
That occasional surge of voice when we simply cannot
                        not say something aloud

                          to ourselves
                    to others
The "listen to this" as we make the story our own.

Vocalization is going on all the time, but reading
is a physical
activity just as open as any other to cliché,
tragedy, grand style,
representation, installation, conversation,
negotiation:
the attempt, the essay, the rehearsal. and the
                    vulnerability of change.

                    to ourselves
               to others
The "listen to this" as we make the story our own.

Vocalization is going on all the time, but reading
is a physical
activity just as open as any other to cliché,
tragedy, grand style,
representation, installation, conversation,
negotiation:
the attempt, the essay, the rehearsal. and the
                    vulnerability of change.

F mlyf rnt r

That Sunday, after the noon dinner at Alfred's, I set out to walk all
e   a   a   o   oo i   ou e. I I a e o   a s, I e -
o ed that I would have covered about ten miles, which ought to
ffs t th ff cts f th m l h d t n. f lt v rf ll, n t j st f
food but of everything that I had seen and sensed in the p rtm nt.
e o e o -a io e u i i s. i's ie e. A i a'
o e,   o a   e, a   i a o ie, a   o e e - a a
s c lds - nth gr nds f g l n.

After I had walked for a while, my stomach did not feel so
heavy. I made a vow not to eat anything for the next twenty-four
ou . I a e o a e , o a e , o e ee o
the tidily rectangular small city. On a Sunday afternoon there was
hardly any traffic, except in the main thoroughfares. Sometimes
my route coincided with a bus route for a few blocks. A bus might
o   i o   oo ee eo ei i. eo e I i o   o
and who did not know me. What a blessing.

h d l d, w s n t m t ng ny fr nds. My friends had mostly
a   o e o e o   ee e   e ie .   a é ou   e a a
until the next day – he was visiting his parents, in Cobourg, on the
a o e n O a a.   ee ou   e o o i e oo i
h s wh n g t th r – n b dy h d t b th r t lk ng t r l st n ng
to. I had nothing to do.

e I a a e o o e a ou , I a a u o e a a
o en , I went in and had a cup of coffee. The coffee was reheated,
a   a ie i a e a e i i a, e a   a I ee e .
I was already feeling relieved, and now I began to feel happy. Such
h pp n ss, t b l n . T s th h t l t - ft rn n l ght n th
i e a ou ie, e a e o a ee u ou i ea, o i
their skimpy shadows. To hear from the back of the shop the
sounds of the ball game that the man who had served me was listening
o o e a io. I i o i o e o I ou a e
about Alfred – not of that in particular – but of the work
I wanted to do which seemed more like grabbing something out of
th r th n c nstr ct ng st r s. Th cr s f th cr wd c m t
e ie i ea ea u o o o . o e o a-ou i
w v s, with th r d st nt, lm st nh m n ss nt nd l nt nt t n.

This was what I wanted, this was what I thought I had to pay
a e io o i a o I a e ie o e.

Family furniture

That Sunday, after the noon dinner at Alfrida's, I set out to walk all the way back to my rooming house. If I walked both ways, I reckoned that I would have covered about ten miles, which ought to offset the effects of the meal I had eaten. I felt overfull, not just of food but of everything that I had seen and sensed in the apartment. The crowded, old-fashioned furnishings. Bill's silences. Alfrida's love, stubborn as sludge, and inappropriate, and hopeless – as far as I could see – on the grounds of age alone.

After I had walked for a while, my stomach did not feel so heavy. I made a vow not to eat anything for the next twenty-four hours. I walked north and west, north and west, on the streets of the tidily rectangular small city. On a Sunday afternoon there was hardly any traffic, except on the main thoroughfares. Sometimes my route coincided with a bus route for a few blocks. A bus might go by with only two or three people in it. People I did not know and who did not know me. What a blessing.

I had lied, I was not meeting any friends. My friends had mostly all gone home to wherever they lived. My fiancé would be away until the next day – he was visiting his parents, in Cobourg, on the way home from Ottawa. There would be nobody in the rooming house when I got there – nobody I had to bother talking to or listening to. I had nothing to do.

When I had walked for over an hour, I saw a drugstore that was open, I went in and had a cup of coffee. The coffee was reheated, black and bitter – its taste was medicinal, exactly what I needed. I was already feeling relieved, and now I began to feel happy. Such happiness, to be alone. To see the hot late-afternoon light on the sidewalk outside, the branches of a tree just out in leaf, throwing their skimpy shadows. To hear from the back of the shop the sounds of the ball game that the man who had served me was listening to on the radio. I did not think of the story I would make about Alfrida – not of that in particular – but of the work I wanted to do which seemed more like grabbing something out of the air than constructing stories. The cries of the crowd came to me like big heartbeats, full of sorrows. Lovely formal-sounding waves, with their distant, almost inhuman assent and lamentation.

This was what I wanted, this was what I thought I had to pay attention to, this was how I wanted my life to be.

The Face, the Mask, and Classical Tragedy in the Household: The Rhetoric of Masking in Recent Work by Alice Munro

WEBLINK http://vimeo.com/18439707

2003 Université d'Orléans (France) "Alice Munro: L'écriture du secret"

2003 University of Birmingham (UK) American and Canadian Studies special lecture

2005 University of California Davis, Arts and Humanities faculty presentation

2006 University of California Davis, Video Performance: Reading/ Writing/Technology symposium with Adrienne Jenik (video record only)

In 2003 Marta Dvorak invited me to give a paper at a conference she was running on Alice Munro. Marta had given me the opportunity to build "Trying Not to Be a Tragic Subject" and had made possible the conference at which I performed "Bodies in Trouble," so I asked if I could build another production. She kindly agreed. My concern with making a piece around Munro's work was that so many people read her writing, especially the earlier writing, in a banal manner. I thought then, and believe her recent writing bears this out, that she is an incredibly skilled craftsperson of the grotesque and of tragedies of the everyday.

This piece self-consciously addresses a query implicit in the previous three explorations in part two: the process of reading/audiencing. If "Bodies in Trouble" tried to involve the audience but in fact kept them at a distance (albeit one that may have engaged them), if "FACE-WORK" explored how the reader installs themself into the text to do situated work, and if the Brossard essay engenders the reader's embodiment of the text through translation, then "Radical Tragedy in the Household," slightly off-centre from the "Classical Tragedy" of the performance, is about the reader re-making the text while they read.

The production started off as a paper called "How Not to Give a Conference Paper." Over the year it took to produce, it morphed into a realization that the reader's work or the audience's work during a performance can *also* involve performativity. I speak about this as a fully formed concept in the opening to part two, but it took the productions associated with the essays in this section to demonstrate to me that this was/is possible. The production "Classical Tragedy" is made up of eight segments of two-and-a-half minutes each. The first two are representational, the second two are super-mediated, i.e., mediated at one remove from the body through digital media, the third two are examples of mediation as embodiment in rehearsal, and the final two explore embodiment as a way of situating knowledge. The second part of each dyad is taken directly from a story in Munro's *Hateship, Friendship, Courtship, Loveship, Marriage* (Knopf 2001).

I prepared for the performance by taking voice classes with Trish Bailey, a voice coach specializing in Alexander Technique at Manchester Metropolitan University School of Theatre. Over several months, working with Trish and training the range of my voice through the Listening Program, I learned about the locations for sound in the body and combined this with my own Lishi Daoist energy work to release tensions and intentions. In the video record on the website, the opening dyad is as conventionally performed as I could make it. The second dyad consists of one part a live voice speaking a critique of liberal social contract politics over an electronic playback of the same words, followed by a distorted live webcam face behind an electronic reading of a section of a short story. The third dyad starts with a live voice speaking a "treatise" on alongside politics over a silent video projection of the same person speaking the same words. It is followed by a video projection of a storyteller silently saying the same story as the live body in front of the projection speaks that story, breaking down into vowel/consonant clusters that grip various musculatures and tendon knottings in the body. The final dyad is an embodied present voice speaking first a section of critical commentary on the value of the alongside embodiments of reading, and concluded by a live, envoiced reading of a story.

The graphic performance of "Radical Tragedy," on which I collaborated with chris lanier and Elena Cid del Prado, is similarly split into four segments with a dyad in each. Elena and I subtly altered the typography of the first dyad to underline the banality of the critical reading, and restored the typography of this book, and that of Munro, to the final dyad. chris's work producing the graphic novel was a surprise through collaboration. After brief initial conversations in which he immediately sighted the piece, we went through a draft that took me to the comment that this had to be "stark" or "dark." chris had already found that place and the graphic novel here is not what I expected but just what I expected.

I would also like to thank Garet Markvoort, the designer at McGill-Queen's, who, with this chapter and several others, took extraordinary care to render the original design. It was not possible to do so in all cases, for example pages 202–5 were to be laid out on two rather than four pages, yet the process of generating the integrity of the page has been a performance in itself.

I am honoured that it was possible to work with two collaborators who built such subtle and engaged renditions of verbal/visual/graphic/digital images for the "essay." It was an intriguing process to build for this book a completely new artifact based on the production, so many years after the event. In the preceding work, I've consistently differentiated between the video "productions" and the essays, even in the more graphically experimental work of the chapters in this book. Yet here it's difficult to know which is the "production" and which is the critical "essay."

Many people at the initial performance in Orléans asked questions, especially about the media interfaces I was using. The most engaged feedback on this production came from the group Danielle Fuller gathered to watch it in Birmingham. Possibly because the production was partly in response to Danielle's own work on reading and readership, the audience was alive to the modes of reading that the piece explores, and generated a valuable conversation about the embodied experience of reading. The video record is of this performance. The "performance" at a technoculture symposium with Adrienne Jenik at the University of California Davis was intriguing because I did not perform live, simply showed a loop of the video and was present to take up any discussion. Performed live, the body creates its own sense of time and place, and I believe the video fails to capture that processual integration of duration and spatial coordinates. At the same time, the looping video of a relatively short twenty-minute piece meant that several people in the gallery came back to look at segments they wanted to see again, potentially creating their own temporality and sensation.

part three

COLLABORATION

At present we have an aesthetic inheritance from the modern period that marginalizes many texts that do not contribute to sociocultural fit. While this may have been predictable under governments that excluded most of the populace from political and cultural power, today's democracies need to respond to the diversity that is now asserted. Art-work is central to the way people adjust their bodies to social and political change.[1] It is vital to a felt knowledge of the diverse views and different ways of life that have been brought far more immediately into everyday experience by transnational rhetorics. Not all people will be artists, but the possibility of engaging in art-work is fundamental to participatory democracy and does much to convey the ethics of a community.[2] I would like to suggest that a case-by-case approach to the support of art-work and textuality is one way of extending these skills more widely and, I would argue, one that shifts the focus from the object made to the processes that produce it. I do not advocate for getting rid of texts, but for unfolding the texuality of the work that happens before the object is realized in a representative form and thinking about the implications for a disunified aesthetics.

CASE-BY-CASE AESTHETIC SUPPORT AND THE NON-AUTONOMOUS SELF

One of the effects of globalization is that ISAs (Institutional State Apparatuses [Althusser]) no longer work in quite the same way that Althusser suggested. The social contract political theory of liberal humanism was based on a simultaneous acceptance of universals and of the autonomy of the individual citizen. G-SAs (Global-State Apparatuses [Hunter 2003]) support global economics, which simultaneously need, yet deny, claims to national universalism, and recast the individual as a consumer in a niche-market group.[3] Art is no longer made only by the individual private artist, caught heroically between representation of the ideological subject, and the transgression or transcendence of that subject – art is part of niche Art, caught ironically between commodity and simulacrum. These effects are complex. As argued in part one, one of the elements carrying the effects is the shift in citizenship that occurs at the same time as early-twentieth-century globalization: the enfranchisement of a broad national populace throughout Western social contract democratic nations. It is even possible to argue that the enfranchisements were responsive to growing individual capitalization brought about by the need for a larger consumer base, in other words, a growing middle class.

Nations today have both ISAs and G-SAs, and these have to be compatible to some extent. Yet if the individual has to relate to national ISAs as a subject, and to the global-national structures of G-SAs as part of a consumer group, what tensions arise? Does membership in a consumer group weaken subjectivity by giving you connections to concepts of subjectivity outside your national ISAs? Or does membership in a consumer group strengthen subjectivity by diminishing the alternatives to that subjectivity? Not all ISAs are compatible with G-SAs; there are, for example, trade embargoes. And even though ISAs and G-SAs are both based in capitalism, ISAs have a vested interest in capital projects that will benefit their own nations rather than others, hence there are bound to be differences of opinion and focus. ISAs are controlled to a greater or lesser extent by governments, and are therefore responsible to citizens, whereas G-SAs are relationships governments have with bodies that have no political responsibilities at all.

Given that art has been recognized socially and nationally in the modern period of liberal humanism only when produced by or working for people defined as citizen-subjects, the widening of the franchise and the doubling up of subject and consumer has had a broad impact on artistic production and consumption and on support provided by arts policy. However, transnational impact, which is not only that of global financial and capital economies but also that of greater movement geographically – economic/political/cultural migration – has also thrown forward a particular aspect of aesthetic work which has always been present: collaboration.

With transnational movements and greater enfranchisement, there is an enormous diversity of lived experience that cannot be represented in the same way as the universal subject (aka usually propertied, white, religion of the book, and male). Indeed, the "transnational" could be a word to describe the differentiated voices marked by globalization, or it could be, like "transculturalism," both compromised in the G-SAs and resistant to them. I would suggest that it releases all three positions and would like to discuss in a little more detail how G-SAs can drive a wedge between the ISAs and the private individual.

Transnationalism has been part of the challenge to representative government that has led to theories of deliberative government, advocacy, proportional representation, and other ways of engaging with diversity (Hunter 2004, 2010b). It has defined the questioning of liberal humanism that has led to theories of democratic humanism. It is inextricable from the formation of G-SAs, through which international corporations and transnationals have an impact on nations, citizens, and workers. It has helped shift the focus from citizenship as symmetrical subjectivity to asymetrical and multilayered models[4] of postmodern pluralisms/responsive universalism/differentiated public spaces (Benhabib 1996). And it has thrown forward a tension between the artist as hero, the artist as commodity, and artistic value as a processual event of particular individuals collaborating.

Transnationalism has realized this agency partly through the curious effect of its ability to undermine nation-state claims to universalism, and if the nation-state cannot maintain that claim, it can also no longer guarantee the autonomy of the individual. The result: the doublethink necessary to capitalism (that one is socially mobile but also constrained to social status – see political commentators from Francis Bacon to George Orwell) cannot be maintained: it becomes suddenly visible and obvious. Under G-SAs national universals are often ironized, even satirized. But most often they are commodified into the simulacrum, that ambivalent knowingness that allows us to live alongside ideology while still inflected by it, which has replaced the repressions of doublethink. Another effect of this undermining is that the private becomes porous because the private is dependent on the individual autonomy promised by the state to its citizens, guaranteed through capital and private ownership, and that autonomy can no longer be guaranteed. A third effect is the breakdown in the modern definition of the artist as the citizen who is the licensed transgressor of representative subjectivity. Because the private becomes porous, the limitations of that transgression are exposed as being confined to liberal humanist subjects, a very small proportion of the population who identify with liberal concepts of representation, and who value art when it achieves cultural "fit."[5] Fit does not simply imply "predictable." It is more related to the experience of something that disrupts the shape of ideology just at the moment that it needs to re-form. Fit delivers the adrenaline surge of possibility and the endorphins of satisfaction at the same time, and ranges from the fulfillment of cliché to a subtle and ambiguous pleasure.

G-SAs de-emphasize the subject/citizen and focus instead on the niche identity of the consumer. They encourage the artist as a brand-creator, corporate team-worker, who feeds the simulacrum, constructs the iconicity of an enfranchised population. This work is different from popular culture because popular culture was never supported by those in power, never recognized as claiming universal values, representation, or the aesthetic value of "fit." Consumer culture claims niche-brands that ally it to the ideological "fit" of G-SA economics in surprisingly knowing ways. The star system, which originated in women's journals of the nineteenth century when they became an illustrated mass media in the 1880s, is one response to the demand for wider representation and static fit from a broader public that is aware of what it desires.

Transnationalism not only foregrounds some of the limitations of nation-state universals under liberal social contract ideology but it has also provoked a wide range of alternatives. Under early globalization, this variety was initially contained by relativism and toleration. But the sheer diversity of alternatives proposed by people newly marked as "citizens" is leading to forms of government that can recognize and value difference – for example, deliberative governance, proportional representation, or community representatives such as the Members of the Territorial Assembly in Nunavut (Hunter 2005b). Hence transnationalism is one element that creates the conditions for the recognition of differentiated public voices and the possibility of a move toward democratic humanism, a humanism not solely confined to liberal subjects.

Under relativism, the one form of valued aesthetic difference is resistance to the universals anchoring that relative. Another form is mimicry. A relativist understanding of masking and mimicry in postcolonial art emphasizes the underlying similarities and the toleration of difference. And, of course, under a tolerant governance, artists may turn their own alternatives into universals. But with governance that is genuinely attempting to recognize and value diversity, people have often turned to focus on the situated, the negotiations among people that *make* difference. Art in these conditions has moved past the "post" to neocolonialism[6] and a mimicry of traumatic difference.

A fundamental argument in this book is that difference does not exist on its own; it is made, it is a rhetorical artifact. Universalism assumes a priori that difference exists, constructed by hegemonic understanding, constituted by hegemonic compromise, commodifed by economic desire – all strategies that ideologically constrain the individual within difference. But difference can also be thought of as being made by individuals and groups in the more immediate work of installation in which it is formed in the process of working with others, or of constellation in which it is formed in the process of participation and recognition. Both involve a collaboration that coexists with the particular individual. This particular/collaborative whole is not confined to human beings but to the ecology of the activity, the interactive netting of geography, time, space, place, food, shelter, plants and animals.

One of the implications of this philosophical perspective is that the work of the art-maker and of the audience becomes more collaborative, more porous. It is not that there is a collective "making" that produces an art object, but a working together with the art-maker's text: engaging in a textuality could be another text. It is helpful to think of this remembering of that "text" here as art-work in process – otherwise it's a script or a score. The situated textuality is the rhetorical stance of performativity that installs in the making. A philosophical perspective that can be read from Nicole Brossard's thinking is one that coalesces the processes of rehearsal and performance. I suspect that it can do so only within particular communities, engaging people who choose some similar positionality, so that the rhetorical contexts for rehearsal are the same as those for performance. This is ethically acceptable if the people involved recognize that the experience is partial, that it excludes others from collaborating in the same way. When collaborators have different positionalities, rehearsal and performance have necessarily different rhetorics.

Difference that is made by individuals in collaboration with others is not private, not based on capital ownership, but also not niche, not based on consumption. Neither is it resistant nor mimic. In the particular/collaborative making of recent kinds of site-based art (Kester, Kwon), or of computer-aided blog interaction (premised in the structure of Frank Davey and Fred Wah's SwiftCurrent experiment of the 1980s [Davey and Wah]), of responsive hypertext (Hunter 1999, chapter 4), of some zines,[7] and throughout many other current media, people have been developing strategies for integration and de-integration rather than production and consumption (Marlatt 1998), processes that highlight the differences that are made and the resulting affiliations and aesthetic/cultural needs that are addressed (Appiah), rather than the authorities and ownerships/copyrights of art. With installation, aesthetic value is less in the product and more in the work of making that creates the difference defined by the object. As such, documentation has become an integral part of this kind of art-work because the object produced is not separable from the process producing it. Collaboration involves strategies of disagreement, trust, *verfremdungseffekt*, that focus on how difference has been made and how it is recognized. In the process, moral choices are made which have ethical implications, but these do not represent difference, rather, they make it.

Situated work opens up art- or text-making to a large number of participants, and this is where collaborative strategies become important. Because there are no universal criteria for aesthetic value, or obligations to commodify, textuality can be valued aesthetically even if it is not undertaken by those designated as citizens or consumers. However, this raises the problem of how it can be supported in a capitalist society, how it can be funded. Art-work needs support, and funding any kind of art-work has traditionally been based on assessing the likelihood that the made object will achieve some kind of cultural "fit." But if there are many and diverse experiences engaged in the work of making a text/art-work, then it is unlikely that the made object will be recognized as fitting into dominant expectations. Situated textuality focuses on the process of the work undertaken by diverse individuals, at times with quite different beliefs and sets toward hegemony, but working with and across them, making possible collaborative strategies.

Collaborative rhetorics can argue for positions that are not made up of unified agreements – a gaggle of differences. And one central strategy for support for collaborative/particular art-making can be to argue on a case-by-case basis for the value of a specific project.

Case-by-case law is in a sense a partial return to the idea of justice that operated prior to the modern period in the Western world. Early sixteenth-century statues of Justice depict a woman staring keenly at the world, but later statues blindfold justice. The phrase "Justice is blind" comes from this later Renaissance period, and describes a shift in concepts of equity, from "justice needs to know all the available details to be able to contextualize the issue" to "justice treats all people equally no matter who they are" (Majeske). Clearly the former is as open to abuse as the latter, and the latter, for the emergent monied class of the sixteenth century who could afford to go to law, insisted on parity between the emergent class and the old aristocracy. What does this have to do with art-work or text-making? I would suggest that we operate with similar attitudes to aesthetic value. For the most part, aesthetic value and arts policy funding is accorded to those objects that fit social and cultural notions of "beauty," and beauty is linked to certain universals, one of which is that we all recognize it. Case-by-case aesthetics would focus more on the texts produced by a widely diverse range of people, making things that would not all be recognized as "beautiful" or valuable, indeed may well not be recognized as art-work at all.

This means being able to argue for funding for projects based on the interactions that may happen, rather than the made text that will result. The made object, once released into culture, may find itself constellated into another process, but it may also be commodified or even defined as representation. What becomes important is the possibility for engagement among the makers rehearsing and among those participating through constellation in the public performance. Art becomes not an end but a way to communicate among human beings, to recognize the differences that are made, and to value them in the knowledge that we have made them.

I think artists/text-makers have usually worked this way, but what we see happening is a marking of the activity by the wider public as aesthetically significant in itself. Poetics, especially through the genre of allegory, has found ways of delineating what goes on before, during, and after installation, in the situated and partial place, the ephemeral (Hunter 2010b). The activity is part of the deep enigmatic experience of partial knowledge, and in installation/constellation it becomes the work of allegorical recognition that forms the not-said of both subjectivity and of niche-identification as well as the not-yet-said of installation. It's why we go to the theatre more than once to see the same show, because the interactions will be different. And it's why so many young people want to be involved in performance. It's also why we read the same poem more than once, because the interrelations and negotiations will be different. Although some would say that the rereading is a constellation, I would argue, and elaborate on this in the case study below, that writers install their words in different ways, sometimes to insist on a participation in the installation procedures, through grammar, verse form, layout. Readers are perfectly capable of responding as subjects, constituted subjectivities, consumers, abjects/victims, but also as particular elements in a collaboration that never ceases. It's why so many young people try their hand at poetry. One could also argue that the proliferation of literary criticism is a response to this need.

Yet make no mistake: We are all still subjects, and can be represented in government and called into being – for example, to fight for our country. We are all still consumers, and are commodified into niche brands – for example, as a double-income empty-nester who likes to read. Yet we are also all situated, and can be advocated on behalf of, can advocate on behalf of, yet remain partially known and that only in the process of making and valuing our differences.

But there is a problem: there is no specific set of poetic forms or rhetorical strategies that will guarantee that an art object is representative, resistant, commodified, mimic, constellated, installed. Both ISAs and G-SAs use stabilizing strategies but for different reasons, since ISAs attempt to build unique national-state identities while G-SAs need to blend them in order to maximize markets. Artists devoted to representation or resistance, to commodification or ironization, still need those stabilizing strategies to work with/against, and they will inflect issues of collaboration to a greater or lesser extent. And given the varieties of difference noted above, and these are only some among many, devices and techniques for difference may overlap and result in unintended effects. For example, partial knowledge may contribute to particular/collaborative interaction that feeds directly into niche-marketing consumer groups. The movement could also go the other way, in theory.

Representative strategies, geared to putting stable identities into place, are usually explanatory, closed, analytical, synthetic, and descriptive, leaving common grounds unexamined, dependent on a priori agreement, corporate in argumentative structure, and tending to the authoritative. They operate in ways parallel to case law, and draw strength from universalism. Corollary resistant strategies often highlight heroic individual subjectivity, focusing on their compromised autonomy, issues of relative empowerment, lack, absence, mimicry, the work of transgression and transcendence, and desire.

In contrast, consumer strategies are constrained rather than heroic, highly responsive to peer pressure, group solidarity and collectivism, branding, bonding, cult-formation, wish-fulfillment, and deferred power. Niche strategies tend to be explanatory but aimed at plausibility, pluralist/relativist, focused on pleasure, on associative similarities, on knowledge based in the simulacrum, and on the constitution of stable but self-consciously fore-grounded identities. Because of the non-responsible status of globalized corporations, plausibility replaces notions of case.

Collaborative strategies at present in constellation emphasize particular/collaborative interrelations, documentation of ongoing process, devices from happenings, improvisation, yin-yang, making choices generated by need, and treat both materiality and presence as continually renegotiated in case-by-case situations. Situated installations are potentiary, today using techniques such as collage, allusion, allegory, analogy, partial knowledge moving to probable grounds, engaged and enacted agreement.

None of these devices, techniques, tactics, strategies, arguments is in itself a guarantee of the poetic it serves. They are each and all historically specific, and may be more or less appropriate in other contexts.

Possibly more important to remember: whom do these activities exclude? The representative notoriously excludes anyone who is not a subject/citizen, simply does not acknowledge them, and resistant work frequently comes from those only partially disempowered, so that a large proportion of people in the nation-state, such as workers or the unemployed or voteless homemakers, are disenfranchised from aesthetic work and the making of value. Both commodified and niche aesthetics also exclude labourers whose work for those in the West is usually at a distance, outside the relations of global power with nation-states and easily obscured from awareness – all too often niche art ironizes such exclusions into commodities in themselves. And situated work can easily exclude those without education (of all kinds), access, or unrecognizable difference. Other people's installations and constellations can be boring, unintelligible, awkward, simply not understood as process.

Globalization supports the increase in neoliberalism because, when many different societies all buy into capitalism, they need to have consistent and transparent rules of engagement. These rules are the reduced bones of what is needed to make profit, and people make no bones about their importance and necessity. Transnationalism is a word being used to delineate some of the more positive effects of opening up communication around the world. As such, transnationalism drives a wedge between the nation-state and the private individual, but comes with its own version of hyperliberalism that evades, hides, and obscures the underlying skeletal relation to its neoliberal cousin. One importance of Afropessimism as a critical approach is that it foregrounds the common bedrock of the two. Nevertheless, transnational rhetorics have been vital to a felt knowledge of the diverse views and different ways of contemporary life. Transnational discourses have disrupted universalist concepts of aesthetic value, yet placed in their stead relational concepts that reinforce liberal structures and continue to exclude. The fact that there are different rhetorics for aesthetics is not the same as thinking about the rhetoric of disunified aesthetics that specifically focuses on collaboration.

Situated work enables a much wider embrace of art and the importance of disunified aesthetic practice. Case-by-case arts policy tied to an appreciation of situated textuality can facilitate much more diverse participation of people in cultural and social action. Art-work/text-making is open to kinds and intensities of analysis and knowledge that are different to those found elsewhere. In particular, situated textuality offers somatic and affective engagement with difference that can be central to transnational cultural recognition – situated thinking is not possible without aesthetics and ethics. So I would argue that we need an arts policy that can maintain the potential for situated articulation when under the institutional pressures of ISAs and G-SAs. Publishers, curators, artistic directors, should be encouraged to do more than nod to diversity, and to take up the far more substantial challenge of advocating for processual art that is at the moment opening up aesthetics to a far more diverse public.

The first chapter in this third part, chapter 8, "What Is an Honest Man? and Can There Be an Honest Woman?," explores some of the national and transnational issues around aesthetics by putting Daphne Marlatt's writing about collaborations with other writers and readers in productive tension with her poetics. Her work consistently engages larger political issues at the same time as it installs the particular and invites collaboration. The kinds of collaboration Marlatt enables through the performativity of her work call on both installation and constellation. This chapter begins with a condensed repetition of some of the material in this introduction to part three, supported by ever-receding footnotes. A playful rebus if you like. It then merges through a performative engagement in process with Marlatt's work, first as a reader and then as a writer. The chapter concludes with a rehearsal of *this tremor love is*, not moving toward articulation and staying always in the process of making to insist on the engaged reader, until the final paragraph.

The ninth chapter of the book pushes the process further by rehearsing bpNichol's *Selected Organs*, de-scripting it into free verse on the page that then becomes a palimpsest for the critical engagement, the constellation. The literary critical work is keen to explore notions of community, inoperative community, dissension, and a range of significance for "we" and "I" and the many other pronouns that people Nichol's text. The performance text online invites the reader to read Nichol's published writing, the rehearsed de-scripting, the superimposed constellation, in different combinations and layerings. The printed text engages with more difficulty the typographic immersions of readings that are at times literally impossible to read. The watermark of the pages in this section, created by artmaker Ilya Noé, consists of my own de-scripting into verse of Nichol's prose work, with my reading of those writings then printed over it.

The tenth chapter and final section of this book offers a series of reflections on collaboration in the context of a case study of a practice of art-making. In this production I deliberately decentred the text by using a long poem of my own and inviting others to rehearse its material reading by rebinding the sheets of the printed verse into different folds, stitchings, gatherings, and cuttings. The essay that I wrote to accompany this production constitutes this introduction to part three.

8

Daphne Marlatt's Poetics: What Is an Honest Man? and Can There Be an Honest Woman?

POETICS AND PUBLIC CULTURE

The first part of this essay explores the changing position of aesthetics in a world of increasingly global influence and argues for a specific approach to public culture, rooted in a democratic humanism, that addresses the ambivalent effects of that influence. The latter part of the essay reads recent work by Daphne Marlatt and her development of the particular/collaborative in an attempt to design strategies for a democratic humanism.

What *Is* Public Culture?

The underlying argument of this essay is that public culture is changing because of the changing nature of the nation. In an economically defined nation-state, culture has traditionally been split between "art" and "popular culture," a split that defines aesthetic objects in terms of their production and reception/consumption rather than what the people who make them actually do. It is a way of defining how aesthetics has come about in Western countries that have established democratic understanding via liberal social contracts – the liberal humanism of the modern period in Western history.

Today the nation is not so economically defined because the economics of state institutions is often inflected, if not organized, by global corporate power. There has been a shift from Althusser's Institutional State Apparatuses (ISAs) (Althusser 1971) of the nation, articulated just at the point that they were losing power, to Global-State Apparatuses (G-SAs) (Hunter

2003). Parallel to the rise of G-SAs in the twentieth century is the movement of enfranchisement and the growth of diverse voting communities (Hunter 2001). National governments have struggled to work out how to handle these developments, and Canadian public culture has been at the leading edge of the exploration, partly because it has been a strong liberal social democratic state affected by G-SAs (from both the US and the UK) in a self-conscious way from the late-nineteenth and early twentieth centuries. Canadian strategies for multiculturalism can be seen as an indication of the nation operating as a cultural rather than an economic unit. Other ways of operating non-economically[a] include strategies such as proportional representation (Hunter 2004). Nations today have become the protectors of the individual against G-SAs: for example, through legal restraints on companies such as McDonalds, but also the conduits through which G-SAs identify and/or shape markets.[b]

Public culture, for the purpose of this chapter, is defined as the culture that recognizes diverse cultural power. If "art" is the culture of the empowered and relatively empowered group with special rights, which has the money to consume and produce, to disseminate and market, and "popular

a Some recent discussion has developed these ideas in terms of the phrase "cultural imaginaries." The stronger a nation-state is economically the more control it can exert over its cultural imaginaries. The more diverse the economic control of state functions the more diverse the cultural imaginaries that result.

b Nations in effect serve to guarantee that all enfranchised people have human rights, despite empowered economic special rights accorded to transnational or global corporations (Pateman 1995). Empowered people within global organizations still retain the structure of the liberal social contract and still control many state apparatuses: for example, private educational providers, based in this instance in the United States, have been employed by local municipalities in the UK to run "failing" secondary schools. What is interesting is that just at this moment of shift, public participation in national institutions is able to become more diverse. This is partly because nation-states no longer have to maintain special rights in a way that excludes diversity, and partly because G-SAs require specified markets for commodities.[1] But it's also partly because people in capitalized countries at least have begun to claim political and cultural power in a different way (Benhabib 1996). Education, driven by national economic needs, has taught people to learn how to learn, to value their lives and work in different ways, more affirmatively using different media for communication and dissemination.

1 There's a curious levelling off that occurs at points in consumption by very large markets that has been responded to by splitting market demand and creating niche markets: *Women's Own/Woman* in the 1930s, Coke/DietCoke/Cherry Coke/, etc.

culture" is the culture of people excluded from that empowered group, then "public culture" could be defined as the culture of people at last included in "rights," including the right to cultural power. The theoretical exploration of diverse cultural power has been furthered and informed by, among others, Canadian philosophers such as Dorothy Smith and Lorraine Code (Hunter 1999, chapter 6), whose work, along with that of writers such as Iris Young (Young 1997) has moved knowledge toward what Seyla Benhabib calls deliberative democracy[c] – what I would call democratic (rather than liberal) humanism, although this may claim too much.

Public culture has to be able to recognize, and welcome, differentiated voices. Strategies for this kind of recognition have been developed in the field of situated knowledge (Code, Haraway, Collins), which offers an alternative to the universal/relative split of the liberal social contract,[d] arguing

c Deliberative democracy (Benhabib 1996a) provides strategies for negotiating the social contract so that the special rights accorded to propertied citizens are distributed more widely among the newly enfranchised population. Central to these strategies is an understanding that newly enfranchised citizens will probably not have the same interests at heart as the in-place privileged citizens, nor will their interests be in common as a group. Because their interests are both different and unlikely to be in common, they will find it more difficult to find a vocabulary that will communicate their value.[2]

2 Communication of these diverse interests will often go unseen and unheard by the in-place governing bodies, so newly enfranchised citizens need to develop a range of techniques that will allow their needs to be recognized, and in-place citizens have a responsibility to learn new ways of hearing and seeing the issues (Mansbridge 1996).

d Getting rid of the universal/relative split prompts a discarding of the split between "subject" and "man." In capitalized countries, it's no longer a split between universal and relative, but between universal and niche, or more accurately between mass and niche, that calls forth an ambivalent identity between "global subject" and "consumer," encouraging a doublethink not between universal and autonomous but between mass and consumer-individual. The global subject is not a subject in the old way because it operates beyond nation and territory. While it is still subject to the nation-state, that subjectivity doesn't work within the same economic restraints because national economies have ceded varying degrees of power to global structures; hence the power of national representation will feel different. Concepts of loyalty will change, as will concepts of betrayal.[3] To focus on the first two categories: consumers are global subjects while labourers become their shadow, acting as did the wife to the husband, or to some extent the working class to the bourgeoisie, in the nation-state.

that living with the split is only workable with a very small population of privileged people from roughly same-interest backgrounds, having economic power over aesthetic objects (both production and consumption). Instead, there can be a recognition of partial knowledge that acknowledges that "difference" is not something that pre-exists, that we "tolerate" in others, but something we make in our interrelations with other people (Hunter 2001b, chapter 6), recognizing their and our partiality[e] and collapsing the power of producer/consumer/maker.

But public culture also has to be able to welcome differentiated voices into social and political agency. In the modern period, culture has been associated with agency primarily through transgression and transcendence (that gothic/sublime binary). The aesthetic difference of modern culture has been founded on representation (pre-existing) and on the (ideological) position of subjects, which has been transmuted by later twentieth-century theorizing into the discursive relations of hegemonic subjectivities.[f] What

3 Under G-SAs it's more complicated.[i] G-SAs are interested in individuals as consumers if they come from Western capitalized countries, but interested in individuals, from under-capitalized erstwhile named third-world countries, as labourers. It's as yet unclear whether they are interested in fourth-world/aboriginal individuals, but I suspect that they are since so many raw materials and resources are tied up in land claims relating to the rights of this group of people.

i Under ISAs this yields a step into materiality (Belsey 1999).

e This is one way of understanding Derrida's notion of "différance": that "difference" is something that we recognize by comparing it to ourselves and assessing whether or not it is "the same," while "'différance" is something we make when we negotiate elements that we have no way of recognizing within our own lives. The pull to recognize "difference" is exceptionally strong and exceptionally helpful in many situations, but it erases the particularities of other people. That pull is one of the reasons that in-place citizens cannot hear or see the interests or "rights" of differentiated newly enfranchised citizens.[4] And "différance," because it is made between and among people actively interrelating through various media, is more time-consuming and requires energy to sustain.

4 Partial knowledge is a position citizens may take up to remind themselves of the need to continually negotiate différance.

f Representations are the way nation-states mediate the possibilities of subject positions for their citizens (Hunter 1999a, chapter 1). Aesthetics in capitalized countries has been based on valuing the ways in which subjects (hence people of privilege) articulate different possibilities for self that lie outwith representation.[5] All aesthetics values the articulation of differences lying outwith representation: modern aesthetics has simply focused this on the privileged citizen aka subject, is difficult is distinguishing between the differences generated by modern culture and those generated by the perspective of situated knowledge in increasingly deliberative democracies, and distinguishing between the agency of subjectivity and the agency of partiality.

Why should this matter?

Because partiality and the situated in themselves are no guarantee of democratic agency. They employ rhetorical techniques often similar to those used by G-SAs to establish representations which, even if they are not representations for the individual in the nation state, are still representations for the consumer in global state structures.

Nations today increasingly work not with concepts of universal/relative but with multiple competing markets, not basing representation on the "same" but on "difference." At precisely this point, where the individual becomes diverse and partial from a situated perspective, s/he also ceases to be economically important as an individual autonomous subject subsumed into "universal man" (aka propertied white capitalist) and becomes a consumer in niche-marketing techniques that are also diverse but in this case relative. The problem becomes: how to tell the "difference" apart. Is the technique generating difference *partial* in respect for people's particularities, making the differences among us in the process of engagement? Or is it *relative* because it is defined as such by global corporate structures imposing representations of difference tied to commodities for consumption – representations of G-SAs mediated via national state structures?

For example: What is the difference between finding/making a democratic community *and* having an ego trip because everyone recognizes and affirms your consumer identity?

What is the difference between being open to intuition *and* allowing representations to take hold?

What is the difference between collaboration of diverse groups *and* corporate structure?

---

both as producer and consumer. With an increasingly larger number of people from diverse backgrounds claiming cultural power, the representations on offer are no longer appropriate. The subject is less predictable, even the more flexible concept of subjectivity is fraying at the edges.

5 Hegemonic political structures encourage a representative art (not realism) that represents and resists the representations of empowered people, thereby incorporating change, effect, compromise, and desire, in order to maintain economic stability and national identity through the interpellation of private subjects.

The difficulty occurs partly because we lack words to distinguish between the differences and partly because there are no rhetorical strategies and techniques that could guarantee one or the other.[g]

What about Poetics?

At present, the "making" art at the centre of poetics is one of the few ways we have of understanding the activity of partial knowledge. Textuality that involves writer/text/reader in one text that they *make* together is a helpful way of thinking about partial knowledge that can distinguish it from the representations of G-SAs. But the distinction is in the *stance*, the process of the event, what rhetoric used to call allegory and others have described as experience "in the moment."

Poetics can delineate the generation of energy[h] that is needed for *installation*, a Brossardian term for the eruption into representation. But this is a

g One could generate strategies that would probably work toward partiality in a specific social and historical context (Young 1996), but the speed with which these are co-opted into global corporate techniques for producing relational markets is increasing (Hunter 1999a, chapter 5). Understanding the slide/slippage (rhetorical drift) from negotiation of partiality, to consensus agreement, to corporate structure, is a needed skill for a differentiated public government and its citizens (Hunter 1999a, chapter 4).

h For many years people worried about the lack of agency written into totalizing theories of the subject, like Althusser's on ISAs. Some, including Foucault, Laclau and Mouffe, and Butler, also invested in a concept of subjectivity that could affect/ effect power, by casting the nation-state as ideological and hegemony as discursive (see Macdonnell). But neither accounts for where the energy for that affect/ effect comes from. Much modern aesthetics, including Brossard's, answered that this energy comes from the erotics of interrelation (Hunter 2005): the idea of the labour on the text that informs installation that erupts through representation[6] rather than transgressing or transcending it.[7] But installations may also be acclaimed as "'beauty," associated with the adrenalin rush of recognition, and if repeated and set into culture as "beautiful," they generate a sense of sociocultural fit. Brossard implies that the acclamation is a warm beauty, and the repeated fit is cold beauty (Brossard 1990, 145–6). Yet installations are often completely "uninteresting" because they cannot be "seen" or "heard" (Hunter 1999a, chapter 6), which is one of the reasons that "rarity" has been important to recent Western aesthetics.

6 The eruption of installation into representation has depended on ISAs and discursively constituted structures of performance through which an installation has to make its way. It is recognized as beauty if it emerges into the representative

particular way of looking at poetics. It is about poetics that comes not from a small group worrying about inadequate representation, which leaves the status quo as such because "inadequacy" implies "adequacy." Rather it's a poetics from people concerned to work on saying what isn't said:[i] Language is not inadequate but limited by the people using it.

The poetics of public culture, as defined in this essay, makes room for the activity of making that is particular to people who claim cultural power

field by simultaneously disrupting that field and fitting into it at the same time.[ii] Fit happens differently under G-SAs but it is still a capital-intensive product and is marketed accordingly, which means to wide audiences, usually niched after a certain cut-off. Earlier readings of this marketing, for example, by members of the early Frankfurt school, read it as popular culture moving inexorably toward "sameness." More recent theorizing watches it move toward a common materiality within which difference operates. What would be interesting would be marketing that encouraged interaction on a common basis, but the problem with this is that it is unpredictable and would disturb the stability necessary for profit. Nevertheless, there is always money to be made in the initial stages.

7   Because what is said about poetics usually differs from what happens in the making, the poetics associated with "art" has described the activity of making peculiar to empowered individuals, or in response to the representations available to empowered individuals, because this is the art that has been widely valued as such. The key terms of transgression, transcendence, and subversion all hint at the sense of inadequacy of these representations for those in a context of relative empowerment and hence in a position to create/organize adequacy. It's a poetics of chagrin, one that demands heroes. In contrast, the poetics of popular culture describes the activity of making peculiar to those with no political power and therefore no representations. The poetics of popular culture cannot be one of transgression because there is nothing to transgress, except through mimicry, parody, clowning, and carnival, which is one reason why popular culture is often judged as banal within current aesthetic terms. But there is the possibility of a poetics based not only on exclusion and disaffection but also on need.

ii "Fit" is essential to modern concepts of "beauty," and has been tied to the representative field of privileged citizens

i   What isn't said is related in installation to either need or desire or both. Within ISAs, need arises from valuing self and community outwith national structures. Under G-SAs need is still associated with installation that arises from valuing self and community outwith both national and global representations in order to locate an agency for participation. It is also partly associated with valuing the possibility of being "token," not basing the unsaid on individually made difference but on the differences made by being self-identified with what one is part of, such as an ethnicity.

within the context of partiality. To address a context of partiality one has to engage in recognition of other partialities, often in collaboration, and have a sense of your own situated location and its particulars. In this poetics we are not dealing in representations as universals, and a loss of self into relativism, but in making and using the energy of the particular/collaborative difference. Public culture is porous. It welcomes both art and popular culture but also recognizes installation – occurring when the particular/collaborative makings that arise from the energy of partiality happen, as they sometimes do, with a density that sends them erupting through the representative layer, installing themselves.

Yet even if we look at poetics as based on partiality, there is the same kind of potential for con/fusion as there is with the potential collapse of the distinction between the partial individual and the consumer individual. Installation may be distinct from transgression/transcendence, but it may erupt through representation and create/constitute a sense of aesthetic fit that is very similar. It may be recognized as "beautiful," instigating short-term change, and either be co-opted into the cold beauty of sublime representation or become banal consumer representation, *or* it may carry the energy needed for long-term social and political change. In this it is often troubling. But also at times intangible, enigmatic, or even uninteresting because we do not recognize its presence, at the very same time that it has present value in the moment for other people.

This reminds me of listening to poetry. Sometimes it works for me and sometimes it doesn't. Or should that be: sometimes I work for it. Or possibly: it happens.

READING DAPHNE MARLATT'S WRITING

One of the tasks to hand is finding a way to talk about these distinctions in poetics, a procedure that I think is important because of the transference of knowledge and understanding that I would like to make from poetics and toward politics and public culture. The readings I work on are engaged with Daphne Marlatt's poetry in *this tremor love is* (2001) and some of the writing on poetics in *Readings from the Labyrinth* (1998) along with one or two later short essays (Marlatt 1998, 2002). Marlatt's critical writing is acutely aware, as it develops, of the issues that result from a shift from an aesthetics of the universal/relative to an aesthetics of the partial. That awareness is drawn from her commitment to a democratic humanism that in turn derives from her concern to put lesbian politics and, more broadly, women's rights on the agenda, not as single issues but as highly contradictory tissues of the body politic. The writing articulates the problem of the infusion between the two kinds, first, of the particular and partial individual on the one hand, and second, of the consumer on the other, as well as parallel issues in poetics such as how to recognize other people as partial not relative, how to tell into words the person who is partial/situated, what images/figures/schemes are available to articulate a self that would displace the double/doppelganger/split personality/hysteric/schizophrenic, etc. that mark out the universal/relative divide of modern Western culture.

The exploration of Marlatt's writing addresses parallel questions in politics. For example, what happens after the "subject"? This has been a problem for neo-Marxism faced with the International becoming the global corporation rather than global democracy. What happens after "subjectivity"? This is a problem for discourse studies faced with the invisibility of poverty within its practitioners, and for ecological studies faced with the "disappearance of history." Yet these are very modern questions, and go hand in hand with postmodern issues that are continually concerned that cultural and social diversity complicate and/or remove structures of "fit," that representations of G-SAs are not fully understood, that representations, like science for technology, have entered a world of "second stage fit."[j]

Through Marlatt's texts it is possible to ask a different set of questions, questions that arise for me in the title of this essay: *What is an honest man? and is it possible to be an honest woman?*

An honest man is one without heroics: the ego isn't in it. It's the person who continually resists allowing the "subject" to be constructed, the one who opens up to representations of social and political multiplicity/divers-

---

j Second-stage science describes the effects of global corporations on scientific laboratories that pursue independently parts of a larger scientific program of which they may be unaware (Rose 1998). This poses obvious questions about ethical responsibilities. Second-stage culture produces fit in bits and pieces. There is no easily recognized aesthetic picture, but either interlocking pieces or the mammoth fit of mainstream cinema, circus, sport. The need that generates the energy for fit is cast differently under G-SAs because the hidden labour force is not domestic and, in contrast to the hidden family in nation-states, is not involved in the moral upbringing of future consumers who may be liable to rebel. The G-SA workforce is hidden in other places, unseen, with no value in the moral economy of the nation's culture. The problem of fit occurring with need but without responsibility is different from the relation of need and fit under ISAs. The need of those not fitting in the UK is not equal to the need of those not fitting in Uganda. Neither is better or worse, simply different and engendering different strategies.

ity and the difficulty of variousness. This as opposed to sincerity: the position of the person who relies on subjectivity to put themselves in touch with "consciousness." And the honest woman? A woman with no ego/id, no subject representation, yes. But what does it mean not to be a hero if you have never been one, or could ever be one? What does it mean to be without ego if ego has *never* been in it? It's the shadowed/woman who can only exist if we believe that the subject is important to realize.

What does honesty or agency mean for women and other others who choose not to value a subjectivity that effaces them? Marlatt suggests to me that the value comes through collaborative worlds of partial knowledge, that agency becomes the way you read/write in a situated textuality. It is appropriate or honest in that particular moment. And it is agential not only in how you affect/effect the hegemonic but also the particular. And perhaps if we affect the hegemony from that particular place there is more chance for democratic humanism.

Tissue of Quotations

The following prose is transliterated from Marlatt's commentaries on poetics. The page numbers from *Readings from the Labyrinth* follow specific critical ghostings into this text.

In Marlatt's early criticism she describes the experience of being a woman in terms of someone outside subjectivity – the "excluded" (15) who has "hidden meaning" (33). Hence for the lesbian, or non-heteronormative woman, or queer person, to speak oneself is to go beyond limits of self as distinct from other (46–7). Women are active, not heroic (65). Later she speaks of salvaging women not into the normal but into a workable new cultural vision (167). The problem is how to tell the story of a self that hovers, as she puts it, "fictively," on the subject/object threshold (205).

Similar to the Brossardian installation that erupts through the subject/object by ignoring them, Marlatt's ficticity may be received either as "beauty," which has warm and cold attributes, or as an "event," a "happening," "in the moment." This ambiguity of reception generates the problem both of distinguishing different ways of responding to beauty and of distinguishing between beauty and partiality. Marlatt quotes Brossard, saying that writing makes women visible in public space (66), and goes on to suggest that such writing also makes more public space for other women to inhabit. From early on, Marlatt recognizes that one needs both reader and writer in order to ask effective political and cultural questions, and thereby defines a necessary set toward the public.

What I find Marlatt helping me to think through is this distinction be-tween performance, the event in public culture, and particularity, or where the energy for the installing comes from – a discussion that she focuses through commentary on the public. She is aware of the way that any pres-ence in public culture is an invitation to the public audience to engage, and they may do so in quite different ways. The early criticism spends a lot of time working through strategies that could ensure long-term effects of beauty and subjective agency. Yet, from the beginning of *Readings from the Labyrinth*, there is an awareness that both the individual and the public have to interrelate in any aesthetic experience, and that this interrelation will affect the effects of strategy. She suggests that, despite the opposition between privacy and the commonwealth (25), collaboration can resolve the binary. She defines the lesbian erotic as transforming the subject when we "touch ourselves into mutual being" (49). Narrative may be survival, but survival is never done alone (62).[k] The commentary talks about the terror and the beauty of the installation that results (147), as well as the collective body that results (149).

Also, this work articulates the problem of distinguishing in itself. It sug-gests a "you" that is a light beam that includes, does not set the other apart in the third person (132). It is a "you" that does not make the other the *same* and hence plausible (as opposed to probable). This "you" goes hand in hand with the small "i" that signifies a multiplicity of presence and absence in different perspectives, speaking through the rigid sameness and in distinc-tion to the "I" (138). Further, there is a "we" that can be a connection and solidarity or can blur differences and exclude others. Nevertheless there is a need for "we," despite the possibilities that it excludes others, because there is a need for hope in community (155). Marlatt later suggests the complexity of the woman writer's sense of community (208) which means that text is not for self alone: it is shared, resonant with voices often inaudible till then, which she resists and affiliates with, affiliation pushing to the collective, not to sameness.

If this is the aesthetic, and political, problem, Marlatt explores it in her studies of writing: narrative, lyric, autobiography, and life-writing. Narrative needs the sensory beyond narrative convention, and the early commentary places "beyond" in another kind of writing, the lyric (53), generating a very Lacanian structure, as if lyric is the way we surface the repressed. Lyric itself

k It is interesting here that stories "resonate beyond the particular," indicating a transcendence and a gesture toward the binary.

is wonderfully examined through "knots" that bend and break the difference between figure and ground, which conjoining preserves hegemony and truth (126–7). Lyric speaks in corresponding differences, not oppositionality (133). And if syntax is where ideology is found (146), lyrical strategies to disrupt it include repetition, litany, run over margins, silence, taking the idiomatic at face value (167), and others. In this analysis we can find a clear description of the long-term effects of installation through lyric.

Installation in narrative is more confusing. The commentary provides a long list of anti-representational strategies: pulling the plug out of our ears, remaking language/genre/symbol, poking holes in the monolithic, reinterpreting old tales, scotching containing categories, crossing boundaries, opening up the unspoken, seeing through cover stories, satirizing transcendental signifiers (82), theatricalizing patriarchal images to foreground and falsify (161), among others. The problem with many, if not all, of these strategies is that in reception it is more difficult to distinguish between the political work of compromising with representation and positioning as consumer, and that of erupting through representation – both being negotiations possible to performance. Furthermore, are the narrative elements erupting toward fit or from the enigma of the particular?

We can't tell without knowledge of the particular. These strategies have a historical specificity that would help us if we are working with the universal/relative binary of the nation state, but they are potentially misleading in their similarity to rhetorical strategies of niche-structure G-SAs. Hence Marlatt insists on context (62) that "bears us in our harrowing complexity" (126–7). It can help us to distinguish the "connectedness" of the syntactic relations (168) from hegemonic syntax in prose, through our understanding of the complexity of many installations happening at once (157).

Marlatt's writing indicates a growing interest in autobiography and life-writing, for this is where text becomes context (127). The looser narrative of journal writing generates connections between narrative and knowing, discerns shape in the repetition of lines, maps contours against the scatter of the daily to locate us differently (68). Autobiography is an affirmation of an embodied multiphasic being from where we stand (147). It drops out of narrative as heroic into narrative as a relating of context, an "honest" rendering of life because it involves both the reader and writer in making the text in the moment. Life-writing is not set toward beauty but works on need: the not-yet-said. And the element of *bios* is what enables us to articulate and recognize need. The reader/writer engagement is a process of "becoming" that Marlatt calls "ficticity": to find something "i" might recognize, to tunnel back to the place of not-knowing to narrate "becoming." If naming is analogous to memory, becoming is analogous to things. Hence, becoming has an immediacy that flares up in the moment (206), a kinetics of identity (206), that sets self in a knot in a larger net of relations: a fire of connection (216) or love.

A reader of the commentary can feel the growth of the awareness through the keywords: conversation (23), translation (28), communal response (114), intuition (114), collaboration (116), relation (117), connectedness (140, 170), dialogue (137), net (216), and compassion (216).

The development is also apparent in her explicit commentary on writing and reading. Writing begins as a connection of language with the world beyond narrative line (50) that threads "touch words" (55). This writing is motivated by the necessity to share, to ripple out to a joint "you" (132). It activates meaning in motion across the skin, across different bodies reading and writing (140), so that the text becomes the trace of body, imprinted in body tissue. The exploration moves to place writing as an erotic where self and other as a binary disappear (218), so that writing recognizes particular need, a testing and contesting of necessity (218).*

Feminist reading is identified early on as active reading "as it arises in your mouth on the page" (28). Reading is allied with transformance, in which meaning "seeps" from writer to reader (72–3). At this stage the commentary also categorizes readers as "male"/normative, resistant, empathic, and merging (84) and talks about the last as a place of danger. The concepts turn increasingly to difference, which describes reading as the place where words "turn" depending on who reads them, gesturing to a relative binary (133).** Yet reading is also cast as a delicate balance of recognizing both difference and shared ground (137), the beginnings of particularity.

The strands of writing and reading combine in a series of comments about a stance that merges or coalesces writer, reader, and text. There is an early comment about the labyrinthine quality of the "inner ear" that catches for both writer and reader the unexpected drifts and currents of meaning (32).

* Daphne Marlatt kindly responded to this paper and commented here: "it's the movement back & forth i was focusing on, not the erasure of self & other, because it's the movement that embraces both while still recognizing difference between" (Marlatt, email, June 2005).

** Marlatt resisted this reading, commenting "i'm not sure how 'binary' arises, even a relative one, from 'the multiple nature of the real.' but then again, i'm not sure i'd use that term 'the real' in such an unqualified way now" (Marlatt, email, June 2005).

Or the "slippage" between what the writer wants to say and what language wants to say (70). This moves to an "active complex" generated when the word as an object in flight wings into the core of being and you recognize what it stands for and shares in (131), and it becomes that testing of necessity where writer and reader jointly make and recognize the gesture of the text. They intersect in the kinematic, make the fire that travels the knots of identity (218). Both work on a "hypothetical ground" where they slip or slide in language, as the image of garden hovers beyond the retaining wall of a street (219), the particular reading/writing altering you/me (222).

The stance, which I would call allegorical, delineates what goes on before and during and after performance. In the situated and partial place of installing, the ephemeral, it is part of the deep enigmatic experience of partial knowledge.

And does this happen when we read (write)? Is this possible?

What Marlatt is exploring, and is being explored through this ghost-writing, is how to articulate self as not-subject, how to do this honestly, without reinsertion into recognized fit (most of us desire this), and how to interrelate with other people/animals/landscape/and other, without treating them as subjects/objects.

The following reading/writing may be read alongside t*his tremor love is* as a group of essays/assays into how those interrelations might occur or feel.

Hypothetical Ground

The opening poem in *this tremor love is* is exemplary. The first section, "ocha words" (11), cascades into small rocks of pronouns and prepositions:

Stir up
Stir up out of what
                  what dreams
                  what cause of communion
  stir up nouns
                  as the honey pours   *your* dream was this
                                  this reading
                                  this poem pouring
                                  this cup of tea
                        proposes *your* favourite word

The cascade generates a narrative "i," one person looking out the window through rain:

you   drop the book, your books
[the poem hangs on]   depends
[& begins again]   pressing days into pages   [back echo]
          & paged, *we* could pull out any *one* this *one*, so young
                                             These

The poem is dealing in memories, and hence in names/nouns/pronouns. *i* to
you through *winter   rice
     tea strain*   recalling the past.
& then in the sweet tongue
          green hope of tea   there's slippage: steam's slip, becoming,
                    now, in the present:
     i & *you* overheard, breathing yourself into sound,
                    as if breath, one's own breath, breathes others into
                    being.

The second section, "touch" (12), ripples along in eddies of assonance and
internal rhyme: river/tongue/tea:
          tea & trout
     tea: sweet steep
               sweet infusion   tipping our lips   at the smallest
                                                  ordinary
Suddenly arrested by then
     crescendo light through dark   [two people into one fusion tipping/
     your eyes [i]   nearly touching, not quite, ordinary]
Scattering the assonance: soft cacophony of   planned
     foot skin smooth startle | to mere | trout lines | unplanned | nothing
     dark trout leap | [water] | | undone
     ichthyic spine rippling | shine | | *our* lines haphazard

"tea" brings "i" back into the pronoun pebbles: i see/your eye/my eye – an
exploration of presence, not memory – through a conversation/infusion of
two people   seeing trout leap:
     "you": crescendo of eyes/i's | as if the words go back & forth
                                    | between you and i
          luminous/luminant | – the trout described as thunder
                                    | inflorescent
          wander/wonder | OR
          amazed/astony | "you" describes self as slow to leap
          touched/touching |

"you" is slow to leap to what is   trout: the budding wonder [of tea]: to leap, leaves [tea], scales: miraculous. As a friend would say "among" [not either/ or or both/and or between (implying only *two*), but *among*]. As if the [self]- description isn't enough: not separate but *among*. But also that human beings are different from the trout: find it more difficult to be *among*.

The third section, "bachi" (13), opens with a little litany
        sea bush
        small tree
        fruit bearing
        salt sprung

in a descriptive net of sound: its own de/scription:

*dr*enched *l*eaves	*dr*awn to *sh*are	a making/
*str*aining to *l*ight		poiein
*s*pume		
*dr*ift of *r*epeated ob*ser*vation		

and "you" offer *tea*: another moment of things in recall, a different page: they sip as yours/mine: *interinflected*.

The poem <u>depends</u>, again. Yet if we break our description of the world, based on repeated and observation of our own thingness, who then is the dreamer/dreamed? Our description becomes another's, so is *our* body ours or all of ours? who's dreaming who? A very human question.

Back again to the windowpane: the past is no longer the past but rain & incessant words make the slippage *between*. Tea is brought to *different* lips, this space where names unfold, like budding wonder: leaf by leaf *we* disappear, into   among. And the nouns: winter/rice/tea strain : unfold like lives : in the tea : as if we too are leaves unfolding, making the infusion.

≈

"Winter/- Rice/- Tea strain" is a lyric exemplary because of its gatherings: the image of leaves particular yet infused, the simultaneity of memory and presence, of noun and becoming, of pages and breathing, of i/you/between/ among. In contrast, the poem "Listen" (24–6) has a narrative about two people quite separate, but at the same time about the recognition of this separation on the part of one of them. The syntax tells the reader from the start:

| *he* was reading to *her* | *he* was standing/reading/ |
| | holding |

>   *she* was making salad
>
> &   *she* was wondering about ... carrots
>
>   [*very funny very sad*]

> [& between them   a lamp]
> her son ... light ...
> shade, in its glow: drawing
> "exact" heroes no one
> had seen except in coloured ink
> [*she* had bought
> for colour / *he* called it cheap
> imitation]

And he's worried about imitation yet he, like his son, is imitating from a book, reading to/at her while she's making/wondering: she's not in this reading.

The poem cuts back & forth between the two: not only making clear that there's little connection but also allowing "her" the poetic presence, *her* wondering swirls around the island of interruption *he* makes, telling the reader something only *she* reaches at the end.

He's talking about loss and excitement, emphatic, stirred: with words not his own even though he embraces them / says *their* dancing has lost the sense of the collective.

She's standing, wondering: making salad, easily – spring stirring (not him now), moving with the rhythm of the rain (not him now), barely knowing it.

He says /caught her eye to make the point: people have lost touch / people dance alone.

She's lifting/pressing/watching: feels accused [infused into the vision of blood in the salad]: thinks of an argument: then remembers back to a party & people together but not knowing each other: only glanced off the meaning in the book.

He's getting in touch with nature [husbandry etc.] through a book, she's doing it in the rain/rhythm.

Then the poetics give us the display of their separating relationship:
>   listen   he was saying / & he read
>   listen   he said / & read
>   she said / thinking: making a statement about fertility and
>   women
>   he said ---------- he means fertility of the earth [his syntax
>   reversing hers]
>   listen   he said

He overwrites *her*, over reads her. they are one/other: no joining, no complementarity, only opposition.

Her response is a series of actions: she scooped, dropped, watched, tossed: the salad, with its dark heart of blood, the dark heart that she suddenly sees in *their* hearts. And she casts back to that other night, after the party, their laughter, conversation, wrapt in warmth: she remembers: the movement to & from each other in the dance, loving others in each other: through & away & toward their separate bodies.
AND BACK : listen   she said: rain's come up
                        salad on the table under the lamp
in the particular.

What she's making becomes an extension of her: blood in the salad as though the carrot against the green leaves becomes a visceral transformation/transport into feeling. It's a happening at the same time as an infusion/interflection of her own. She held a fullness he didn't feel: she didn't know that till the carrot hit the salad. Memory needs at least one other person to be valued and suddenly she's just lost hers. And now they eat that dark-hearted salad under that troubled lamp. But she's dealt with the lamp and will deal with the salad.

The writing feels early for various reasons, but one of them is that the becoming self infuses itself with the natural rather than the human, separating between the two as if there's a choice.

≈

Another kind of relationship is imaged in "hands on the table" (14–17), a
    poem partly about a dream, troubling, and the associative chaining
    through which dream becomes memory and words/writing. But it is
    also about the relationship that makes this possible.
The speaking presence opens, saying out hands from a dream: a dream and
    hence part of her body: & the cry: whose hands? whose cry? has it
    become part of her?
Set against the action of someone with her, "you," wiping the table bare of
    prints/hand prints: to bare, make spare, so to make visible that which
    "comes up out of nothing, & lifts me, like wind, into recognition" (14).
The chaining is released by this making bare/spare: bare swept church:
    beggar: child, moving to the other side of "the law." The child is in the

dark of dream: the dark getting larger as the law "held on": for both
her mother and her self. Till there's another church: remains: child's
hands: her mother's hands: child asleep in death.

The dream: the hands of the mother/child. The cry: on the other side of
dreaming: where our bodies become part of the world, where our
bodies become memory and words, where the child/mother is born
into the world made visible.

Both set back into: this world where the living still live: where the table
is not your/mine but a table where *we* sit and *our* hands are on the
table. Hands rest/move. Words speak out of separate quiet, speak of
strangeness   *our* hands cannot re/move. Words make present the
other body and make different and strange at the same time. "you" as
a reader.

And this is the centre of the strategy of the particular: that the reader
makes the body of the poem and builds their differences to/from it at
the same time.

≈

Particularity with another is imaged in yet a different way in "meant" (23):
to give up intent, for words to "utter what they offer":

rush on us two   apart: happening to
give to   each but differently

words/waves break forever crashing & pulling on the	particulars being suspended	on the coast of our
difficult particulars of two very different people – makes them apart + a part of the world in their particularity	each noun "awash": nouns being here floating pebbles the result of a wave collapsed	astonishment

words (waves) run on – break (like waves) on their particular astonishment
[intent/meant]

> break: pebbles crash and pull – articulating the difficult particulars
> > of the two people
> > making them apart from each
> > other but also a part
> the breaking wave is the energy that imparts our particularity, at
> once one & many

but also in the "washing" "awash," the pebbles lose their separateness at the same time as they lose their coastal sameness: released into particularity and oneness at the same time.

a yin-yang expression*

≈

For me, reading, these opening poems are exploring ways of telling that particularity and wholeness so that it is no longer a binary but a becoming/ process. And because of the partiality of each, of reader/writer/text (but also) image, the process is enigmatic.

Many of the following sections of *this tremor love is* explore the feeling of "love" as an image central to understanding the simultaneity of particularity and wholeness. & understanding what it is not. For example, "Small print" (58–65), a poem NOT about: what does it mean to lose love? BUT : what does it mean to have love? When you are in love the other reads you, your writing, and makes actual. But it's not *you* they make actual although you could deceive yourself into thinking so. It's something else that is part of this world. But they also read *you*: mingle with you and rearrange the text. The removal of their voice also means that "you" no longer reads the other

* Marlatt reads through to: "this is a significant poem for me. a very knotted one (its reach too large). it took me years to arrive at this version, & it may be too convoluted. please indulge me as i try to work through the knots. you work at a different set of analogies than i 'meant' (ha!) yet you arrive at the same overall sense of it. first of all, the last line 'astonishments' is in the plural (one coast, many astonishments, for each of us in the poem). i hear 'stone' in astonish, a false derivation i know (& probably too obscure) but an echo of 'astony' in the 'touch' poem. so, moving from pebble (that stony particular) towards the shared 'stone' of 'stoned' – that sense of wonder & its link with love. being stoned takes us out of the usual boxed-in categories of particulars we're so attached to as a means to identity. it's not 'astonishments' that i associate with your 'intent/meant' (nice, that compound), but the singularity of the building wave, the singularity of individual intent before it crashes & disintegrates on the many particulars of others – each noun then awash in possible meanings for the 2 who occupy the same coast or site of listening-to-wave-disintegration, even in their separate astonishments. so when you say 'released into particularity and oneness at the same time,' yes, exactly" (Marlatt, email June 2005).

[left with a carbon copy]. It's the dream of an undifferentiated body, that [dangerous] merged empathic reader – "we" – a collective body that becomes imagination's scrap.

Love allows us to connect the body with the word – allows us to read: allows us the intimacy & immediacy of the word: a physical textual engagement in the present. Yet here's the warning: reading is making something together, but both reader & writer remain particular at the same time. you/i never fuse: they infuse and are not "each other."

≈

"Sea Shining Between" may be read as a journey to the particular. "booking passage" (69–72) announces the surprise of isolation "poised ... for the wall to break // the wall that isolates, that i   so   late   to   this: it doesn't, it slides apart – footings, walls, galleries, this island architecture" (70). It "islands me   in the night, fear & rage the isolate talking in my head. to combat this slipping away, of me, of you ..." (71).
A corollary of isolation is the overwhelming hugeness of peripheral vision, vision with no focus: "central to the periphery" (63–4) contains, "look right through an old horizon ... on & on we are learning how far we extend," as if this is a meditation in preparation for aloneness. "the shape grief takes" builds on the feeling of becoming enislanded, an archipelago, "each one alone in what can't be said," "islands drifting further and further away," "in a shifting sea of emptiness."
"passage between" (79–80) reads like a response to Brossard's *Green Night in the Labyrinth Park*, with its exploration of: to leap, "to bite into risk," "to land in some new place." But what if this "new place," "this you unknown & isolate," is the same old footing? the "you" here both an other and herself. But also the need to break the passage of the life, of becoming, for "some place to be": the arrest of self in love. Just at this point the voice gains distance on the "stranded isolate," commenting "(omitting mountain's joint footing under water, o joined jouissant, the world is round she sang" (81).
"in the current" (81–2) moves on to the passage: "it is the passage ... that can appear ... most difficult" but "It happens in a flash. In a leap. Without transition ...." There is "welcome streaming out of your eyes. & risk. all the bodies we have loved pass their shadows in transit between us," "impossible & yes, in trust" (82). And "is love enough?" (83–4) arrives as a sense of "Chi equally in / the salt sea and fields thick with bloom/ inner channels & rivers // a sea full of apparent islands, no jetting-off point, no airborne leap

possible // without the body all these bodies / interlaced" (84). Again the imaging: apparent islands joined beneath the sea, chi in every particular thing. The journey to the particular simultaneously encompasses the world.

≈

A concatenation of particular/whole imaginations is stored in "Impossible Portraiture," which offers a series of (im)possibilities, reconceptualizations of particularities in love, of self, of being-with-others not as subjects. The face of the other composes itself in this impossible particularity of "love." The lashes open, flare, close, on the particularity of "you": but what "eye"/I sees? what "you"? The intense visuals are carried by assonance/alliteration/ the clamour of consonant and vowel: "curve of your / lips mine tilts to meet, bee-quick –." "you" is not a "literal love" but "i recognise in cheek, lash, light / holds us within it / characteristic, i // see you deep in the unexpected ..." (92). Nor is "you" myth alone, or the "storying delight" (94). There is contradiction in the relationship in "the / shine the keeping words can't speak de-light de / cision   (click)." But the relationship is also a list of possible particular/ whole images:

"our histories / exclude, elude the exact shade ... we balk at,
eye-identifying whole oceans between" (95)
"to want / you (converse & particular, this-time-eyes // solo note" (96)
"this tremor love is, all premise / promise, fold- / over – // – no hold anywhere" (96)
"particular grace" "to keep us strange under one roof"
"home is nothing" (99)

Nothing, or for a Buddhist, Everything.

≈

The final poem in the collection, "Tracing the Cut," also traces the possible particular/whole. Figures and syntax coalesce throughout the poem, surfacing and resurfacing as it flows along. For example, light:

the splendor of light's appetite
eating up detail in this
dark fist of mountains
          we inhabit, momentary
          detail, a piece cut off from
          détailler, to cut (thoroughly
          _____PHAT _____ (103).

Language, like light, "opens its connect- /ing points, com- /panion in this / eating of light" (104). Both eat detail, cut from the whole, but do they leave it detailless or whole? To cut is to recognize by making particular, not a cut that "insists itself // a part / a parting" (105).

In "rain," "i"

> hears the solid *beat*
> lift, in a *wave*like motion
> wrist turn & lift the *drum*
> fluid, of the heart's enlarging (105, added italics)

bringing together the point and the wave of quantum physics. Meditation becomes "a grace-note held / in attention, someone's / thought to set" (106) – "or no, just grace / drops / evenly all round" (106) as if grace cannot be held, even in attention/intention/in tension. The whisper of memory is a "bless'd / fold after fold in time's warp / sand // which'd – " (107): the fold as if body and time fold over one another, even felted, recalling "this tremor love is, all premises / promises, fold- / over – / – no hold anywhere" (96).

And again, the waves,

> ... crash wall
> after wall of green
> disintegrate, each
> smash on stones'
> thunk the resonant
> well of the drum
> we carry   (108)

Waves make particular, they dis-integrate, so each person becomes a

> ... particular
> step on shingle, glide
> of the solitary ones
> or the hummers, quick
> humourous ones ...   (108)

Each put together differently in their particularity, yet all with that resonant well of the drum. All part of the "familial body stuck in / time's warp" "a ruin clung to, for memory's sake"— the "ghost wreath" of mother: is it appropriate "at this particular / age ..."?

> the story the body still
> clinging   (109)

or do we

> ____cut____   (109)

To cut away from the particular story is to enter the empty, and how do we know whether to do the one or the other, to cling or to cut?

Yet perhaps that is not the choice: the poem concludes with breath, and self "fragile and changing / with each breath," combining one concept of body and heart (drum) with another concept of body and breath (wave). She has "mothers all around," the wind/lake/- pine, "all breath-beings & non-breath-sky," and all "offered thus" (110). You "cut" yourself away from the particular that insists on itself and become/enter the particular of the much larger world. You become "offered thus" as they are. And language/light/rain/- lake/- waves help lead you to the cut/fold/empty:full/grace-not-held.

≈

Reading through these poems allows me to deal with the difficulty of distinguishing things that may appear/sound the same but are not: in Marlatt's versions of love, of the cut, the fold: and to find ways to make more probable the particular that does not insist on itself, the pebble/wave, drum/breath, the infusion of tea, the beings in the landscape. The particular and the whole, because they may appear autonomous and connected, can be mistaken for (or be) a binary. They may also be the particular/collaborative needed for installation and its incredibly politically effective short-term strategies. And they may also hold and release the long-term energy of the pebble simultaneously dis-integrated by the wave as it becomes part of the wave's resonance.

Transferring

Marlatt speaks about the way figure and ground, foreground/background, the emptiness at the heart of every particular, stem from "a mode of thought that can hold in mind 2 levels at once," both silence and words. The short line which she explores in this collection lets "more space in, lets the words sound against the space of silence," so that "the prose comes in short bursts that keep returning to the left margin as if to an unspeakable potential the words themselves spill out of and then fall back to" (Marlatt, 2002). As she puts it, "the question is, how to bring it live into the poem if it lies outside language?" (4) But that's not what the poetry does. In Marlatt's poetry, language leads you in, like light, to the particular of emptiness/of the larger world. It leads you to the hypothetical ground, slipping/sliding, the enigmatic allegorical stance of partial knowledge, to energy work.

The poetry is a way of reconceptualizing identity/individuality not as private, nor as subjected, but as particular/whole. That simultaneity is experienced only in the moment. Yet the understanding of particular/collaborative as a conceptual structure drawing its energy from the moment, makes it available for assessing the appropriateness of action, and discourse inflected by this kind of agency is potentially more open to democratic humanism. There is always the problem of the slide from the appropriate to the consensual, from the consensual to the corporate, from the corporate to the authoritarian. Poetics helps public culture to distinguish between these, between installation toward fit and from the moment, to locate the moment, to become conscious of and arrest the slide. NOT by defining specific strategies but by making possible a particular stance.

Democratic humanism depends on diversity and valuing the differences we make among ourselves. It depends on people acting together and apart at the same time. It needs a different kind of public culture, one that certainly won't work for all people as they are at the moment, and it's going to be difficult to fund because modes of production and consumption will shift. But also, because it's only interested in beauty as a sign of discursive efficacy, much of its aesthetics may not be recognized as "culture."

Marlatt's work reminds us that makers, reader/writers, listeners/speakers, have probably always done something like this: it's not postmodern, or modern, or classic. "Postmodern" and similar critical sets are temporary structures for describing and understanding the relation between agency (sometimes artistic) and ruling power. Yes, it is vitally important to address them, which I do in most of my work, but it is also important to remind ourselves they will change.

and why.

PERFORMANCE 8
What Is an Honest Man? and Can There Be an Honest Woman?

WEBLINK http://vimeo.com/18439707

2005   March: "What Is an Honest Man? and Can There Be an Honest
        Woman?" Keynote to the conference "Poetics and Public
        Culture in Canada," University of Western Ontario.

The printed essay that makes up chapter 8 was written for the conference celebrating the work of Frank Davey, whom I knew to hold Daphne Marlatt's writing in high regard. It was delivered as a spoken paper at the end of the conference to a stalwart group of "stayers," including Frank Davey and Daphne Marlatt. Marlatt was kind enough to send me a series of notes on the essay, part of which I've reproduced below.

This script was delivered orally in a conference style one degree off. Indeed, I think many people thought it was dead on. The first third of the piece, the theoretical engagement, was conceived of partly as a joke. I did not read the footnotes, and without the footnotes, which engage the conversationalists in this to and fro, the slick, rather glib theory-rant is a simulacrum at best. Many people afterwards felt completely alienated by it, but there were some in the audience who had worked with me on precisely these issues and they recognized its dance along an argument about the lack of any rhetorical guarantee for formal qualities.

The central part of the script, "Tissue of Quotations," merges the usually footnoted material right into the critic's writing. There was an attempt here to tell a palimpsest of Marlatt's writing about reading/writing experience as a critical intervention, which she may or may not have imagined but which nevertheless is released from listening to her text, making my own differences, and re-telling the story as needed for the conversation the piece has with politics and the personal philosophical. Marlatt responded directly to this with the observation that she liked

> how you situate the push towards what you call the "particular/
> collaborative" within such a political framework. it's your reading of
> the perceptual/philosophic & how you relate it to the political that
> astonishes.

It was difficult for the audience to follow conceptually, but it offered a rhythmic bridge to the final section.

The last third of the script, "On Hypothetical Ground," was a rehearsing of several poems in *this tremor love is* (2001). I pushed the experiment with Alice Munro's prose further and used the poetics of the verse to generate grammatical structures and rhetorical strategies shaping a differently versed conversation with Marlatt's work. When I read this aloud at the conference, people told me afterward that they thought I was reading Marlatt's poetry aloud. I worried about the ethics of this, but Daphne Marlatt herself seems to recognize the intimate and alongside positioning that I was attempting. The listeners engaged with the final section in various ways, leaning their bodies into it. I could hear them repeating words like "compassion" with surprised familiarity. Afterwards Fred Wah came up to me and said "'among,' that's an important word in another poem." I expected him to tell me which one it was he was thinking of, but he never did.

The excisions from Marlatt's notes below are mainly to do with misquotations introduced by the publisher, which I had failed to pick up in proofing. Rather like the French printers who printed Joyce's *Ulysses*, setting the words that they seemed to be reading, and creating a text that generations would attribute to a single author, this essay became a collaborative event. I am grateful, as ever, to Frank Davey for retyping the material so that it could be generated as camera-ready copy for a volume of *Open Letter*. I am also grateful to Elena Cid del Prado for inciting me to redesign the footnotes into evermore elaborate pediments, and for the many conversations – live and digital – in which we engaged during the design of the website materials.

Email from Daphne Marlatt: 07/05

Dear Lynette,
... i'm not going to respond much to the theoretical
section about public culture – i haven't read your sources – but i
do like your leaping-off point, that public culture is "culture that
recognizes diverse cultural power," "the culture of people at last
included in 'rights' ... " i have to confess that i had some trouble
reading sentences with the word "outwith" in them, having no idea
what this coinage is in reaction to or how to read it (some critical
history here that i'm unaware of?)

first of all, thank you for reading so closely a major impulse in my
work. quite personally, it serves as a compass point when i get lost
– as i frequently have to, it seems, to write at all (those periods
are very difficult to traverse & i often experience one at
conferences where people are busy situating themselves in
oppositional binaries).

i love the immediacy of the way you break down each poem in your
reading & through this fragmenting carefully reconstitute what each
is saying.

just to continue the dialogue i was having with you while reading
your essay (this is an intense form of interaction!) i'd like to
look at places where i felt some resistance to your paraphrasing.
in the discussion of Readings from the Labyrinth, p. 8, your

paragraph about my commentary on writing and reading: your phrase "where self and other disappear (218)" – is this in reference to my "to oscillate in the space between self and other"? it's the movement back & forth i was focusing on, not the erasure of self & other, because it's the movement that embraces both while still recognizing difference between.

in the following paragraph, "gesturing to a relative binary (133)" – i'm not sure how "binary" arises, even a relative one, from "the multiple nature of the real." but then again, i'm not sure i'd use that term "the real" in such an unqualified way now.

also p. 10, your discussion of "meánt" (its actual title, not "for Roy in La Push") interested me. this is a significant poem for me, a very knotted one (its reach too large). it took me years to arrive at this version, & it may be too convoluted. please indulge me as i try to work through the knots. you work at a different set of analogies than i "meant" (ha!) yet you arrive at the same overall sense of it. first of all, the last line "astonishments" is in the plural (one coast, many astonishments, for each of us in the poem). i hear "stone" in astonish, a false derivation i know (& probably too obscure) but an echo of "astony" in the "touch" poem. so, moving from pebble (that stony particular) towards the shared "stone" of "stoned" – that sense of wonder & its link with love. being stoned takes us out of the usual boxed-in categories or particulars we're so attached to as a means to identity. it's not "astonishments" that i associate with the singularity of your "[intent/meant]" (nice, that compound), but the singularity of the building wave, the singularity of individual intent before it crashes & disintegrates on the many particulars of others – each noun then awash in possible meanings for the 2 who occupy the same coast or site of listening-to-wave-disintegration, even in their separate astonishments. so when you say "released into particularity and oneness at the same time," yes, exactly.

& finally, to "Tracing the Cut" (i still don't know how Karl, Christy & i all missed the capitals in that title, the only one that is capitalized – meaning nothing beyond my random use of caps in draft versions).
... & i

love your statement about "combining one concept of body and heart (drum) with another concept of body and breath (wave)" yes, quantum physics again. i don't know how much you know about Tibetan Buddhism, but your articulation of the back-&-forth between clinging & cutting is an accurate reading – it's the habit of attachment (clinging) to fixed notions of identity & being that PHAT (literally, "cut") works against. an echo of the film director's "cut" which cuts short the continuing story being filmed/told.

well, this has turned out to be a rather long e-mail, Lynette. thank you for such thoughtful reading & analysis. & thank you for the opportunity to continue our conversation.

Daphne

9

De-scribing Performance in bpNichol's *Selected Organs*

The writing here reads bpNichol's *Selected Organs* in two movements, and asks its reader to see with the third eye, listen with the third ear, and feel with the third hand – the second hand being there in the present, in the process, ticking away. One movement is to commentary, as the writing performs the critical reading, forms through the commentary a constellation and a constitution of my own "critical self." It's a constitution insofar as it's inflected by the ideological powers of politics and the society that make me up, and it's a constellation in the Brechtian/Benjaminian sense of the audience/reader re-making the text in reception, finding the narratives of the grammar, phonology, and so on. The other movement is to de-scribing the writing, following the language to the poetry the reading writes. It's a process that opens out the pun, works from prosody and poetics, and it's an installation in the Brossardian sense: of an eruption into and disturbance of the ABC (bpNichol 2002, 392; all references to Nichol's criticism are from this book).

Nichol frequently talks about the way that if writing is reading, reading is also writing. Reading is a slowing down through commentary, which he illustrates in "When the Time Comes" (317), his exploration of Gertrude Stein's *Ida &*. This kind of commentary opens up, like the process of opening up through the pun into another world of "thots" (298). It is an invitation to collaboration, the moment when the fictional flickers with the real. That flicker is an experience that Nichol also connects to the sacred activity of language (334), an activity which has tremendous power and if respected, leads you "to things that I would not arrive at otherwise" (334). You have to give up on the self guiding the poem, yet keep your technical skill in the midst of language's power. It becomes a unity of me: the moment of writing, and of language: that's leading me. This combination gets to the flicker of the sacred. Just as there's a political and emotional reality to the world, Nichol says there's a sacred reality; so the process of writing is analogous to the sacred, and both to the deconstruction of the "I."

The deconstruction of the "I" in the process of writing *Selected Organs* becomes a sacred meditation, becomes language that leads you somewhere. I myself would hesitate to use the word "sacred" because I do not have any particular faith in/on which to base a concept of sacrality. But the process of which bpN speaks, of allowing the language to lead you, or working in collaboration with the language, is close to the concept of installation being used here: the place you arrive at "otherwise" being the moment of installation that your audience will constellate within its own context. The book is a sacred meditation that the commentary here, my commentary, follows on the grounds of the English language context of late-twentieth century Christianity. The commentary reads bpN's deconstruction at the same time as it constitutes its own "commentator self," yet works within the constellation of that deconstruction in a far more intertextual, collective manner. At the same time it installs a de-scribing of the writing, not a re-writing but a de-scribing that allows the writing to lead you to those "things that I would not arrive at otherwise," in a manner analogous to Miwon Kwon's differentiation of the community from the collective, I call it not description but de-scribing (2004, 154).

So, for example, *Selected Organs* begins with "The Vagina," parts one and two building the male body. It begins, "I never had one," not "I don't have one" but with the language of "never" and the implied hope of the past tense "had": in other words, not "I will never have one." In part two, the repetition of "'I'" builds up so that "I" becomes the name for a body, an entity with an identifiable body. Balanced and rhythmic syntax carries the prose:

> **I lived inside a woman**   it's a brief history of relationships in enclosed
> **for nine months**   domestic space, full of his needs, his wants, their
> **& inside this male shell**   use and abuse (poking, kicking) & their self-
> **for all of my life**   **self-chosen exits.**
>
> **I floated around on that side of the wall**

And here I've been for years running after me,
trying to catch up
shouting   poking and kicking her
it's the real   not looking for exits till I needed them
it all depends on the real

There came a time I needed you   at my bibliography   Then the story begins, almost "Once
                    the many books & pamphlets
vagina   saying with painful accuracy   upon a time," and it's still his need,
to get thru   that b   moving from "that" womb-space to
    into this world   "this" world – "that" housing the past
Th   tense, and "this" suddenly the present
    of "say" and the daylight so different   First thing I say
but   that   from the darkness of women/womb.   at the light of day
    Yet the moment he opens his mouth   is Waah
They said   he's recognizing that difference as complementary   Ma
so you learn   in the inversion of W/M, of genders man and woman.
they cut things off if they might swell up

The breathless part three, punctuated only by the repetition of "I thot" that
travels through the details of ordinary life to the bewildered "somewhere,"
resolves itself into "I thot they were all hairless and they weren't," implying
new knowledge. There's a sense of everything spilling out, rushing out, as
if it's too embarrassing to talk about but you need to say it, to exit from
internal perils – at the same time, bpN has placed this organ first, as if to
open the whole thing up. The fourth part begins to layer the organ onto the
social words that reference it, interact with it – or not. The voice begins
to break the word "vagina" apart. It began with a "v" and went "g" in the
middle: the women he knows, his mother and sister, they never mention
"it" by name. The mouth and the tongue suddenly work like the vagina and
womb, giving birth to words and babies, and he ends by saying "vagina."

Oh I said that   the "oh" adding a pause, a gasp of body breath, "that" being the
    I said that   unspoken vagina/mouth, desired "again & again."
    I said 'Waah Ma' again & again after I was born

In a narrative structure that the following organ parts also offer, sections 5
and 6 narrate an older boy becoming man. The first is an anecdotal story
about the assumptions wrapped up in vaginas, that are "bound to open,"
and the second, in a more generalized story. It is explanatory and has the
drive and gentle relentlessness of a "proof" that by the final sentence doesn't
prove anything. The statement "When sex happened / I realized / it was all
a matter of muscles" is undone first through the balance of "I liked …" / "she
liked … " and then the suppositions "It wasn't one thing *or* the other / *but* the
way the two of them worked together" [added italics], moving to the logic

of "And," yet concluding with the disruption of the folk song "alive alive oh," that "oh" that both opens and closes.

The final section starts with the architectural/physical collation of "Doorway. Frame. Mouth. Opening. Passage." It opens with a "trick": "to get from there to her thru her," not once but again and again, to keep on "getting there." This is followed by a misreading and the introduction of "Ellie," the name of bpNichol's wife, the misreading being between "exit'" and "'exist,'" which is followed by a conundrum — "the exit's the entrance." He exits Ma and must exist, but is only *en*tranced/*en*tranced when he "feel in love" with "Ellie." This entire part of "Vagina" is about that intermediary time between the world from which "I" came and the world into which "I" was *en*tranced – a passive verb, but also transferring the power away from the "I": a world, the world, but also "this" world, hence the ideologically and socially present, "Our world" and therefore collaborative, and at the same time "Worlds" of difference. It's a world that gets progressively more complex, a world ineradicably heterosexual but also given a queer twist by its transfer of emphasis to "*en*tranced," to the gendered woman. It's also a meditation on the Alpha/Omega, the beginning and the end in a non-teleological structure where exits are also entrances.

Selected Organs: Parts of an Autobiography is neither fiction nor non-fiction, ten chosen parts of a projected twenty. It presents a series of studies, conversations, poetic analyses of his body parts and one he does not have, which are overtly to do with re-membering, trying to articulate his response/feelings toward a particular member or organ, trying to work together the body and the words. Nichol takes apart the scripted language for the body, the social cliché or the institutional system of the individual's stories, all of which are narratives of the body that the text forms again. Sometimes it's a narrative of history, sometimes of story, sometimes of logic and of figuration, sometimes it's a narrative of grammar. Precisely because narratives are there to help us interact with the grounds of social and political reality, they are frequently about crisis, suspense, action, things happening or going wrong; they are often about violence and always about power. If you want to change the story, or if you want to re-member it in a different way, you have to loosen its structures, deal with the grounds of its representation in language, shift the terms, remove the a priori: Nichol uses the visual metaphor of pun, a word that has fallen through the ground, which is in effect a constructed floor, gone into free fall until a set of other

I miss my tonsils
I think my throat used to feel fuller
now my throat feels empty too
& maybe
that's why I eat too fast
filling the throat
except food is no substitute for tonsils
the throat just gets empty again
I was told I didn't need my tonsils
Maybe this is the way it is
Maybe
Maybe they just like cutting them out
Maybe the tonsils are a delicacy doctors eat
Maybe this is just paranoia
I bet if I had a lobotomy they could cut this paranoia out
What cutting remark!
What a cutting wit
What the dentist
Ah cut it out
cut it short
He can't cut it
You said a mouthful
Therefore them
they hang there in your throat
There are two of them in sacs
they swell up
Gosh these words seem empty!
You obsessed obsessed obsessed
Carol Wing
You couldn't take your eyes off it
Everyone (who was your age) had a chest
But then
You turned thirteen
& your chest was puny & he really had a chest & she was chesty
& all the bad puns began about being 'chest friends'
& it was 'chest too much'
or   two much
or   two for tea anytime baby

(which you always said to a guy coz you were too embarrassed to say it to a girl)

& suddenly you had discovered chests as if they had never been there before

& they were everywhere

associations appropriate to the present needs forms a new net to catch it into immediate common ground.

& you were obsessed with them

Each section of *Selected Organs* is also underlaid with a meditation which emerges from the word/body/text interaction and acquires gravity, ground, flesh. For example, there is the section "The Hips" which has several elements of the Noah's Ark story as generation after generation walk by on their two legs supported by their hips into family history. But the focus on the family history read through the hips moves the section into a "begat" study about being the same yet being different. The family similarity which begets each different generation with the asymmetrical Workman hips ties them together despite their individuality. Every "begat" listing in the Bible, culminating in that for Christ, emphasizes the family group connections at the same time as preparing for the unique difference of the last generation. With Christ the difference is his divinity, and divinity is the spirit of difference, the Holy Spirit within the human being, defining its difference. Similar meditations are encouraged from the vocabulary set and phraseology of each section and play off against narrative and linguistic change/mutability.

you kept getting chest colds
Once a year for three weeks
you'd be sick in bed
your breathing shallower (which you hated)
your nostrils redder
your face whiter
mutter for mother muttering for her
you'd say   I'm getting bedder   over & over again like a charm
clutched to your hopeless chest
I'm getting bedder   til the bed & you were one pale
continuous tone
I'm getting bedder   bedder

To loosen the ties of written narratives the de-scribing is carried out often through oral storytelling devices (*Selected Organs*, 5) that alter our expectations about plot structure, temporal consistency, register (colloquiality/formality), about the function and extent of repetition and redundancy, about stylistic features such as metaphor, pun, and allegory, about genre, about logic including connectives, syntax, conjunctions, and contradictions, about rhythm and stress, about the significance of grammar. Yet it is not to valorize the oral storyteller over the writer, but to play one set of narratives/conventions within a different medium to un-do or loosen the accepted links.

It was lo...
It was what you played your cards close to
It was one of the few body parts rhymed with the furniture
& held hope
or linen
It was a clear noun
didn't seem somehow smaller thru naming
It had ...y names or dirty names

& it was the largest part of all

For example, I'd like to look first at pronouns, verbs, and conjunctions.

You stuck it out
You puffed it up
It was chest
What it was was chest

Pronouns

The sections of the text are each focused on particular sets of pronouns in relation to each other: I/he, I/me/it, he/they/it, and so on. One of the curious events that happens in "The Mouth" is the nominalization of "I." The first section begins with a series of clichés that distance common experience from the self by way of the collective "you": "You were never supposed to talk when it was full. It was better to keep it shut if you had

You didn't think of the chest as sensitive
until   you dance with her
You were ... crossed
& tho the moving bodies of your friends pressed you together
you would only allow your chests to touch

& there was heat   & pressure   & movement
& pressure   & movement between you & your chest
& your chest was ten times
more sensitive than your hands felt
felt more than your eyes could see
& your trapped heart pounded as if you would die
explode, right there before her eyes
disintegrate from the aching

"nothing to say" (13). However, section two moves into the personal with a repetition, from "Probably there are ... " to "Probably my mouth ... " The phrase "my mouth" alternates with the pronoun "I" for three sentences as if "my mouth is something separate from "I," before shifting to an alternation between "My mouth" and "my life": "life" displacing "I." Section three continues the dislocation of "I" from "mouth," externalizing "I" through excessive repetition and reversing of the expected description "smashed his knee into my face" to "smashed my face into his knee," so that the body part is separated from "I" and becomes an object that is "rearranged." Section four continues this objectifying momentum by way of a cumulative series of stories about what dentists did to his mouth. The stories get longer and longer yet increasingly controlled as they get more and more violent, until he reaches dentist number six. Here the sentence unfurls into phrases and clauses that describe his relief that his mouth will not need to be operated upon, at the same time as bringing back "I" as a noun, a character: "I'd begun to see that every time I thot of dentists I ended the sentence with the word 'me.'" It's an I who concludes "My mouth was me." As a result, the final cliché "my heart in my mouth" acquires an immediacy and physicality a long way from the opening collective banalities.

If section three offered a short story and section four a series of cumulative remembered stories, section five can be read as a retrospective account of memory from the needs of the present. The long sentences locate the substantial "I" not in specific events but in actions. They take off on sound, association, pun, yet retain a narrative momentum because they move chronologically through a human being's life from birth to adulthood and sexual embrace. Although the techniques engage with ways of articulating common experience, they refer less to the crisis and violence in story than to the patterns made out of daily life. For example, the collocation of "nipple/rubber nipple/bottle," or the sound association of "tongue & flung," or the rhythmic stress of "reach him, kiss her, get my tongue ... ," or the expansion from the list "words ... , meals, sex" into "belt out a duet, share a belt of whisky, undo your belts & put your mouths together," pattern the narrative on the strategies of sound, stress, and semantic association between and among words as they construct connection and cohesion rather than crisis. The final sentence of this section varies "In the beginning was the word" to "it begins here, on the tongue, in the pun, comes from mouth to mouth where we all come from," layering the Christian phrase over with a humanist mimesis of life and sexuality.

Six or eight or ten of us not breathing while he walked down the line
holding our breath while he looked us over
while he chose one of us to punch in the gut. to see how
tough   waiting
A breathless line   I said
I was staying at Bob and Smaro's place in Winnipeg
I was sleeping on the floor in Smaro's study
I was getting up early and reading   I was
getting up early and going into the living room
I was sitting down in a chair and reading a copy of a new book on literary theory or literary criticism Smaro had
just brought back from some recent trip   as she tends to do
I was just beginning to get into the book
when Bob appeared at the top of the stairs
                                                                        came down the stairs anyway
Bob muttering to himself   Life the great tyrant that makes you go on breathing
And   I thought about the
I thought about it
I thought   about   the lung poems I've tried to perfect in various ways
                    the lung poems Bob's written
                    when we got out
And
I thought about the lungs sitting there   inside the chest
                                                the mouth
                                    exhaling
And
I thought to myself
        to myself because Bob was in no mood to hear it
I thought 'Life's about going the lung distance
                                                just that
And   His
We were all first
        It was just the way you read it
        It was authentic
And   All the past tense   just like in all the other stories
If only we'd attempt
If only we'd had the stories read to us
        we'd have known then how the whole thing had to end
        but we didn't know   what part
But   we didn't
And   we did
        we really should have known
        we didn't
But   we made us
And   we didn't want ...
        I never really wanted   again
Even when I was a teenager   except that
Even though
        even though   just when I thought about it
It didn't you know
Look what happened   This wasn't supposed

From this section, which coheres and gives substance to the "I," the concluding section six moves back and tells a personal history. The opening sentence elides from the speaking pronoun "I" to the nominalized character "I," "I always said I was part of the oral tradition," using the conversational and including device, "I always said," which is quite different from the autocratic "you" ... generalizations of the first part. This device is repeated with increasing extension and excessive interruption over the following four sentences, from "I always said I ... ," to "I always said poetry ...," to "When I went into therapy my therapist always said I ...," to the memory he wants to reach: "At the age of five when Al Watts Inr was still my friend, I actually said, when asked who could do some thing or other, 'me or Al.'" The repetition ties together "I" and "poetry" and "oral," so that after the pun "me or Al" there comes a "realization" line – a line, and there is usually one in each part of *Selected Organs*, where suddenly the words seem to make sense – "only years later realized how the truth's flung out of you at certain points & runs on ahead." This truth, flung out by the tongue, becomes the nominalized "me" that the "I," here anchored down as "bp" or "books and pamphlets" [Nichol], runs after shouting "it's the oral" for years, so that people say "that bp – he really runs off at the mouth." The section "The Mouth" ends with a cliché, yet the reader has been taken along not only to learn the personal life behind a banal comment, but the strategies we can use to re-construct the "truth" that's flung out in the phrase.

Verbs

If pronouns move strangely into the substance of nouns, verbs too acquire unusual responses from use atypical for written prose. The section "The Tonsils" opens with relentless past tenses and goes on to alternate with the present. All the past tense verbs but one, "hung," refer to what people were doing to the tonsils rather than the tonsils themselves, while the present tense verbs attempt to describe them, represent them. Yet they are absent in the present, cut off and without memory. In the past they were there having things done to them, in the present they are absent, permanently. The section is a discourse partly on power and the powerlessness of the child to object, but also about despair. "The Chest" also subtly uses alternating verb tenses to locate a response, as it moves between the active and the passive to describe who has a "recognizable" chest and who hasn't: girls and boys, connecting that fact that you "had" a chest with the ongoing implications of the boy who was "obsessed" by it. "The Fingers," more openly and with a combination of humour and concealed threat, is dominated by imperative verbs, commands wagging their fingers at you, reprimanding, correcting, and controlling.

A far more self-conscious use of verb tenses is found in "The Lungs," which opens with three sections overladen with participles and imperfect verbs. Section one starts off differently with a series of short sentences that radically break up the syntactical rhythm by shifting abruptly between short lines "This is a breath line," and even shorter "I said," and asymmetrical repetitions such as "I said," "Line up, he said," "He said," or "this was a no breath line," and "A breathless line." The section moves into a lengthy sentence that plays off the tension of the men, static in an inspection line-up, with their stomachs "pulled in" and their lungs "pushed out." They are "not breathing" "holding" "waiting," while the inspector is relaxed: "while he looked ... " "while he chose ... " "while he paced ... " "while he paused ... " The response is to associate the participles with a self-consciousness of breath, as well as to tell a story about the petty cruelty of someone trying to exercise power by controlling breath.

The second section of "The Lungs" elaborates on this connection by opening the first five sentences with an imperfect verb: "was staying" "was sleeping" "was getting up" "was sitting," "was turning," and connecting these verbs of on-going state with the resonating sound of nouns such as "morning" and "living," and participles such as "going," "getting," and "beginning," as well as cognate phrases such as "like I tend to do," "as she tends to do." The carefully regulated rhythm, which builds up density as the sentences lengthen, is halted by "when Bob appeared," "when Bob came down," then softened by a repeated "came down" indicating on-going movement, into "muttering" and finally "breathing." Given that the section describes people waking up in the morning, the following shift into the repeated phrase "I thought about..." mimics the more contained and aware control over rhythm of the wakened person, and the phrase is focused more and more upon the word "lung," both as "the lungs" and as a pun for "long." The excessive patterning that results slows the reading down as the reader deals with a multiplicity of overlaid connotations, rhythmic and semantic waves that lung and long together and come to rest in the refracted cliché "I thought life's about going the lung distance." The section reproduces the effortless habit of breathing as well as the uneasiness that comes about when we begin to think about it. Re-membering the lungs is useless without the "air" they contain. They are not there in themselves but as on-going necessaries for some other action,

This wasn't supposed to be the way the story goes

But it was
as if the lungs wanted
as if the lungs had a memory

Not commands
but a primal puff, primal smoke from a primal prairie fire

as if the whole childhood episode has been like one of those moral tales

where the reader takes a different lesson from the one the writer intended

or like one of those shaggy-dog jokes where the punch line comes way after
the joke should have ended   way after the person listening has
lost all interest in what is being

Lung time   different from the head's

When do you first start to think of your lungs?
when you're young ... like my mom told me it happened to me?
when you ... like the first time ...
when you ...
Does it happen when you're young or old?
trying to remember,
In a moment like this   can you ever say 'I remember this about my lungs'?
NO NO
Almost no memories at all
feel the earth that they're pumping away
just beneath the surface of these lines

One of those parts you can't do without
Two of them
he bellows
The bellows   airing his opinion
covering up some divine
bellowing our prays, our songs
bellowing our lung-ings

A draft he calls it
pulls a new rhythm through a crack in the mind   just a bunch of hot air
trying to force air
get the cadences to fall
syllables to the past the eye and ear
just enough to de-scribe
As the mind tapped the lung and each that hung there in its proper place
It's just... I'll get it
he feels the breath heave
he hears the words start
to take
all that air
and squeeze it harder
it   brought life's about the mind
NO   next time
the lung   when the lungs stop
Like that last sentence on the tongue
hangs in the air after the lungs have pressed their last square
only the body left

I'll get it right next time

Even tho …   he knew he was human

life, that eludes us when we think of it, only being reminded of the "breath of life" at the "moment of absolute death."

Even when …   . he knew

He flexed his fingers
He twiddled his thumbs

Conjunctions

I'm human he said and   he knew

The vast array of ways words can be joined together allows conjunctions to work with unusually sophisticated strategies that Nichol asks the reader

In all the early photos he is holding his sister's hand

to recognize. The writing slows down the speed of habitual reading so that

his fingers wrapped around her fingers

minimalist changes of "and" to "&" become significant: the former have the

grabbing hold

force of logical joining while the latter become a connective device for a list

hanging on

that takes the junctions as more self-evident. Even punctuation comes to the

He is

the left hand usually
the left fingers

fore as a device of conjunction. Many sections have little punctuation, but "The Lungs" is heavily punctuated, accentuating the arrest or halt, however brief, between the breath in and the breath out. Not only And/But/Or

pushes his brother away with

are foregrounded, but also adverbial connectives such as which/whether/

his right fingers
what his sister fingers

whereby, or relative pronouns working as connections, such as "who" or

And these are his write fingers too

"which." "The Tonsils" is replete with connectives describing loss: almost,

grasping the pen he uses to describe this as he stares at the fingers of his left hand

even tho, ever, just, maybe.

open now and empty

his sister

hundreds of miles away

"The Hips" presents sections of prose that are skilfully crafted to offer pairs

grabbing hold

of representations around a conjunction, yet leave the clauses on each side

hanging on   full of these descriptions

unbalanced in length or syntax: the name "Boxcar Annie" is paired with "who

was also called Queen of the Hoboes," as well as "she had the biggest hips

hangs at his side

I'd ever seen." Several pairs work around "and": "and whoever finished first

Take his hand   they'd say
c'mon give him a hand

was the winner" is connected, as it might be in oral conversation but rarely

It's very handy   they'd add

in written prose, to the new clause "and he told them all to wait." Similarly,

when he'd find a hand   they'd say   backward left?

"and afterwards Annie went off to drink beer with the men she'd beaten" is

And

connected with only indirect causality to "and I got back on my bike and

If he couldn't grasp what they were saying

rode it all the way back up the hill to home." Other connection strategies

drawing circles with their fingertips

work through repetition such as "beat every man in the place," "beat them

touch their fingers to their brows

all easily," or "I'd ever seen" "and will ever see," the "and" reinforcing the

and him reinforcing the

connection. At the same time the repetitions and conjunctions work subtly

fingering him as mental

to shift the pairings as in "until he yelled go" reinforced by "and he yelled

And
softer mad   fingers   pointed

go," yet shifted in weight by the immediate connection to "and I watched the

bang bang you're dead

whole contest."

Raised to ask questions
raised to answer them

stuck out to signal   Fingers like sharks   Fins   GRRR

"The Hips," of course, is about similarity and difference, both in family

They held him in the front line in front of Moose.

history and in the personal body. The hips not only connect our head to our

They put him in the front line in front of Moose.

feet, but work similarly yet differently on either side of the spine's axis. The

They put him in the front line in front of Moose when no one else would stand in front of

section that underlines the joy of this combination extends the conjunctions

and connectives into syntactical inversions. It begins, "We tend not to think

balancing on his fingertips

as the Q called the signals

as the ball was snapped

as Moose trampled over him rushing to follow the ball in

They put him in the front line and Moose trampled over him again and again

game after game until the day his finger broke

snapped

snapped, as he tried to touch Moose
as he tried to lay a hand on him
tried to carry out, somehow, the rules of the game

He wore a cast for weeks, covering his wrist and sticking out along his broken finger like a hook
and then then asked who had he pressed
how had he broken his finger,
he told them ... playing touch football

of them as different. We tend not to think of them as unique," and continues through phonemic connections of "say" "hey" "sway" "away," of syntactic elisions such as "interesting/interested," or of paired yet different clichés "what a caboose" and "nice pair of hips." These pairings end with:

because nobody else would get in line in front of Moose
no one else could or would   touch him

But then one day someone places their hand on your hip, lovingly, expectantly, and the hip they touch is different, unique, left or right, and it carries you away as they lay their hand there and you let it stay, you place your hand on their hip, press your bodies close together and say okay. Let the hips carry you away.

The thing was he couldn't control his fingers properly
And he was told to …
And he learned to …
And they wanted him to …

He could contain the fingers but he couldn't control them
like later with the model plane kits – balsa wood, plastic

Here the pairs of "lovingly/expectantly," "different/unique" "left or right" act as combinations which join each clause to the next. The clauses invert each other as "places their hand on your hip" becomes "place your hand on their hip," and words with contradictory semantics convey some of the significance as the hips both carry you away and let you stay, together. The part on "The Fingers" is a complex mixture of unpredictably weighted balances and the frustration of the perfect match. Several sections in the part are dense with interlacing and cohesion strategies, including variations on combinations of words but also multitudes of homonyms. Section four, which is full of homonymical play on "front" "touch" "line" "snapped," begins with five sentences opening exactly the same way. The first three are short and establish the storyline and crisis point. The fourth sentence sets the scene and the fifth tells the event. Both the fourth and fifth sentences elaborate in the same way moving from the opening clause to a relative clause to three parallel phrases. The last phrase of the fourth sentence contains the violence of the projected crisis "as Moose trampled over him rushing to follow the ball in," which is held in suspense by the grammatical structure that insists that it is all contained within the one written unit. The fifth sentence sustains the suspense by duplicating the syntax almost exactly, so the force of the corollary movement overrides the actual crisis that his finger "snapped" and comes to rest now predictably in the third phrase that underscores the inevitable way that following the rules of a game means that crisis must happen to somebody: that connection and causality can be part of a set of structures that claim sense and inevitability yet are merely a game invented by human beings so the significance of crisis is defused into bathos.

trying to be so precise
and he couldn't
his finger kept fumbling things
snapping them
Clumsy in one attempt to apply it
glue
and he would finish these models
he'd then use his fingers again later than
but they wouldn't
didn't
never would
fly
they event ...   on his shelf
making him feel guilty
assess
as if they were pointing the finger at him
at his failure
his inability to control his fingers

This is the way it went
He was ... to move ... to overtake ... the
He was to keep his fingers to himself
He was not to finger himself (which made his fingers sticky)
or stick his finger in his nose (which made his fingers sticky)
He was to keep them out of the cookie jar
inside the car
around the golf club
before the table
But
He was supposed to get a grip on himself

A rather different effect of connectives is conveyed through the effort of trying to get the fingers to do small accurate finicky things. A series of

get a good grasp of languages
problems
situations
a good grasp on reality
be able to reach people
to touch them
get a feel for them
put his finger on the solution almost instantly
And you have to hand it to him

he handled the whole thing like a five finger exercise

kept his fingers on the pulse of the notion even when his reach exceeded his grasp

even when he was losing his grip

even when his head was whirling with more conflicting messages than you could count on the fingers of both hands

carefully exact words and phrases controls the movement of the writing so tightly that the representation becomes simultaneously frustrating and reductive. Word and phrase pairings include "bits fit," "so careful, so precise," "couldn't, wasn't," "fumbling, snapping," "wouldn't, didn't," "never had, never would," "on his fingers, on his shelf," "guilty, useless," and culminate in a triptych of lengthening phrases "at him," "at his failure" "his inability to control his fingers" which encircles the section and sends it back, yet again, to the opening statement. "He couldn't contain the fingers but he couldn't control them." The part "The Fingers" again and again tells the story of potential helping and co-operation that frequently fails when we try to match too exactly, yet it also tells of the sense of another presence when the hand, holding another hand, does achieve communication.

he handled them

he kept them in hand

he was always trying to control his fingers

First
Later

he learned the fingers controlled everything

Early on

he learned the fingers gave you pleasure

Later

he learned his fingers could give other people pleasure too

Other fingers could give him pleasure

in the reaching

even

evenhandedness of love

AND when she married him, he took the ring that they had bought and place it on her finger

And he cried
And she cried
And Now

Of the many larger de-scripted structures in *Selected Organs*, logic and written narrative are the two I'd like briefly to look at.

there was something there

this was the first step in beginning to grasp it

and maybe

Logic

What he wanted to do was play a musical instrument

The concept of order, with or without causality, is de-scribed and per-formed primarily by setting written devices alongside the oral. If the basis for logical persuasion is to gain agreement to a set of common grounds from which to journey out, the attempt at neutrality, often depended upon by written statements, is undermined by conversational openings that make the ethos of the logic at times more intimate, "I miss … " or "The thing was … ," and at times quite formal in etiquette. The devices openly both include and at times distance the reader so that the common grounds for initial agreement are not taken as a priori but examined in relation to each individual's response. The whole procedure of cohesion and redundancy in the written is set off against the tacit organization of the oral. For example, in the spoken story, chronological time can proceed more swiftly than in the written – or, the written allows one to proceed more slowly. In *Selected Organs* one paragraph can take you from "First" to "Later" to "Early" to "Later" to "Now" in an unexpectedly speedy denouement of a logical progression, almost a narrative postcard. Conversely, the written is expected to progress, however slowly, from beginning to middle to end, while the spoken can unabashedly offer lengthy variations upon stationary lists through numbers "The first," "The second," "The third," etc., through descriptions of states such as the seven repeated "It was … " openings in "The Chest," or the more variable "You were," "It was … " "You were … " "It was … " "It got … " "You were," or through forward and backward chaining "I don't remember … "

so he took up the violin
he took up the violin because they had one at school

and they offered it to him
a real hand-me-down

got his hands on it
and off he went

Except
everyone at home hated it when he played it
hated it because he couldn't get the fingering right no matter how hard he tried
in a manner of speaking
to wring the right sounds from the strings
and he couldn't
he didn't
he never will make that violin sing
because he was all thumbs
because his fingers fumbled it
his digits
didn't

All that talk of reaching and touching
All those barriers his fingers seemed to encounter between him and some imagined other
And there one day he realized that of course
he was staring at his hand when he wrote
was always watching the pen as it moved along

gripped by his fingers
his fingers floating there

floating there in front of his eyes just above the words
above that single white sheet
just above these words i'm writing now

his fingers between him

between him and all that, like another person
a third person
when all along you thought it was just the two of you talking

And suddenly he realized it was the three of them
handing it on from one to the other
his hand translating itself
his words slipping thru his fingers into the written world.

"I remember ... " "I don't remember ... " "The mouth remembers ... ," and
many other devices.

You.

Much later he began to write for puppets
and there he was

Nichol explores the possibility of logical ordering through "chaining" or the repetition of verbal structures. He reiterates the same kinds of grammatical or syntactic changes from section to section, the similarities insisting on perfect logical parallels where the semantics may not. He uses excessive patterning of habitually used words that moves toward reification. The reasoning process itself is often set out in conversational rather than analytical modes, with apparent digressions and elaborations. Several sections go quietly around the narratives, in order to reach and/or construct their "realization" lines as in "The Mouth." The process underlines the notion that the "sense" of logic is to put things in a recognizable place, and that we don't' recognize the "sense" until we have prepared our environment for it: not that all "realization" lines are "true." The realization in "The Vagina" that "it was all a matter of muscles" is specific to a period of adolescent understanding and is overturned as the chronology of the autobiography moves on and the "place" changes. Akin to this process is the way cliché and banal phrase are continually reconstructed into immediate significance. And underneath the conversational lies the body logic, the order being built by the smaller connectives, the verbs, the pronouns, the sound, syntax and morphemic connotations, the rhythm and stress that perform the breath beneath the bones of grammar.

watching his words come out of the mouths of his fingers
watching hands turn to each other say the lines
the hands insisting on perfect

And one day one of the hands turned to him and said: 'Hey, bp, what do you think?'
And it had always been his fingers talking
his fingers shaping the letters
the words
that ran my grip around the pen
the tongue
and he lifted his hand up, opening and closing his fingers, and said: 'Nothing'

nt hp

Maw called them 'the Workman hips.'. Too bad,' she'd say to me 'you've got
the Workman hips. Too bad,' she'd say to my sister, 'you've got
the Workman hips. Too bad,' she'd say to my brother, 'you've got
the Workman hips. Too bad,' she'd say to my nieces, shaking her head in dismay. 'you've got

'the Workman hips,'   she'd say, as generation after generation of family swayed past

ee o a i   ee a a e e a i o a e e e a i o o a i y a e a

Narrative
th wrkm n h ps   sh d s y s g n r t n ft r g n r t n f f m l sw y d p st
Whether with history, story, logic, figuration, or grammar, narrative is the way the words articulate the body. Narratives in response to history, specifically official history, are for people in Western liberal nation-states ways of situating the individual in response to subjugation by the stare or, increasingly, the transnational economy. Those concerned with responding to cultural story are dealing far more with the civic and with the popular. Those articulating the body in response to the social deal with other stories but more pertinently with cliché. Selected Organs situates its narratives in response to all these structurings, yet its focus is not upon competitive alternatives. Rather, given the set of other narratives that are generated by the communities around the individual, the writing offers ways of loosening their structures and re-membering the personal within that set, making possible collectivity, performing both the differences and similarities of the self.

on their way into history 'you've got
o e a i o o i oy 'oo o
v g t

We tend not to think of them as different
We refer to them by direction – left or right – and when they're really wide
we say "hey, what a caboose" as the hips   sway   away
brother right and left
disappearing into the distance
We tend to think of them distantly, something that's there when the body gets interesting
interested

the way the bum shapes itself
the belly
the crotch

we're referring to

But then one day someone places their hand
on your hip   lovingly
expectantly

and the hip they touch is different
unique
left or right

"The Chest" emphatically engages with the process as a meditation on "The word made flesh." As with other parts, its first section opens by looking at the way that recognition of the "chest" is an introduction into language that describes it. Section one surveys the social phrases and the speed with which young people learn the cliché as a way of entering society. At the same time, as indicating the static positions offered by cliché, it demonstrates skill with pun that releases the individual into action – these adolescents move quickly from "she was chesty" to "chest friends" to "two much/too much."

However, the second section de-scribes a different attempt to understand the body by sinking under the significant plot, losing the crisis of the story of illness which usually leads to recovery or death by smoothing out the words into a continuous monotone that mimics the loss of colour in the child's face.

By moving away from simile and metaphor and controlling the words away from the visual image into the significance of sound, the story fades out through "your voice getting deeper (which you like)," to "your breathing shallower (which you hated), to our nostrils redder, your face whiter, saying matter for mother muttering for her. The sentence is alternating between the clarity of retrospective memory and the increasingly overlaid comparatives, and ends with the alternation between redder/whiter, mutter/mother, muttering/for her. Following this, the child is re-presented as having things done to him, as if he's no longer able to be self-consciously aware, neither liking nor hating, but only able to repeat over and over "I'm gedding bedder." This sentence alternates not within the child's mind but between the increasingly desolate repeated monotone "gedding bedder," and the retrospective narration. The narration briefly reintroduces both simile and metaphor as artificial figurations, contrasting heavily with the child's speech, "like a charm clutched to your hopeless chest," before eliding into the literalisms of "sinking further into the sheets," and the minimalist description "you were one continuous tone, white on white in white."

Section three swiftly returns the reader to words and phrases that tell the body in the public world. The list controls the words away from the physicality of the body into substantiating names, clear nouns, that hover on the border of the nominal and the reified. For the adolescent boy who is discovering these alternative words and phrases, there is satisfaction in "what it was was chest, and to this small extent there is some plot here. But the section resists the elaboration of story to focus on figuration, so

---

and it carrries you away
    as they
        lay
and you let it stay
    I was just a kid
We were the way that
and it was Saturday afternoon
and I had nothing to do …
        and there was this big crowd …
and we were in the middle
        and there was a woman standing
there in the middle of the crowd who had the biggest hips we'd ever seen
It turned out her name was Boxcar Annie
At least that's what she said to us about two much/too much
and Boxcar Annie
who was also called the Queen of the Hoboes   was the lone woman contestant
The idea was to see who could sink the most
and whoever finished first was the winner   and he told them all to wait until he yelled go,
and he yelled go   and I watched the whole contest
each   into a continuous monotone
and, of course, Boxcar Annie
who had the biggest hips we'd ever seen   and will ever see
and Boxcar Annie
beat every man in the place   beat them all easily
and
everyone cheered and said how terrific Annie was the really neat part of the story
and afterwards Annie went off to drink beer with the men she's beaten
and I got back on my bike and rode it all the way back up the hill to home
And saying matter for mother muttering for her
                precisely
                rhythmically
                    hips flying
                    hips swaying
        the biggest hips I've ever seen
It was because of my hips I started writing.   I was in Grade 4.
It was fall or early spring, I can't remember which
but I remember the ditch and one near the school
and it was full of icy slush
and a friend dared me to jump across it so I did
    my left foot
    my right leg …
and I landed like some bad imitation of a ballet dancer
    struck, my left leg …
    stuck, my right leg …
My hips kept me afloat
Or at least that's what the firemen said to my Ma when they brought me home after rescuing me
    visible just above the freezing sludge to everyone who saw me while my friend ran and told the teacher
    who phoned the fire department   who came and laid ladders across on either side of me
and pulled me
    and the firemen said that the ditch was so deep and the sludge so like quicksand
        I would've drowned if it hadn't been for the strange position of my legs and hips
and they kept me there …
and during that time I wrote my first novel …
It was all about a Martian sailor who came to Earth
        went to work on a sailing ship   and
                along the way fell in love with a girl called Luna who
    I remember writing,
                        was 'not of this world'
    I can't remember now how the novel ended
        or even how it went   and

My Maw thru it away by mistake three years later so there's no way I can go back and refresh my memory   but

I do remember that when I went back to school I showed it to my teacher   and

she read the whole think to the class, a bit a morning for a week or two   and

that the sudden development of story in section four comes as an explosion   and

she said she liked it

the kids said they like it   and

of plot that is thick with semantic tension. If the words substantiate the body in part three, here the body rushes into the words with an energy that makes each clause constantly offer progressions that are then clawed back

I was alive   and   I was a writer too

into new clauses. For example, the clause "there was heat and pressure and

And whenever people ask me 'how did you become a writer,'

movement" appears to belong together, yet loops back into ""[there was] …

I always tend to say 'I just fell into it'

movement between you and your chest," which loops into "your chest was

right into my hips

ten times more sensitive than your hand, felt," loops into "felt more than

Relieve me

your eyes could see." When the loops stop, the grammar explodes into "as if

Hip hip hooray?

your would die … explore … disintegrate." The loops continue, with retarded

Two hips, hooray?

movement, to the end of the section.

There had to be some meaning in it somewhere, some symbolism

Hip hip hooray   hip hip hooray

which meant someone had done something

The fifth and final part of "The Chest" is a desolate performance of the social

outstanding

insistence that we separate the word and the body. In therapy, where we are

in day to day

Close to the structure of the medical institution, "all the language changed"

But later, when I was sixteen and in Grade 13 at King Eddy in Vancouver

I joined the Jazz Club and began to hang around jazz clubs with Sandy, whose brother was a jazz

and the writer is told that the chest is "a vessel & feelings held there grew

musician

And in all those clubs I went to

stagnant, festered, expanded under pressure until released into air." The

In one of those clubs I went to I learned it was not hip to shout hooray

chest is where "deep lay," the grammar eliding a missing word that cannot be

It was not even hip to continue to

given a name: deep what. Again and again the speaker is told simultaneously

not to "be too heady," not to be "dead from the neck down," and not to move

single

unique   that was okay

So we danced below the neck, below the chest, and "dump shit on anyone" or "talk a

load of crap." The writer should speak from the heart – where the chest is: "It

when the soloist was transported away in an

improvisation

was the chest. It had to be the chest." This chest is not the substantial "chest"

of section three but a reified "the chest," with a socially approved role. The

we nodded

maybe grinned   tho even grinning was suspect in those days

speaker should get "everything off your chest, just like you were supposed

to." Explicit in this series of forbidden feelings and forbidden actions is the

just hip

No hooray

command to separate head from body, word from body, to stick to the social

You can never outlive the hip

story and keep the body out of it. Implicit in the tedious and easy listing of

My maw was always aware of her hips

the banal phrases is the conviction that this is all wrong, that word and body

She'd put on a dress and turn

are one.

and look at herself in the mirror

and sigh

and you knew she was sighing about her hips

Because "The Chest" does not go on to rebuild a performative positive narrative,

it ends sadly. However, it is immediately followed by "The Lungs" which

the sheet pulled up to her waist

and the nurse came in and said 'my aren't you petite'

mimics the describing of the story yet moves on to other narrative devices.

My maw couldn't resist laughing what til you put down his one

The split between body and word is replicated in the split between lung

because she wouldn't forget about her

hips

And now most days I feel this pain in my left hip

time and head time. Head time offers stories whose narratives get usurped

by rhythm and recognition just right. Section three in particular focuses on

I feel this pain in my left hip   and I think about Maw

the story of the children who want to smoke, and when caught doing so by a

I think about Grandma

parent, are made to smoke a cigar, whereupon they are violently sick from it.

nagging little pain saying I won't let you forget about me

And you don't let me forget about you do you?

You're there reminding me every time I stand too long

reminding me every time the chair's too soft or too hard or too wrong

You're never going to let me forget about you

Are you   hip?

It is   an   us   & yes we all have them

And as far as I can tell

I never was able to see much difference between them

Just that little pucker among the cheeks

the start the remembered personal narrative is littered with "If only we'd read the stories. If only we'd had the stories read to us" – "But we hadn't," the inevitability of the ending constituted through the redundancy of "We should have known" "We really should have known" "We didn't." Yet once the expectation of the story has been set up, the social narrative is taken apart. It should conform to a particular humour which the reader begins to recognize and follow, yet then the story sense runs out, the plot diverges: lung time takes over. Instead of putting him off smoking, the memory of the cigar creates an intense desire in the older man to smoke them. The second half of the story slowly takes apart the first, mainly by keeping up the rhythmic repetitions but substituting different words and sounds so that a whole new tenor is introduced. "Even when" "Even though," "This wasn't supposed" "This wasn't supposed to be the way the story goes." The earlier "just the way" "just like," becomes "as if" "as if" "As if the whole childhood episode had been like one of those moral tales where the reader takes a different lesson from the one the writer intended" "or like." The plot is replaced by a joke which offers a different "sense," a different construction of narrative coming from the body, the lungs, into the words, articulating the self to replace the social convention of the isolated "dead" mind.

My mother stuck a tube up it to give me an enema

I remember it really cleaned me out

I remember lying over her knees with my pants down

& her sticking this tube up me

& me screaming 'that's ENOUGH!'

I remember thinking ma was the enema and the anus us

That's what confuse us say

Continue us say

don't make me wee

We didn't so much name it as allude to it

My maw said 'wherever you may be may your winds blow free'

My maw said 'whoever makes a smell like that must be rotten inside'

It was one of the big connections with the inside & thru it she knew whether you were sick or healthy &

whether or not you needed an enema

You always looked to see if messy

You never referred … except to say the bum

and to wonder really whether you had wiped it

When I read my first porno comic I found the word poot

People would be making love & fart & the sound effect read poot, poot, poot

Just like the joke about the fireman's big red fire engine going

in & out of his wife's firehall Hoot, hoot

The violence of story is here overtly contained and handled by pun, the work of which expands in section four of "The Lungs" into the exuberant associations of ""The bellows,' he bellows, airing his opinion. Because to air is human. To forgive the divine. Bellowing our prays, our songs. Bellowing our lung-ings." The naive silliness of these associations displaces the social, political, and religious plots just as thoroughly as the intellectually engaging pun. Through sound, rhythm, etymology, and syntax, Nichol provides devices and strategies for dealing with the systemic power and often daily violence exercised by the plots of history and story and genre. Not that pun and grammar are not have their own systemic power, but we have to work on it more carefully. We take its narratives less for granted, even sometimes thinking of them as natural. Currently, metaphor and other figuration is the primary device working between the conventions of history and story and the naturalness of grammar and language. Metaphor is the focus for most literary and critical interpretation. As such, it is extremely useful but also continually falling into its own convention/the janus-face of "nature." Nichol's work is extraordinary in its ability to release language, pun, grammar, syntax, morpheme, phoneme, rhythm from the natural into the constituted, where, just because it is so unexpected, they work with great

I was trying to figure it oot

I came out of the movie with some friends & there was a christian recruiting group singing hymns across the street

& this car drove by with this guy's ass stuck out the window

hanging a moon for the world to see

The body is sacred

The moon isn't green cheese

The last rose of summer is impossible to determine but when he drops it you known he's been there

then he dropped a rose that smelled like green cheese & my brother woke up yelling

'get your bum out of my face'

I just thot 'there's two many rymes in this piece'

I just thot the anus rhymes both men and women

I just thot it little guy I knew who often reacted 'he said he used to like enemas'

& this woman I knew who objecting to her lover's advances said 'he used me like a man'

I just thot about the anus & wrote down an icon

I just thot the anus is extraordinary in its ability

I just thot that & now here I am writing this sentence's anus

coz that's where a certain process in the body ends

I was lying … staring … & thot how ugly

I was fifteen   & really depressed & the clouds … & and I stared … of flesh & bone

& thot how ugly & how maybe I should kill myself

I lay   & thot about killing … & the ugliness of my toes & decided …

This was the first time I ever really looked at my toes & boy they were something else
They were really ugly

In Port Arthur ... & shoved our feet

& stared ...

It was like the peepshow movies we saw

impact on the conventional. It's hard work, but Nichol makes you want to do it because, unlike the impact of a lot of poetic writing which is sad, desolate, courageous and suffering, this poetic is also funny, strong, and humorous.

where we ...

but we ...

The writing performs ways of looking at and loosening the grounds of narrative, and ways of reconstructing narratives with humour.

& there were no sets of bones

& there were no lead shields

& we did it

The performance of "The Fingers," in its recognition of a third presence there at the moment of communication, is most clearly about the Trinity:

Maybe they mutated

Maybe. Maybe. & ...

not just "me but "you" and the recognition of the outside, the written world.

Maybe postmodern writers like me all have post-atomic poetic feet & that's what makes them ugly to the pre-atomic eye & difficult to notate

If "The Mouth" introduced bp, running for years after "me," "The Fingers" introduces Nichol's own lower-case "i" in the penultimate section of the

Maybe this is the way we're always saying to the words 'take me to your reader'

part. This is the most difficult for me to read – even more so than "The Toes" – for it comes at the end of the enormous frustration about the lack

It was okay to talk about feet

It was okay to talk about toes

It was never okay to talk about toe-jam

of words for over his fingers and ends in the potential cynicism of "hey bp what do you think?" "Nothing." Yet this has also to do with the enclosed

I've never even seen the word spelt before

I think I like it best just the way I've spelt it here,

circuit that destruction of bp words always tied into the I/me, not running after anything. The closing de-scriptions speak about the way the fingers connect the body with the temporal articulation of memory: just above these words

written particularly one word only & just

like the dark gringy hyphen you were embarrassed to discover there

I'm writing now, his fingers between him and all that, like another person, a third person, when all along you thot it was just the two of you talking.

between your toes

inside your sock

your shoe

The fingers release "bp" from the doubleness, the continually reflecting mirrors of I and me, by reminding him of "You." On his own he is nothing,

Where you were never able to figure out how the toe-jam got

but recognizing and writing in response to the outside he becomes part of a collaboration.

When Ellie & I moved in together we bought a house with six other people on Warren Rd

& the next door neighbours had a dog named 'toes'

Neither the individual nor the groups of which they are part can act in

It was a joke

isolation. Nichol's writing offers a mimesis of both the extraordinary way

I felt fifteen again

that our lives are manifolded in vocabularies that define our bodies to us

& the stupid dog chased me every time I walked from the house to the coach room

and tie us to the world in particular ways, and the way that recognition of

& back again

It was like a bad dream where the repressed returns

difference, of "you," keeps the self performing, keeps the writing coming.

& there I was,

You aren't isolated but you aren't the same as those you're together with,

toes yapping at me

or, you're part of a collectivity and different at the same time – you're

toes wanting to step on me

collaborating (see, for example, Green 2001). Given that the great theoretical

ugly & depressing

gaps in philosophy at the moment are to do with the lack of vocabulary for

difference within the group, Nichol's way of proceeding with de-scribing

I forget when I first noticed my toenails grew funny

and per-forming the various narratives of writing and language offers a set

& then the big toenails were the worst of all

of valuable strategies and learnable skills.

flaky & fragmented

& the little toe-nails

The sacred meditation of this collection moves appropriately from the

almost non-existent

& the ones in between

alpha and omega, through "The Mouth" and its investigation of the biblical

curling around the stubs of the toes

hugging them

so that even now

except for the big toe (which gets sharp

& jagged

& rips my sock)

I don't have to cut them for months

unless of course

I feel like it

But it is easier if you keep them cut because of all the dirt that wedges under them

statement "In the beginning was the word ... ," to the consideration of powerlessness and despair that is "The Tonsils." "The Chest" explores various ways that "the word is made flesh" and "I feel things" wrestles with "breath of life." Curiously, the meditation on "The Fingers" ponders the experience of recognizing the third person, the "Trinity," and "The Hips" investigates genealogy and the transfer of humanity. Yet the final three sections shift the ground from specific theological phrases leading to sacred sites to focus on language itself. Perhaps this is an analogy for God. Certainly these parts are obsessed with naming.

And toenails are dull like this paragraph
& in writing we're warned to cut the dull short
except that in dreams short things they're still dull
& lately I began to think that maybe all you are saying when you say "it's dull"
The slips & differences
And I really stuck on the way the toenails cut around pressed flat against the stubby pink surfaces of the toes
as if they were hiding from me
fighting for air like
feeding on the dirt & jam accumulate there
in the dark of the shoe

"The Anus" muses on problems of unnameability. It's clear that the "anus" and the "bum" are related but different. The anus is both unseen, between the bum cheeks, yet heard by its "whistle," its poot/toot, at the same time as it is a source of invasion – by the "enema"/enemy, and by other unwanted penetrations. Its strange/alien location in the bum results partly from "not naming" it. "We didn't so much name it as allude to it," perhaps because you cannot see your own anus very easily, but whether bum or anus, the writer ends up rhyming as if substituting for significance. When one of a group of boys "hangs a moon" out a car window, the bum/anus has a strange power, a power that's wrapped up in language's inability to grasp its significance. This insight leads to the surreal section six, in which the bum/anus, the moon/green cheese, get melded in "The last rose of summer" as one of his brothers "dropped a rose" into the sleeping face of another brother, whose response was "get your bum out of my face," not "stop your anus letting go a fart." The part is about miscommunication, about not enough being said about an important part of everyday life, about being together and a part at the same time.

growing
Why were the toes piggies?
Why did one of them go to market
how come he did it all the way home?
this little piggie went "wee wee wee"
We all know pigs become sausages
& your sausages look like toes
Where do these metaphors & similes
these symbolisms
Who makes up these resemblances
these languages
Why is it some days the works look so strange?
so other, almost as if someone
somewhere is speaking to us from behind them
trying to make me understand
instruct me
maybe even
warn me
you know
trying to keep me on my toes?

However, "The Toes" is a part all about significance, and how when it is negatively by the social meaning comes to dominate our lives. The first section makes a parallel between recognizing "ugly toes" and thinking about "suicide." There there is no aimless, meandering day-dreaming in the syntax such that the second section converts from potential self-pity into a series of increasingly bizarre "maybe" phrases that conclude "Maybe this is THE ATTACK OF THE MUTANT POST-ATOMIC FEET. Maybe this is why we're always saying to the words: 'take me to your reader.'" Most of all, this and subsequent sections ask where significance comes from. Why else would we transfer fear through a word, so that a dog called "Toes" turns into a "bad dream where the repressed ... comes ... massing ... until consciousness is ... ugly and out of control"? Which begs the question: what is "ugly"? "Where do

So many things inside me I am not in touch with
So many things with such strange names
pray I never see as in the horror movie spleen
the sound of them is enough to make me vomit
And when did there become a something meandering-day and the syntax
without it, can smell it taste it feel it
praying I'll never have to again praying it will stop
the contraction in the throat the sound from beyond the tongue more in touch with my insides
than I really wanted
If you're unlucky you get to meet them if you're lucky you never get to meet them at all
while you go about your life oblivious
And this is the real organ music the harmony of the spheres the way the different organs play together, work
the real unconscious the unseen

It's the old problem of writing about something you know nothing about
I can do the research   read the book   but it's not the same   It's not the same

Tho they name the organs and the names are the same they're not the same organs as the organs sitting there inside me the bpNichol liver the bpNichol kidney the bpNichol bladder

these metaphors & similes these symbolisms come from? Who makes up these resemblances these languages anyway?" Implying that if we had other words perhaps the ugly would not be so, and dull would be different.

collected workings I think of as me

which is why I worry if the doctor may be a real collector a completist

so you never say to the doctor 'Doctor please save me' No you never say that

The concluding "Sum of the Parts," meditates on the way that names are not things. The second time the Doctor says that if you work in a "discipline" the words you use assume a direct connection with things – disciplinary words, like medical words, such as "spleen," "are not metaphors." But hovering around this insight is a corollary: that disciplines are where words get invented or found, words for the things we don't usually see. And we do not usually "want to see" these parts of yourselves" because the individual being within the unseen body is prayer. But the unseen is "before the tongue, literally and metaphorically." It's inside us the prior to language the unconscious. And do we need it the hand of collaboration, to see, listen, and touch but not name these organs. We know they are there because they need consciousness not to making organ music, "the true harmony of the spheres that is the tune of the third man. The third in anything the thirdness the binary standoff in an important issue in the language/critical world of the 1980s in which bpN is writing. Whether it is God, the Holy Spirit, the other, the different, it's the thing that we know and cannot be named.

You say 'what's wrong with me?' or 'I'm in rotten shape' or better 'I'm worthless'
downplaying yourself devaluing yourself making yourself as miserable and undesirable as possible the Doctor says that if you
which is how you wants things to be.
I almost forgot to meet my self
I had been to see the Doctor & the Doctor said well it really looked like my thyroid was enlarged
& really I should get a thyroid scan and before you could say goiter there I was in this tiny room
strapped down under this big machine
so the technician was giving you self to worry. O because the thing that being is whether
I only had to lie there as still as possible for fifteen minutes or so and then I could get up and leave
I lay there as still as possible thinking about my thyroid thinking about my nose
couldn't see the technician who even then was looking at it picture of it aware of my unseen
thyroid aware of the unseen technician who had so carefully left the room after she strapped me down
worry. And of course I worried I always worry.
Even tho you say you'd like to see it, you always worry there's a chance you might finally get
your finally finally seeing off into an important
turning inside out a raw feeling of See
you don't want to see

After I threw out my back where and X-Rayed X-Rayed the lumbar sacrum region
Only the Doctor that day was giving a lecture to these two trainees and as the technician shoved me
around on the cold steel table he would whisper his commentaries

It was the sacred meditation where the bpN somehow evel the studio audience take him to a naming of the sacred itself. It's a process, what he calls an "underpinning," something that precedes our writing which books was a bitter you that I believed in process (336). Just so, the writing or a reading has led me to palimpsestic installation, constellating into the narrative of this essay. The nice thing about Nichol is that what he says actually happens. He's a man of his word.

and the trouble was I didn't know you see
You live your whole life making do with only the reflection of certain parts making do with
people who have seen them, know directly what you only glimpse third-hand
Like your back
Every single part of you has been taken to look at it you only know through mirrors,
photographs that other people take of you. And there are Doctors and Nurses who have cut you
open watched your blood flow seen your heart pulse know the inner woman or man
And these aren't just metaphors you know these aren't just similes
It's a discipline
We learn to see with the third eye
to listen with the third ear
to touch the unknown with the third hand
to walk down dark streets in search of the hidden the mystery
while in the air around us invisible presences pick up their zithers and begin to play The Third Man Theme.

WEBLINKS

1 The text as here in the book, overlaid
   http://lynettehunterperformance.com/htmls/de-scribing-overlay.html
2 The two texts here in the book, unlaid
   http://lynettehunterperformance.com/htmls/unlaid.html
3 The two texts here in the book in parallel with Nichol's *Selected
   Organs* (courtesy of Ellie Nichol)
   http://lynettehunterperformance.com/htmls/comparison.html

January 1995   University of Calgary Visiting Professor, lecturing on
        "De-scripting Performance in bpNichol's *Selected Organs*"
"Describing Performance," edited by Lori Emerson, *Open Letter* (April
        2008): 115–32

Back in 1995, at the start of this series of productions, I was asked to give
a paper on bpNichol by the University of Calgary, which I was visiting
on a fellowship. I was told that people were worried about him not being
helpful to "feminism," and since I'd just completed a study in which I followed his profound commitment to what I call the imagination of the non-
autonomous self – central to the possibilities of democratic humanism – I
thought I'd take it on. What I ended up doing was rehearsing into verse one
of the few texts he had published as prose, *Selected Organs*.

When asked ten years later to contribute to a collection on his work, I
returned to this study and re-rehearsed the text within the quite different
context built by the intervening productions. Nichol's work has been central to my work, as it has to so many Canadian writers, since the 1970s. He
released me from the tyranny of the line-end only to open up its joys. He
exploded grammatical rules into the glory of anarchic logic way before the
historians of rhetoric got there, and in the midst of the debate about the
biological essentialism of language. He performed the written text in a way
that did deconstruction before Derrida hit the English language scene, and
taught me deconstruction's moral and ethical value as the beating heart of
social change.

Nichol's work inspired me. Literally breathed energy into me. Made me
realize why I worked with words when so many had turned to bodies, and
helped me materialize the body of the text. My rehearsing of *Selected Organs*

in 2006 developed into a laying out of prose onto the page, but that is too morbid a metaphor, no matter how accurate in typographical terms. The prose carried itself through my musculature with a spatial rhythm ending up at the fingers and pouring onto the page. It was this performativity that moved me to write the critical commentary, and I couldn't separate the one from the other. So I literally overwrote the one with the other, with help from the artist Ilya Noé who completed the overlaid PDF layout and design and the ever-patient editor and publisher Frank Davey.

The resulting digital transcription of the prose and ghostings of the text can most simply be seen on the website, where you can superimpose any of them onto each other to read the suggestive combinations. Yet the printed text has the format I initially intended because it becomes increasingly more difficult to read for verbal sentences as it proceeds – leading some subscribers to *Open Letter* to return their copies because of "misprinting." But this is a visual art-making as well as a verbal performance. One of the publishers' readers of the typescript of this book commented that it becomes "impossible to read" on the printed page. At the same time another reader enjoyed the effort involved and claimed that "with effort, [it] can be read." The suggestion from the former reader was to use, for example, onionskin paper to overlay one text on the other. However, as the second reader noted, the graphic presentation of some of the essays,

> stage[s] the scene of their own reading, juxtaposing and overlaying fragments of the successive moments of their own production. I am thinking of the many instances in *Disunified Aesthetics* where someone else reads a version of the text I am in the process of reading, where the process of revision is evoked and discussed. Lynette Hunter is a performance artist as well as a critic; the difficulty, in the context of the manuscript, of separating these practices turns out to be an effective way of exploring the interactions among writer, reader, critic and text.

Key for this book-based performance is the experience of the typographic performance critique amalgamating with the critical essay and morphing from a written text into a visual text. The essay becomes a piece of visual art that creates differences between and among the texts it engages and opens the possibility for audiences also to do so, especially because it works outside generic expectation. The website records are not performative in themselves, but simply digitized records that lay out elements used to build the graphic/visual performance and, possibly, to enable a different kind of engagement with the printed essay in the book.

The piece is collaborative in many ways. It arrives and becomes a text from the collaborations inspired by Nichol and by my own history with Canadian texts, from the collaborations of material production in 1995 with the University of Calgary, in 2005 with Ilya Noé and Frank Davey, and in 2011 with McGill-Queen's University Press, and it continues to create ecologies in which readers (both silent and oral) can find points of dissonance resonating the body. It continues in an ongoing collaboration with Noé and some young digital artists.

10

Roget Falls in Love

PERFORMANCE 10

"Roget Falls in Love: Crossing Margaret Atwood with bpNichol"
   2007   Birmingham University (UK), "Beyond the Book" conference
   October 2007   "Case by Case Arts Policy in Canada," TransCanada 2
      plenary paper, University of Guelph

WEBLINKS
   1 The video record of "Roget Falls in Love,"
      http://vimeo.com/18439763
   2 The text of *Roget Falls in Love: How Analytical Thought Stops
      You Thinking*, http://lynettehunterperformance.com/htmls/
      analytical-thought.html

The rhetorical flow of installation and constellation with culture and society can be read from the vocabulary of this book in a number of ways. Working alongside hegemony with strategies of installation, like-minded groups collaborate in the process of making difference, of becoming. They constellate moments of ar(rest) in which becoming takes shape and erupts into/ merges into culture and society where it is either unseen and unheard or recognized as fit. Fitting art-makings often get co-opted fast into hegemony and turn into objects of satisfaction, the experience of enough. Other art-makings retain, for a set of innumerable reasons that has kept critics/readers/audiences fascinated/spell-bound, the ability to trigger desire, the adrenalin surge, and endorphins of fit again and again – but not for ever.

People experiencing the felt presence of need, often the denial of their own value and/or values – the reasons for them to keep on living – get to a point of until: the moment when they know they have to engage, or in many cases re-engage, with other people in working alongside. This is the critical labour of until. The labour of the critic is to know when we've had enough: to recognize those moments of need, and to devise strategies for re-engagement such as, in the twentieth century, defamiliarization, the *verfremdungseffekt*, deconstruction. At other times that felt moment of need is made present in alongside work itself, and offers us a choice. This is the art-maker's labour of until: to know when we don't know, to recognize the total aporias of nothing, of things that cannot be said, and the other moments when we set in motion processes that make present through the making of difference. It is a wave that gathers itself to throw itself forward on the shore, only to gather again.

Collaboration, the Critic, and the Non-autonomous Self

Throughout this book potentially autonomous entities or activities have been moving into process with each other. Situated knowledge, which promises the recognition of knowledge alternative to hegemonic knowledge, has been shifted into a necessary textuality of process, a rhetorical stance of allegory or performativity. Performativity itself, which distinguishes between rehearsal and performance, has been cast as a movement in which installation and constellation are fused into a rhetorical flow that can occur in either. These rhetorics of situated textuality or performativity necessarily work alongside hegemonic structures, in collaborative groups of non-autonomous beings. Directly related to "fiction theory," Brossard's "utopian," her refusal of transgression, her location of the lesbian body as one porous to other lesbian bodies – with the imagination to pose the "lesbian" as a non-hegemonic relation – and her suggestion that in rhetoric is hope, could be read as a conversation with what Spinoza called "multitudinousness," what Emmanuel Levinas called "substitution" and "trace," what Étienne Balibar has called "transindividuality," and what Brossard and Marlatt collaborate on "in-between."

Some of the primary areas of concern for performance studies, along with phenomenology and various epistemologies, are how to maintain an engaged process in the alongside, often in small collaborative groups, in rehearsal, or when to arrest or rest in a moment to offer an invitation to a larger group of people to have an effect or affect on society and culture; strategies for knowing when to re-engage, or how to recognize need, disentangling it from want and desire, and then, how to adopt those strategies for re-engagement that people in critical studies of all kinds have developed and refined for the past two centuries at least.

If this book began with a critique of the Artist, arguing for democratic access to the valued activity of art-making across many diverse peoples, generating a disunified aesthetics, here I'd want to posit the implications for the Critic. In the modern age of Western liberalism, Critics just as much as Artists have worked for privileged elites who owned the modes of production of their labour. Any critical work involves ethics, since it brings two or more people together, often through the makings and objects of one of them that are being evaluated for sociocultural fit by the other. Critical work can be normative, underlining the tolerant ethics of liberalism that hide universalist assumptions, and generating opinion that satisfies. It can be oppositional and resistant, arguing for, negotiating for cultural and political fit through a responsive ethics. It can also work on positionality with respect to liberal hegemony that insists on a partiality, or on a particularity, or indeed on a position of nothingness. These latter alongside sets toward hegemony recognize need, or events and conditions where the assumptive logic of liberalism disallows, represses, ignores, evades, cannot see or hear the values of many people's lives.

Critical engagement, critique-making, involves the making of value, and hence the making of difference that asks us to take responsibility for the changes we make in ourselves when we make the other person different. This making sets up the possibility for a return, the process of friendship I attributed earlier to Derrida, that enables the feeling of the non-autonomous, the transindividual. If memory is an individual body processing the past for what the present needs, the return of the other person and the collaboration with them as a non-autonomous individual initiates the group memory that processes the past for what the present needs that we call history. If this critical engagement sounds like the earlier discussion of art-making, that's because their difference is in many ways a matter of emphasis.

The Installation: Roget Falls in Love

The art world has tended to use the word "installation" to define the piece that ends up in a gallery or on a site, whereas my use of it here broadens the word to also focus on the process of textualizing. In other words, it is a noun that refers both to an object and a process and might better be thought of as a participle: installating. Constellation/constellating is in many ways the process of textualizing with the installed piece. Perhaps it is on a continuum with it, but I'd like to use this brief critical documentation of a recent installation to explore these relations more carefully, particularly the differences between live performance and reading – which is another kind of performance.

In August 2007 I brought a performance to the conference "Beyond the Book" held in Birmingham, England. The performance resulted from a decade of text-work that became a place to examine passion and subsequently turned into a performance about passion. All the performances that I have worked on have as their central energy the need to open up a particular vulnerability to those participating, either by their taking part in the installation or responding to it. So the task of the installing, over the following ten years, was to make a form that insisted on its own vulnerability. This time, however, I the performer was not vulnerable in the same way because it was the book the poem had turned into, the body of this book that was the place of engaged process.

The installation was initially textualized in the late 1990s simply as an opened-book, a book cut to open in flexible ways.[1] Then, when a printing press became available in 2003, and because I'd taught printing for many years and was obsessed at the time with the semantic field in Shakespeare overlaying printing with passionate sexuality (Thompson and Thompson), the installation shifted. It was to be realized in the well of a library that held a printing press, and the performance would involve people by making and handing round keepsakes from Shakespearean references, and by demonstrating the embossing of pages of the poem's text with unseen words that created a tactile textuality, the folding, sewing, gathering, and binding of the text, and then by cutting it in unexpected ways. The performer had to be highly sexualized. But the library I wanted to work in refused permission despite appeals over three years. So when I was invited to the conference in Birmingham, I hoped to perform this version there.

In the meantime I had got a lot older. I thought about dyeing my hair. I thought about Shakespearean sonnets and age and passion, and how this shifts. And I thought about the relation between installation and constellation, something not on the horizon when the textualizing began. The passionate body of the performer was morphing into the empassioned body of the book.

Birmingham could not in the end offer me a printing press, which turned the performance into something quite different. I realized that (1) the performance was a rehearsal of a reading and (2) readers needed to be involved – not only in the reading but in the rehearsing of process, and in the process itself. If the reading involved engaging with an opened-book, then where did the reading begin? It could begin simply by sitting down reading a series of "opened" books, but I decided to begin with the single printed sheet and engage the reader into the folding, sewing, gathering, binding, cutting, and opening that the early version of the performance had only been going to demonstrate, and encouraging them to drop into the activity at any stage of construction.

This is what happened. As an improvised event involving a range of quite different people in installing text as they worked on tables doing different activities, the performance action was offered as a collaboration. Among the participants were four people who had seen some of my previous performance work, but I was unsure how they would react because in that prior work there had always been a central vulnerable body, and this was here laid aside, displaced into the book. The performer's body was instead interacting in a low-key way, trying to establish lines of connection, difficulty, discussion, negotiation. It was installing and constellating at the same time. A lot of work was used to build energy around the four-square table, and an arc of space was created by the presence of Alexander Lichtenfels videoing the installation. Except for five or six minutes at the start, Lichtenfels maintained the same position, and the radius of the camera line laid up an invisible semicircular screen like a rebound wall that bounced the energy back into the performance space.

Each table had a card sign announcing what activity took place on it, and three cards scattered throughout said "please help me." Some people felt they were participating in a classic "this is how you make a book" activity. These participants had usually some kind of book history or librarianship background, and most of them had not "read" the various opened/cut books that had been prepared in advance, so they were not aware of the flexibility in the material object that underlay the reading installation. Those who did look at the books first responded by making their own in very different ways, folding the sheet only to find that the pages were not consecutive because the folds they had made were not regular, and either enjoying or being frustrated by the experience. One person carefully ripped the sheet into sixty pages, severed the excess, collated the leaves, and stabbed a single hole through to ensure consecutive reading.

The sewing was fraught with problems. There were two activities. The first consisted of machine-sewing the folds to anchor them, and the second of stabbing the sewn fold to hand-stitch the gatherings into a binding. Most participants were women, some despairing and saying they hadn't sewn "for years," and many bypassing the activity altogether, redolent as it is with women's suppression. The two men who started binding the gatherings with large stitches gave up in embarrassment – it was the most difficult phys-ical activity in the installation, yet they seemed to assume that it was their gender that defined their skill.

And the opening: the cutting of the pages, or tearing, or twisting, or re-arranging, despite and because of the sewn backbone of gatherings: this was, with the folding, the place where people engaged the most. Some resisted using knives to cut except along the edges of the consecutive pages, even saying it was too painful to do. Others produced origami-like engineering, or released the text into loose leaf so that it could be re-arranged or tucked into other pages.

A few people then sat down to read their books, or some of the others that had been pre-prepared. Even fewer read aloud, as I had hoped they might and had indicated on the card on the reading table. But people gathered. They talked to each other about the problems they were having, and ways of doing the activities. They helped each other out, became proprietorial about "their" copy, or simply left it for others to read. They formed their own par-ticular/collaborative installation. Those who were involved gathered around the tables, talking to each other, joking, exchanging life details as they worked. I think they each had a particular commitment to getting engaged with the activity, as I think all collaborative work does – whether it was be-cause they were familiar with making books, as two librarians were, whether it was because they picked up on the political dimension of the labour in-volved in making the objects at the centre of the conference, whether they were my friends trying to figure out what I was doing, or whether they were just passing and got pulled into the tactile and haptic, the mathematical and spatial problems the work poses.

The other people in the room were eating lunch, buffet style, and food is, like dogs and children, a difficult presence to negotiate alongside. Many came up to the tables, looked on briefly, and then passed by. It's hard to know what they got out of it. But this is the point about disunified aesthet-ics, any art-making will make sense to some people and not to others. There was a feeling of a "workplace" around those tables that holds within it the way this book got written. I go to my desk, sit down and write. It is quite different from the bravura of the initial performances, there is little lumin-osity about the performance, we were not in it for the "fit." It was almost as if people had decided that rehearsal was all you need, with its frustrations, lovely moments, disappointments, and being among others.

Email follow-up responses to the art-making:

Gillian Roberts

I remember being very bad at the sewing, and being surprised (though I shouldn't have been) at just how difficult it was to do. I suppose I also feel self-conscious doing new things in groups (plus Alex was filming, was he not?), so that no doubt emphasized, for me, my lack of sewing skill. (I heard someone say once that sewing skips a generation; it certainly did in my family.) But I really enjoyed it all the same. I'd never seen a physical book in that state before, the layout of the pages, etc., which was also humbling, considering what occupies most of my waking hours. I did read the book [that I made], yes – I think you sent me one of the copies. I may be making this up now (!) but I think I read it on the way to TransCanada 2 in Guelph (or else shortly before? after? my chronology is a bit muddled now). At some points the pages were difficult to separate, so there were bits of the book that were physically difficult to read (which, in some ways, seemed to make it more of an "art object," but I guess also makes me think again of the materiality of the book).

I remember you alluding to the Birmingham piece in your TransCanada paper and saying you hadn't thought it worked very well, and I wondered why that was the case, I suppose I wondered what you had hoped would come out of it at the same time as thinking about all the things I myself had got out of it.

Catherine Bates

My first reaction to this piece was that it was exciting to get to make a book – and to participate in the physical making in a way which expands the reading experience (or perhaps is part of it?). There was the physical putting together of the book but then you emphasized to me that we could cut it up in any way we wanted. This made me read the contents in a different way, as I was keen to try and make it mine by cutting around particular words to change the shape of the poems and somehow track my own reading experience. To do this properly I would have needed more time so I am worried I didn't do a great job – but it did make me really think of the Barthesian theory I am so attracted to which emphasizes the role of the reader's participation in making the text.

It is interesting to think of the whole piece as a performance event – the performance relied upon people taking part and so many people walked past (partly, because it was a conference and people wanted to eat/drink but also i think because people are worried about getting involved in something they don't already know about – especially, perhaps, if it involves crafts they might not be good at). I enjoyed participating in collaboration – I discussed what I was doing with others and watched what they were doing (I remember noting with you how messy mine was and how neat Emma and Gillian's were and having that regret i used to have so often in Art lessons at school – I had enjoyed my own process until seeing the results of others). It was also great as an event at a conference called Beyond the Book. We were getting an insight into the materiality which brings the content to us – it did highlight how often we just think of the content as something transferable. Cutting up the content made it more noticeably material, somehow.

Possibly, the part that I remember the most is when we had to say how much we thought making a book would cost. This was interesting as my instinct was that we were being asked to consider the cost of the labour (I was somehow considering the question figuratively) whereas actually you were asking for an actual monetary value. I cannot remember what that was but it was surprisingly high. Afterwards, this made me think of the economic power publishers hold and so the reliance writers have on them. I have thought about this since, having got to know writers who have contracts with Vintage and having worked with *Moving Worlds*.

Finally, I realise I must have left my copy of the book in Whitley Bay, but I often think of the title. The reference to Roget makes me think of our relationship to thesauruses – the fact that they are books that we investigate for synonyms, words which cluster around each other with varying levels of intimacy. This puts the reader's participation in a different light but also made me think of the multiple different but similar copies the participants made and the way we compared and contrasted, looked on with envy, admiration and delight.

It was great to have an activity in a conference which gave the opportunity to do something with people and go through an experience (as opposed to hoping to share ideas but often having superficial conversations or failing to connect). I loved it.

Danielle Fuller

I didn't want to rush too much re. the thoughts about performance, so I let it all swish around in my head during the week. There are some images I remember vividly and some of these I have just seen again because I just watched parts of three performances (Roget Falls in Love, Trying Not to Be a Tragic Subject, Bodies in Trouble) online. The moment I was really searching for turned out to be about a third of the way into "Trying" when you let your hair down. To be honest, before I watched the video it was the *only* thing I remembered about this particular piece and I couldn't for the life of me recall the title, although I knew it was a piece about Lee Maracle's work. I think the reason that this moment stayed with me was partly because it was unexpected (this is not a performance with many "props" and there is not a huge variation in physical action and gesture), but also because it was quite breath-taking. And I remember that Colin Nicholson said to me (maybe afterwards) how erotic it was when you undid your hair – then I understood why it felt like watching something that was rather beautiful but a bit unsettling at the same time. Now I think it was very honest of him to say that, at the time (1997 – it was just 2 days after my PhD viva so perhaps my emotions were particularly heightened and I was probably feeling a bit raw) I may have been a little shocked at what Colin said. Maybe I was a little shocked at myself for agreeing. In any case, this is an abiding image for me. Watching part of the performance again, I realised how little of the content and argument I had recalled: the hair trumped everything for me.

Watching Roget Falls in Love was different: it wasn't so long ago, and I could remember quite well how people had gradually joined in the book-making but also how quite a few people skirted around the edges. It was fun to spot people i knew in the filmed version. I kept thinking: well, of course that person (book historian) or that person (reading activist) would dive in and make a book alongside all the other Leeds graduates. And who is that woman in the green dress? And is that the person I emailed just yesterday? And look! there is Julie (not my partner then, but now) and Joan (her then partner, now my friend). And, blimey, I gave those trousers away over a year ago because they were way too tight around the waist. All very personal and rather mundane. I wonder how someone who wasn't there would feel about this film? Would it be very boring for them because there is no commentary or voice-over or overt interpretation within the film? Could they even figure out what was going on? For me, there are great feelings of affection attached to this performance because it was at the Beyond the Book conference and I was so grateful and glad that you could come and do it there. Looking at it now I can see something communal and community making about that piece.

People are very immersed in activity, but they are in there, making something, making it alongside others, facilitated by what you have put before them.

And then there is Bodies in Trouble. I didn't really need to watch it – it's the one I remember most vividly. But there was something almost painful about watching us lifting that cage structure. I remember that Julie M spliced her finger at some point. You can see even in the film how awkward it is to get it through the door and up that pathway. But that fits the performance in a way: the cookie making was arduous, the slow-getting-faster walk from lab was physically demanding, and the breath-work you did emphasised that. People were very unsettled: partly by the fact that the whole thing disrupted their frame of expectations about "the conference" [all that palaver about "should we start the plenary now"!] and their ideas about "Lynette," but also because some of them read it very autobiographically. I remember Margaret Beetham was really upset and almost in tears and even when I suggested that maybe it didn't *have* to be read autobiographically, she was inconsolable. Also, it's just plain weird to see yourself 15 years ago, isn't it? – it's the first time I've seen old footage with me in it. And then you had to walk out of the box in front of everyone which wasn't supposed to happen at all but people just wouldn't move away. I think they would have sat there all night if you hadn't left the box!

I think I remember the parts I recall quite viscerally really – that, and also emotionally. It's more about how it felt (heart and body) for me than what it was all about. I often look at visual art that way: I almost want to resist interpretation. I just want to see what happens. I don't want some fancy vocabulary or theory to come along and stop the sensation or over-complicate it. Serendipitously, one of my students wrote about that online for our class (Reading and Popular Culture) this week – about how she didn't want her pleasure in reading to be killed off by university study but in some ways it had been. She values the intense feelings of enjoyment and she felt that pleasure wasn't part of reading lit in the university that was valued, or given any space to be. I've had students say and write these kind of things before, of course, and also (of course) I deliberately set up ways in which they feel they can articulate these things within a group that will understand them. And maybe I wouldn't be thinking about how to do that if I hadn't seen these performances?

Although the installation doubled itself as a rehearsal and a performance of reading, I would have liked it to have offered more time to engage in the installation of the words, the passion let loose into the folds, cuts, openings, torques, arrangements of the affected paper and ink. Because the book is a technology for extending a complex interweaving of time and space sensed by our bodies, the engaged book can be a way to extend our capacity to sense the presence of passion, just as much as eye glasses extend our sight. The textual performance of the vulnerability of the body taken over by a foreign biochemistry could have made it more of a point of improvisation for the reader. But the temporal is a factor difficult to know beforehand, and this was a time-bound performance different from placing a book on a shelf where the reader makes the time they need.

Writing is so often thought of as individual, with the particular/collaborative happening in some kind of interpretive event after the words on the page are there. Book art/artist's books are a good example of material collaboration, as are hypertexts[2] and many differently mediated verbal scripts, in their ability to suggest that the reader read not only for the story on the page but to constellate the text into their own process. The opened books are points of departure for other processes, but the work of situated textuality that led to them in the first place has to be performed in an appropriate medium. The reader could constellate this for themselves over time, but the audience of a time-bound live performance needs it devised into the performed activity. Both reading and live performance are aesthetic, somatic, and affective activities, but quite different temporally and spatially.

My failure to recognize this before the performance is a good indication of the lack of training institutionally available for the processual elements in reading as constellation. I intend to work the piece more particularly toward another sense of temporality. This makes me suggest that in this long-vision argument for case-by-case arts policy, we could begin where all social change usually begins, by diversifying education. Either in primary schools where there is often more disciplinary flexibility, or in universities which should respond to the combination of new research and pedagogy, there could be specific learning about processual textuality.[3]

The Passion of the Text

The interaction of the critical essay with performance made here by *Disunified Aesthetics* is part of a recognized Canadian literary tradition. It may be found throughout bpNichol's writing and Nicole Brossard's, it surfaces time and again in the work of critics, for example, Frank Davey's *Cultural*

Mischief and Lola Lemire Tostevin's *Subject to Criticism*. It emerges across a wide range of Canadian fiction in both French and English, enacting that emphasis on "fiction" in the interactions of "fiction theory." Performance critique draws on this experimentation with genre and signification, pulling from it the focus on process as a textuality in itself that is promised in the articles that make up *Tessera 2*. This kind of processual textuality, a diffraction from Brossard's *installation*, invites the reader or audience into the event not simply to receive a pre-formed story but to engage in the making of the art that is needed by the particular ecology of the moment.

Nicole Brossard says of reading, in her contribution to *Tessera 2*, "Nous avançons vers une femme subtile et complexe qui reflète le processus et les forms du développement de notre pensée" (40), and concludes, "Toute lecture est une intention d'images, une intention de spectacle qui nous donne espoir." What gets her there, in a reading of a "critical text" (43) by Claire Texte, is the constant re-writing as she reads, the underlining, the commentary. She says that having spent the night reading this book, "J'en ai fait mon livre" (41). These writings are the only way she can bring herself to that text, for it is impossible to say precisely what she likes about it, even if she wrote for a month. Reading is a "paradoxe," an "étrangété," "un malaise d'écriture'(41). The article is entitled "Certain mots," calling on Wittgenstein's "what is the case," that we can only say things that already lie within the language of our culture and society: these are "certain" because they already fit. "Certain mots" writes the impossibility of pinning made-art down to cultural fit and invites us into the process of art-making that goes on in the alongside world of collaboration. At the same time, *un mot/*a word is what her writer chooses to place alongside the body and the world. Brossard again, more recently, "Words honed over years and novels, words we spoke with halting breath laughing spitting sucking an olive, verbs we add to the pleasure of lips, to success, to sure death" (Brossard 2007, 81). In performance, I think of the body as a word, just as in language I think of the word as a body.

The performance critiques in part one led to essays that posited particular differences I had made between myself and other people, in a self-reflective learning process that explored gender, ethnicity, class, and privilege, and brought those made-differences into cultural articulation, as is common to the essay genre. In part two the performance critiques attempt to interact with the audience, generating embodied and graphic performance, turning the process of making difference into made-art that erupts into culture – through the embodied, through the visual, through the translated – and emphasizing the emergence of made-art into cultural fit.

The essays in part three move into the process and try to stay there. The result is that the differences are not coalesced into a made-art that easily articulates in culture. This makes them more difficult to read. They may generate engagement but they also focus on the elusive feelings that arise when collaborators work on saying some thing that can still need to be said once the work of collaboration is over. In the case of reading/writing Daphne Marlatt's *this tremor love is*, the page translates the grammar of her poetry into the rhythm of the performance's spoken word, allowing them to sit side by side, not choosing one or the other, so that the readers can experience making a difference for themselves. With bpNichol's *Selected Organs*, the essay superimposes a performance translation of his poem with a critical reading so that each becomes unreadable typographically and morphs into visual art, morphing the reader into an audience of the sensuality of the eye. The final chapter is a descriptive account of readers/writers working collaboratively in the moment, and an attempt to convey the difficulty of "making sense" of such disunified work.

In "Roget Falls in Love" the book is a word/body. During the collaboration we were doing reading/writing, and what we were doing was making difference and the way it changes everything. If performance critique reminds everyone taking part that everyone is taking part, it does so in an attempt to reach an engaged ethics of the text, a process of agency in democratic claims on culture from many diverse groups. In the disunified aesthetics I have outlined in this book there is an attempt to offer another way of thinking about art that acknowledges the possibility that all people may collaborate in, through, and around it in re-imagining their lives. The process of this aesthetics imagines people as non-autonomous yet situated through the textuality that makes up their positionality with regard to the larger sociocultural and political systems alongside them. Yet this is no relativism, or pluralism, nor is it relational. It asks for an engaged ethics that signifies a recognition that we make difference, change ourselves, value and take responsibility for that change.

coda

The reason I chose Roget, Nichol, and Marlatt for these final essays was in my body. I retained a passion for their work, passion that reminds us every moment of every day that we are making difference.

What would happen if Roget fell into a passion with the words he carefully separated and arranged, so they melted and merged and molded into each other instead of standing up for themselves? What does the human body do with passion? Passion is somatically durational. It lingers in the body. According to opera, it destroys us. The word is linked into roots about suffering and patience, the willingness to endure or undergo. What happens to passion when it becomes textualized? In a book, in a film, in a song, it can enable containment as well as release. To be impressed, folded, sewn, gathered, stitched, bound, cut, opened, read: each material action an empassioned move. Can one read with passion? Or is reading an endurance, a patient willingness to open to affect? And what happens when we re-make the impassioned event?

bpNichol. I never knew him. He loomed and looms so large over writing and reading I feel the energy released by his actions as if he were present. I felt I was rehearsing his text. The hearse, the harrow that carries the dead body. To rehearse, to harrow again the body that has left this life, to turn over the soil of the material words, the body of the text, to grow again. Plato's fourth lover, the one no one reads, the one past the imagination of the philosophical lover, is the writer and the gardener. The writer who tills the soil of the earth of language, loves beyond payment, exchange, and imitation, loves for the difference it makes, the changes it makes to the self.

Daphne Marlatt is my friend, but I do not know her. She is a friend found on the page, a texuality that is always an absence/a difference that gifts back to me the possibility of changing my self. The friend is bound to love, to woo, to caress – from the pre-Teutonic *priyo* or "dear," and further back in the Sanskrit *priya* or free, beloved, goddess, woman, not-subject, the unbound lover. Her words open a resonance to the world, never being able to drink a cup of tea without slowing down, watching the leaves release the stories among us, as a friend would say "among."

This is a moment of ar(rest)

INTRODUCTION

1 See the opening section of chapter 8 for a detailed argument on relevant political philosophy.

2 It would be possible to examine the entire literary history of women's writing in this way. Marie de France, Margaret Cavendish, Virgina Woolf, and Gertrude Stein come immediately to my mind. The Western academic take on the process coalesced for many white middle-class women of the 1970s through the work of Hélène Cixous, Madeleine Gagnon, and others, in particular through the jointly written, with Annie Leclerc, *La venue à l'écriture* (Cixous et al. 1977) containing "La venue à l'écriture" by Hélène Cixous, "Mon corps dans l'écriture" by Madeleine Gagnon, and "La lettre d'amour" by Annie Leclerc.

3 See the introductory commentary to part one for possible connections with this kind of performance critique.

4 She attended the conference "Borderblur" co-organized by Lynette Hunter and Shirley Chew at the University of Leeds, School of English, 1991.

5 Produced at The Traverse Theatre, Edinburgh, 1976; directed by Peter Lichtenfels.

6 http://publish.uwo.ca/~fdavey/c/newvispoems.html

7 This vocabulary is garnered from several different sources, and I have brought it together over the past ten years. In other words, little of it is new, but the particular array into which it is brought here is particular to my own theorizing. For one application, see Hunter 2011.

8 See chapters 1 and 2 for an initial foray into "what is said."

9 See chapters 1 and 2 for initial thinking on "fit"; I also write extensively on "fit" in chapter 5.

10 See chapter 3 for further discussion of the concept of "alongside" and "beside." I write further on "alongside" in chapters 7, 8, 9.

11 This is a concept from Desmond Murray's daoist practice, Hunter and Murray, forthcoming.

12 For example, see Nicolas Bourriaud 1998, where he articulates relational aesthetics as aesthetics within social rather than private space, and uses the situationists' definition of "situation" in a similar way, quite distinctly different from the "situatedness" articulated by scholars in the feminist study of science and technology.

13 There are a multitude of writers and artists in this field from Homi Bhabha to Joseph Roach, and from Stelarc to Keith Hennessy.

14 One of the most challenging on this specific point is Patricia Hill Collins' work *Black Feminist Thought*.

15 Toleration as a central principle of liberal politics is carefully explored in Rieff 2007.

16 See Wilderson 2010 for a full exploration of Afropessimism over the past decade.

17 One could cite, for example, the work of Ernesto Laclau and Chantal Mouffe, of Jurgen Habermas or Hans Gadamer, of Seyla Benhabib, of Jared Sexton.

PART ONE – COMMENTARY

1 There is more on the connotations of "outwith" in chapter 3.

2 "Pomo" is the term I use for reductive postmodern critique of power that generates the melancholy and cynicism of an age in which people are relatively empowered but do not really have an effect on the structures of power.

3 Rationalism, isolation, and the simultaneous autonomous/universal "man" are the primary rhetorical elements of the ethos of nation state ideology. See Hunter 1999, chapter 1.

CHAPTER ONE

1 See Lynn Segal 1990 for a clear appraisal of an early 1990s' social construction of masculinity. Segal's subsequent *Straight Sex* (1994) also offers pertinent and helpful analyses.

2 See Rosie Braidotti's list of questions in *De la parenté à l'eugénisme*.

3 Pomo, as the ahistorical game proposed by Jacques Lyotard (1986), can be distinguished from the historical postmodern outlined by many Canadian critics, particularly Linda Hutcheon (1988) and Frank Davey ("American Alibis").

4 This is argued at greater length in Hunter, *Outsider Notes*.

5 The groundwork in these fields has been done by, among many others, Laura Mulvey on the male gaze and film, Juliet Mitchell on feminism and psychoanalysis, and Hélène Cixous' early writing on alternative women's sexuality as hermaphrodism.

6 The fleetingness of acting which misled early structuralist critics into privileging drama, or the prevalence of memory in performance studies, is parallel to this valuing of food ephemerality.

7 See Terence Cave 1988 for an illuminating replacement of the oedipal with the hunt.

8 For a discussion of lesbian erotics that helped to propel a queer awareness of hetero-erotics, see Valerie Traub 1992.

9 For further theorizing, see Hunter 1996, "Bodily Functions in Cartesian Space."

CHAPTER TWO

1 I have written in detail about some of my own engagements with these texts in Hunter 1996.

2 I owe an incalculable debt of gratitude to Margaret Beetham and the reading group she belonged to in the mid-1990s, and to many members of the English Department at the University of Calgary where I visited on a fellowship and on various other occasions from 1994 to 1997. Rebecca O'Rourke of the Adult Education Department at the University of Leeds was also key to my reimagining of the way it is possible to teach and think with colleagues.

3 Roland Barthes is a good example of the way that detailed critique circles back into the canon; Foucault resists the movement by locating his criticism in isolated nodes of discourse that defy connection with the daily lives of people, yet begins to engage with these issues in his later work; Derrida performs the difficulty itself.

4 See Code et al. 1991, 19, for the proposal that the merging of ethics and the political is a particularly feminist approach.

5 C. Mouffe and E. Laclau locate the word "articulation" within "discourse" in *Hegemony and Socialist Strategy*. They seem unconcerned with any activity that occurs outside of hegemony, yet on pages 135–6, they appear to allow for both "antagonism" and "articulation" to occur without hegemony. The agonistic rhetoric of their political theory claims that co-optation into the normative is inevitable, as does the later development that theory concerned with consensus communication is a threat to democracy (Mouffe, 6). However, rhetoric is not inevitably agonistic.

6 Debate strategies are elsewhere commended by Benhabib 1996, 76.

7 As Benhabib (1992) notes, treating someone in accordance with norms is to treat them as a "generalized" other, while to recognize and confirm someone as "a concrete, individual being with specific needs, talents and capacities" (281) is to treat them with friendship, love, and care.

CHAPTER THREE

1 "Autobiographie/Autobiography," Université de Rennes, organized by Marta Dvorak.

2 For example, Dvorak spoke about this issue at the "Moving Words/Moving Worlds" conference in Leeds in 1994, printed version Dangeroo Press 1995; but one could say that Maracle has been excluded. For example, she is not within the selection *Writing the Circle: Native Women of Western Canada*, compiled and edited by Perreault and Vance.

3 All quotations are taken from the following editions: *I Am Woman* (1988) and *Sojourner's Truth and Other Stories* (1990).

4 See, for example, D. Beetham, *The Legitimation of Power*; see also the general discussion of legitimation in Hunter 1999, chapter 4.

5 For a more extensive background, see Hunter 1999, chapter 1.

6 Hunter, *Modern Allegory and Fantasy*, 17–27.

7 One site that has explored this tangentially is postcolonial theory: from Margaret Atwood's *Survival* (1973) to Homi Bhabha's (1984) readings of "victim" theory elabo-

rated on the position of unitary tragic subjects; seeing beyond the issue is T. deLauretis (DeLauretis 1990).

8 See the clear summary in the "Introduction," Lennon and Whitford 1994.

9 Rhetorical drift moves from presence to consensus to the corporate and the authoritative, and can move to the totalitarian.

10 These interviews were established through introductions by Peter Kulchyski who was running the Trent University summer school in Panniqtuuq (in its fourth year). The interviews were subject to the regulations of the research licence, and each interview was paid for. The interviewees spoke Inuktitut and the translator, Lizzie Karpik, conducted simultaneous translation between that language and English. Karpik was also paid the suggested rate and was responsible for translating the finished transcripts and this article back to the interviewees for their critique and comments. The interviews were conducted in the homes of the interviewees at times of their choosing. I explained that I was a researcher from the University of Leeds in England, and that I was interested in hearing their views on if and why they told stories, and whether stories might be effective for social change. The one exception to this process was the collective meeting at the Angmarlik Centre in Panniqtuuq, to which eight Elders in the community came. All were paid the suggested rate, and my questioning and the translation followed the main pattern.

11 The delineation runs parallel with a comment from Louise Profeit-Leblanc on the concept of stories being "responsibly true." Jim Cheney reports a conversation with Profeit-Leblanc during which she uses the term "'t i anc oh' (usually glossed as 'what they say, it's true') and defined as meaning 'correctly true,' 'responsibly true' (a 'responsible truth'), 'true to what you believe in,' 'what is good for you and the community,' and 'rings true for everybody's well-being'" (Cheney 1996).

PART TWO – COMMENTARY

1 See Marvin Carlson, *Performance*, for an account of the connection between anthropology, ritual, and performance that cites the work of Victor Turner and Richard Scheckner.

2 "Bodies in Trouble" (1997).

3 "FACE-WORK: Coming to the End of the Line. A Study in the Poetry of Frank Davey" (1999, 2000).

4 "The Face, the Mask, and Classical Tragedy in the Household: The Rhetoric of Masking in Recent Work by Alice Munro" (2003–2005).

CHAPTER FOUR

1 LH: "Bodies in Trouble" as a title, in case you're interested, comes fom the song by Mary Margaret O'Hara and I think her voice is ...
SR: *There's a song called "Bodies in Trouble"?*
LH: Yes. Her voice is extraordinary and she has never done anything since like she did in the Miss America album, that song. I think it's called "Miss America." I can't remember what it's called now. And I don't like singing generally, I don't like opera.

I don't like choral voices, but I don't listen to pop songs and I don't listen to much vocal work at all, but her voice is truly an instrument and she plays with her voice so that it does what language parts do on a page and you'd have to listen to "Bodies in Trouble" to understand what I'm saying.

ṢR: *I'd like to.*

LH: It's a wonderful, wonderful piece of music, the whole tape is, but her ability to speak through her voice so that what you hear is not the conceptual content of the words, but the physicalization of sound through the vocal box is, I think in a way, what I was trying to do with the body. She is fantastic. She has never done another one and that is eight or ten years old and she did a short CD for kids for Christmas, which I have been trying to get hold of but haven't got, and she did something else that I've got a very bad recording of which was a film soundtrack, but her voice sustained me through a particular period of my life in which I felt my body was gong through a lot of trouble, my physical body was going through a lot of trouble.

CHAPTER FIVE

1 All references are to Frank Davey's books listed in the bibliography.

CHAPTER SIX

1 Also in "Memory." All references to articles are followed by the bibliographic reference in brackets; all references to articles and books are to those listed in the bibliography. The first citation of any text will include the first date of its publication.

2 OED INTENT a: *Intent* and *intense* are etymologically doublets, *intentus* and *intensus* being two forms of the L. pple.; but already in L. *intensus* was (like the simple *tensus*) more restricted to the physical sense "stretched, strained," hence "intense, violent," while *intentus* was extended to the notion of "mentally or nervously on the stretch, intent, eager, attentive." In the modern langs. this differentiation has been made more complete. So with *intention, intension.*

3 Many of these texts are interwoven; for example, "Memory" is infused into "Trajectory." I have tried wherever possible to indicate double sources, but there will be many I have missed.

4 Much of this theorizing is focused around the work of Michel Foucault after 1976, and the political theory of Ernesto Laclau and Chantal Mouffe in the 1980s.

5 See, for example, the play with "fiction culture cortex" in Marlatt 1985, 98.

6 See the insistent and chosen repetition on "presence" in *She Would Be the First Sentence of My Next Novel* (1998), for example 109, 115, 129, but also note the concern with "an introspective I increasingly isolated from history and solidarities" (91).

7 For example, Brossard 1996a, 332, and "Aut*her*," 2 from typescript provided by Susan Rudy.

8 See Brossard (1989) 1997 for a series of experiments with word resonance and vibration.

9 See romeoandjulietedition.com

10 "Les corps en première ligne" (forthcoming 2013).

1 During Margaret Thatcher's prime ministership in the 1980s, one of the responses to her cutbacks in the arts was a study of the support for the arts in Germany which demonstrated that access to art led to less psychological disturbance in the general populace.

2 For one among many detailed discussions of the way art and sensibility connect with democracy, see Rancière and Rockhill.

3 I have written about this elsewhere: for example, nations are less economically authoritative but still the legally and ethically responsible bodies for maintaining financial systems and issues such as corporate social responsibility and governance (Hunter 2002). Nations need "identities" to operate in global terms culturally/economically/politically. These identities are performed (Hunter 1999, chapter 1). Nation-state ethos used to be addressed to subjects and identity-formation of universals, as well as to difference-making functions with respect to other nation-states. Now it has to respond to transnational similitudes as well (Hunter 2001). Whereas the subject of ISAs was "subjected," the citizen today is invited to collude with the nation-state in producing identities recognizable to the global, i.e., the simulacrum, and that citizen is commodified into brand identities of consumer groups. Whereas the worker/non-citizen of ISAs could always aspire to be a citizen, workers now are "elsewhere" in a state of ongoing financial poverty and increasingly looking to other economies for capital, such as religious economies.

4 See, for example, Kamboureli 2000; or Diana Brydon's contribution to the last Trans-Canada conference in June 2005, and her elaboration of multilayered citizenship; or Marjorie Stone's presentation to the Tenth International Metropolis Conference, October 2005.

5 Cultural "fit" is another way of thinking about "beauty," chapter 6 above.

6 Thanks to Jill LeBihan, Sheffield Hallam University, for this.

7 J. Radway, plenary to the "Beyond the Book" conference, University of Birmingham, 2007.

CHAPTER TEN

1 The book artist Deb Rindl was key to this development in my thinking, and attended the Verbal inter Visual: Poetry and Art conference and arts festival I ran with Robert Vas Dias and Mark Leahy in 2001 at Central Saint Martin's, Birkbeck College, and Gresham College in London.

2 In my experience, younger people trained in these devices are far more able to engage in their flexibility.

3 A movement toward this has been happening at the tertiary level in the UK, Europe, and Australasia, called "practice as research" (Riley and Hunter). And there are a few, very few, places in North America which have begun to pursue it.

bibliography

Aaron, Jane, and Sylvia Walby, eds. 1991. *Out of the Margins: Women's Studies in the Nineties*. London: The Falmer Press

Acoose, Janice. 2008. "Honoring *NiWahkomakanak*." In *Reasoning Together*, edited by The Native Critics Collective. Norman: University of Oklahoma Press

Agamben, Giorgio. 2005. *State of Exception*. Chicago: University of Chicago Press

Ahmed, Sara. 2004. *The Cultural Politics of Emotion*. London: Routledge

Alexander, M. Jacqui, and Chandra Talpade Mohanty. 1996. *Feminist Genealogies, Colonial Legacies, Democratic Futures*. London: Routledge

Althusser, Louis. 1971. "Ideology and Ideological State Apparatuses: Notes towards an Investigation." In *Lenin and Philosophy and Other Essays*, translated by Ben Brewster, 121–76. London: New Left Books

Andalzua, Gloria. 2007. *Borderlands/La Frontera*. San Francisco: Aunt Lute Books

Anderson, Patrick. 2010. *So Much Wasted: Hunger, Performance, and the Morbidity of Resistance*. Durham: Duke University Press

Andrew, Caroline. 2005. "Multiculturalism, Gender, and Social Cohesion: Reflections on Intersectionality and Urban Citizenship in Canada." In *Insiders and Outsiders: Alan Cairns and the Reshaping of Canadian Citizenship*, edited by Gerald Kernerman and Philip Resnick, 316–28. Vancouver: University of British Columbia Press

Appiah, Kwame. 2006. *Cosmopolitanism: Ethics in a World of Strangers*. New York: W.W. Norton

Aptheker, Bettina. 1991. *Tapestries of Life: Women's Work, Women's Consciousness and the Meaning of Daily Experience*. Amherst: University of Massachusetts Press

Atwood, Margaret. 1973. *Survival*. Toronto: McClelland and Stewart

Auslander, Phillip. 1999. *Liveness: Performance in a Mediatized Culture*. London: Routledge

Austin, J.L. 1975. *How to Do Things with Words*. Edited by J.O. Urmson and M. Sbisa. Cambridge: Harvard University Press. First published 1962

Bannerjee, Himani. 1995. *Thinking Through: Essays on Feminism, Marxism and Anti-Racism*. Toronto: Women's Press

Beetham, David. 1991. *The Legitimation of Power*. London: Macmillan

Belenky, Mary Field, Blythe McVicker Clinchy, Nancy Rule Goldberger, and Jill Mattuck Tarule. 1986. *Women's Ways of Knowing: The Development of Self, Voice and Mind*. New York: Basic Books

Belsey, Catherine. 1999. *Shakespeare and the Loss of Eden: The Construction of Family Values in Early Modern Culture*. London: Macmillan

Benhabib, Seyla. 1991. *Situating the Self*. London: Routledge

– 1992. "The Generalized and the Concrete Other." In Frazer et al. 1992, 148–77

– 1996. "Toward a Deliberative Model of Democratic Legitimacy." In Benhabib 1996a, 67–94

– ed. 1996a. *Democracy and Difference: Contesting the Boundaries of the Political*. Princeton: Princeton University Press

Benjamin, Walter. 1985. *The Origins of German Tragic Drama*. Translated by John Osborne. London: Verso

Bhabha, Homi. 1984. "Of Mimicry and Men." *October* 28 (Spring): 125–33

– 1995. *The Location of Culture*. London: Routledge

Bordo, Susan. 1993. *Unbearable Weight: Feminism, Western Culture, and the Body*. Berkeley: University of California Press

Bourriaud, Nicolas. 1998. *Relational Aesthetics*. Paris: Presses du réel

Braidotti, Rosie. 1987. *De la parenté à l'eugénisme*. Paris: Éditions Tierce

Brennan, Teresa. 2004. *The Transmission of Affect*. Ithaca: Cornell University Press

Brossard, Nicole. (1984) 2000. "Installations." In *Installations (with and without pronouns)*, translated by Erin Mouré and Robert Majzels, 4. Winnipeg: The Muses' Company

– (1987) 2000. *Mauve Desert*. Translated by Suzanne de Lotbinière-Harwood. Toronto: Coach House Press

– 1988. "Memory: Hologram of Desire." In "Part I: Memory/Transgression: Women Writing in Québéc." Special issue, *Trivia: A Journal of Ideas* 13 (Fall): 42–7. From typescript provided by Susan Rudy

– 1990a. "Poetic Politics." In *The Politics of Poetic Form*, edited by Charles Bernstein, 73–80. New York: Roof Books

– (1990b) 1997. *Typhon Dru*. Translated by Caroline Bergvall. London: Reality Street Editions; includes *Typhon Dru*, previously published in French in 1989, and "La matière harmonieuse manoeuvre encore," previously published with a different translation by Lisa Weil, 1990

– 1992a. "Labyrinth." In *La nuit verte du parc labyrinthe/Green Night of the Labyrinth Park*, translated by Lou Nelson and Marina Fe, 23–38. Quebec: Les Éditions TROIS

– 1992b. "Writing as Trajectory of Desire and Consciousness." Translated by Alice Parker. In *Feminist Critical Negotiations*, edited by Alice Parker and Elizabeth Meese, 179–85. Philadelphia: John Benjamin Publishing Company

– 1994. "Écrire la société: d'une dérive à la limite du réel et du fictive." *Philosophiques* 21 (Autumn): 303–20

– (1995) 1997. *Baroque at Dawn*. Translated by Patricia Claxton. Toronto: McClelland and Stewart

– 1996a. "Fluid Arguments." In *Onward: Contemporary Poetry and Poetics*, edited by Peter Baker, 315–46. New York: Peter Lang Publishing

– 1996b. "Only a Body to Measure Reality By: Writing the In-Between." "Ravenscroft Lecture, with Daphne Marlatt," edited by S. Chew, special issue, *Journal of Commonwealth Literature* 3 (2): 5–11

– 1997. "Aut*her*." From typescript provided by Susan Rudy

– 1998. *She Would Be the First Sentence of My Next Novel/Elle serait la première phrase de mon prochain roman*. Translated by Suzanne de Lotbinière-Harwood. Toronto: The Mercury Press

– 1999a. "I like to say we and look elsewhere." Translated by P. Joris. In "99 Poets/1999: An International Poetics Symposium," edited by Charles Bernstein, special issue, *boundary 2*, 26 (Spring): 60–2

– 1999b. "The most precious things in the future will be water and silence and a human voice." Paper presented at a graduate student conference, University of Western Ontario, 1999, and at the English Department, University of Alberta, October 2001. From typescript provided by Susan Rudy

– 2000. "Avant-Propos." *Globe: Revue internationale d'études québécoises* 3 (2000): 11–16

Brydon, Diana. 2005. "Metamorphosis of a Discipline: Rethinking the Canadian Literary Institution." Plenary address to the TransCanada Conference, Vancouver 2005

Brydon, Diana, and William Coleman, eds. 2008. *Renegotiating Community: Interdisciplinary Perspectives, Global Contexts. Globalization and Autonomy*. Seattle: University of Washington Press

Bubeck, Keimut. 1998. "Ethic of Care and Feminist Ethics." *Women's Philosophy Review* 19 (Spring): 22–50

Butler, Judith. 1993. *Bodies That Matter: On the Discursive Limits of "Sex."* London: Routledge

Buttigieg, J.A. 1995. "Gramsci on Civil Society." *boundary 2* (Fall): 7

Calhoun, Craig, ed. 1992. *Habermas and the Public Sphere*. Cambridge: MIT Press

Carlson, Marvin. 2003. *Performance*. New York: Routledge

Cave, Terence. 1988. *Recognitions: A Study in Poetics*. London: Clarendon

Chapman, Rowena, and Jonathan Rutherford, eds. 1988. *Male Order: Unwrapping Masculinity*. London: Laurence and Wishart

Cheney, Jim. 1996. "The Moral Epistemology of First Nations Stories." In Jickling 1996, 88–100

Cixous, Hélène, et al. 1977. *La venue à l'écriture*. Paris: Union générale d'éditions

Cockburn, Cynthia. 1998. *The Space between Us: Negotiating Gender and National Identities in Conflict*. London: Zed Books

Cockburn, Cynthia, and Lynette Hunter, eds. 1999. *Transversal Politics*, an issue of *Soundings* 12 (Summer): 88–190

Code, Lorraine. 1988. "Experience, Knowledge and Responsibility." In Griffiths and Whitford, *Feminist Perspectives in Philosophy*, 187–204

– 1995. *Rhetorical Spaces in Gendered Locations*. London: Routledge

– 2006. *Ecological Thinking: The Politics of Epistemic Location*. Oxford: Oxford University Press

Code, Lorraine, Maureen Ford, Kathleen Martindale, Susan Sherwin, and Debra Shogan. 1991. *Is Feminist Ethics Possible?* Ottawa: CRIAW/ICREF

Cohen, Jean. 1990. "Discourse Ethics and Civil Society." In Rasmussen 1990, 83–105

Cohen, Joshua. 1993. "Moral Pluralism and Political Consensus." In David Copp et al. 1993, 270–91

Cohen, Joshua, and Joel Rogers. 1994. "Solidarity, Democracy, Association." In *Staat und Verbande, Politisches Vierteljahresschrift*, edited by Wolfgang Streeck. Opladen: Westdeutscher Verlag

Collins, Patricia Hill. 1990. *Black Feminist Thought: Knowledge, Consciousness and Politics of Empowerment*. New York: Harper Collins Academic

Copeland, Rita, and Peter T. Struck, eds. 2010. *The Cambridge Companion to Allegory*. Cambridge: Cambridge University Press

Copp, David, Jean Hampton, and John Roemer, eds. 1993. *The Idea of Democracy*. Cambridge: Cambridge University Press

Cotnoir, Louise, et al. 1994. "Women of Letters." In *Collaboration in the Feminine*, 9–19. Toronto: Second Story Press

Cruikshank, Julie. 1999. *The Social Life of Stories: Narrative and Knowledge in the Yukon Territory*. Vancouver: University of British Columbia Press

Davey, Frank. 1965. *Bridge Force*. Toronto: Contact Press

– 1970. *Weeds*. Toronto: Coach House Press

– 1972a. *King of Swords*. Vancouver: Talonbooks

– 1972b. *Griffon*. Toronto: Massassauga Editions

– 1973. *Arcana*. Toronto: Coach House Press

– 1974. *The Clallam*. Vancouver: Talonbooks

– 1979. *War Poems*. Toronto: Coach House Press, Manuscript Editions

– 1980. *The Arches: Selected Poems*. Edited by bpNichol. Vancouver: Talonbooks

– 1982. *Capitalistic Affection*. Toronto: Coach House Press

– 1984. *Edward & Patricia*. Toronto: Coach House Press

– 1985. *The Louis Riel Organ and Piano Company*. Winnipeg: Turnstone Press

– 1991. *Popular Narratives*. Vancouver: Talonbooks

– 1993. *Reading "Kim" Right*. Vancouver: Talonbooks

– 1994. *Karla's Web: A Cultural Investigation of the Mahaffy-French Murders*. New York: Viking

- 1994. *Postnational Arguments*. Toronto: University of Toronto Press
- 1996a "American Alibis: A Search for Kroetsch's Postmodernism." In "Kroetsch at Niederbronn," *Open Letter* 9th series 5–6 (Spring/Summer): 241–51
- 1996b. *Cultural Mischief: A Practical Guide to Multiculturalism*. Vancouver: Talonbooks
- 2002. *How Linda Died*. Montreal: ECW Press
- 2010. http://publish.uwo.ca/~fdavey/c/newvispoems.html

Davey, Frank, and Fred Wah. 1986. *The SwiftCurrent Anthology*. Toronto: Coach House Press

DeLauretis, Teresa. 1987. *Technologies of Gender*. Bloomington: Indiana University Press

Derrida, Jacques. 1972. "Signature, Event, Context." In Derrida 1988. *Limited Inc.*, 1–24. Chicago: Northwestern University Press

- 1993. *Aporias*. Translated by Thomas Dutoit. Palo Alto: Stanford University Press 1993

Diamond, Elin. 1997. *Unmaking Mimesis: Essays on Feminism and Theater*. London: Routledge

Diamond, Irene, and Lee Quinby, eds. 1988. *Feminism and Foucault: Reflections on Resistance*. Lebanon, NH: Northeastern University Press

Dietz, Mary. 1991. "Hannah Arendt and Feminist Politics." In Shanley and Pateman 1991, 232–51

Flax, Jane. 1992. "Beyond Equality." In *Beyond Equality and Difference: Citizenship, Feminist Politics and Female Subjectivity*, edited by Gisela Bock and Susan James, 192–210. London: Routledge

Foster, Susan. 2010. *Choreographing Empathy: Kinesthesia in Performance*. London: Routledge

Fraser, Nancy. 1992. "Rethinking the Public Sphere: A Continuation of the Critique of Actually Existing Democracy." In Calhoun 1992, 109–42

Frazer, Eizabeth, Jennifer Hornsby, and Sabina Lovibond, eds. 1992. *Ethics: A Feminist Reader*. Oxford: Blackwell

Frye, Marilyn. 1993. "The Possibility of Feminist Theory." In *Feminist Frameworks: Alternative Theoretical Accounts of the Relations between Women and Men*, edited by Alison Jaggar and Paula Rothenburg, 103–12. Toronto: McGraw Hill

Garber, Marjorie. 1992. *Vested Interests: Cross-Dressing and Cultural Anxiety*. London: Routledge

Godard, Barbara, Daphne Marlatt, Kathy Mezei, Gail Scott. 1986. "Feminist Fiction Theory." *Tessera* 3: 6–12

Gould, Carol. 1988. *Rethinking Democracy: Freedom and Social Cooperation in Politics, Economy, and Society*. Cambridge: Cambridge University Press

- 1990. "On the Conception of the Common Interest: Between Procedure and Substance." In Kelly 1990, 253–73

Green, C. 2001. *The Third Hand: Collaboration in Art from Conceptualism to Postmodernism*. Minneapolis: University of Minnesota

Griffiths, Morwenna, and Margaret Whitford. 1988. *Feminist Perspectives in Philosophy*. Bloomington: Indiana University Press

Habermas, Jurgen. 1973. *Theory and Practice*. Translated by John Viertel. Boston: Beacon Press

– 1991. *The Structural Transformation of the Public Sphere: An Inquiry into a Category of Bourgeois Society*. Translated by Thomas Burger and Frederick Lawrence. Cambridge: MIT Press. First published 1962

Hall, Stuart, ed. 1997. *Representation: Cultural Representations and Signifying Practices*. London: Sage and Open University Press

Hansard. 2000. *Official Report of the Legislative Assembly of Nunavut*, 3rd Session, 1st Assembly, 17 February

Haraway, Donna. 1984. "A Manifesto for Cyborgs: Science, Technology and Socialist Feminism in the 1980s." In *Feminism/Postmodernism*, edited by Linda Nicholson, 65–107. London: Routledge

– 1988. "Situated Knowledges: The Science Question in Feminism and the Privilege of Partial Perspective." *Feminist Studies* 14 (3): 575–99

– 1997. *Modest_Witness@Second_Millenium. FemaleMan© Meets OncoMouse™.* London: Routledge

Harding, Sandra. 1986. *The Science Question in Feminism*. Milton Keynes: Open University Press

– 1991. *Whose Science? Whose Knowledge? Thinking from Women's Lives*. Milton Keynes: Open University Press

Hardt, Michael, and Antonio Negri. 2000. *Empire*. Cambridge: Harvard University Press

Hartmann, Saidiya. 1997. *Scenes of Subjection: Terror, Slavery, and Self-Making in Nineteenth-Century America*. Race and American Culture. New York: Oxford University Press

Hartsock, Nancy. 1983. "The Feminist Standpoint: Developing the Ground for a Specifically Feminist Historical Materialism." In *Discovering Reality: Feminist Perspectives on Metaphysics, Epistemology, Methodology, and Philosophy of Science*, edited by Sandra Harding and Merrill Hintikka, 283–310. Dordrecht: Reidel

Hekman, Susan. 1990. *Gender and Knowledge: Elements of a Postmodern Feminism*. Oxford: Polity/Blackwell

Holquist, Michael. 1981. "Politics of Representation." In *Allegory and Representation*, edited by Stephen Greenblatt, 163–83. Baltimore: Johns Hopkins University Press

Huggan, Graham. 2001. *The Postcolonial Exotic*. London: Routledge

Hunter, Lynette. 1978. "Form and Energy in the Poetry of Michael Ondaatje." *Journal of Canadian Poetry* (February 1978): 50–70, and *Bulletin of the British Association of Canadian Studies* (May 1978): 33–51

– 1984. *Rhetorical Stance, Allegories of Love and Death*. London: Macmillan

– 1987. *Modern Allegory and Fantasy: Rhetorical Stance of Contemporary Writing*. London: Macmillan

– 1995. *Outsider Notes: Feminist Approaches to Nation State Ideology, Writers/Readers, and Publishing.* London: Macmillan

– 1996. "Bodily Functions in Cartesian Space." In *Borderblur*, edited by Shirley Chew and Lynette Hunter, 150–73. Edinburgh: Quadrega and Edinburgh University Press 1996

– 1999a. *Critiques of Knowing: Situated Textualities in Science, Computing and the Arts.* London: Routledge

– 1999b. "Civic Rhetoric 1560–1640." In *Sir Thomas Gresham and Gresham College: Studies in the Intellectual History of London in the Sixteenth and Seventeenth Centuries*, edited by Francis Ames-Lewis, 88–104. London: Ashgate

– 2001a. "Listening to Situated Textuality: Working on Differentiated Public Voices." In "Gendering Ethics/The Ethics of Gender," edited by Linda Hogan and Sasha Roseneil, special issue, *Feminist Theory* 2 (2): 205–18

– 2001b. *Literary Value and Cultural Power.* Manchester: Manchester University Press

– 2000. "Considering Issues of Rhetoric and Violence." *Parallax* 6 (2): 2–8

– 2003. "Unruly Fugues." In *Interrogating Cultural Studies: Theory, Politics and Practice*, edited by Paul Bowman, 233–52. London: Routledge

– 2004. "Video Cicero: The Problem of Peace for Modern Political Rhetoric." In *Oratory in Action*, edited by Christopher Reid and Michael Edwards, 186–209. Manchester: Manchester University Press

– 2005a. "The *Inédit* in Writing by Nicole Brossard: Breathing the Skin of Language." In *Nicole Brossard: Essays on Her Works*, edited by Louise Forsyth, 209–38. Montreal: Guernica

– 2005b. "Equality as Difference: Storytelling in/of Nunavut." *International Journal of Canadian Studies* Fall: 51–81

– 2006. "What is an Honest Man and Can There Be an Honest Woman? The Poetics of Daphne Marlatt in Context of Global Economic Pressure." *Open Letter* 12, no. 8 (Winter 2006): 156–83

– 2010a. "Allegory Happens." In *The Cambridge Guide to Allegory*, edited by Rita Copeland and Peter Struck, 266–80. Cambridge: Cambridge University Press

– 2010b. "Internationalism, Performance and Public Culture." In *The Local Meets the Global in Performance*, edited by Pirkko Koski and Melissa Sirha, 21–40. Cambridge: Cambridge Scholars Press

– 2011. "A Logic of Participles." In *Artistic Research in Action* CARPA2, 11–22. Helsinki: Theatre Academy Publications 42, 2011

– 2013. "Installation and Constellation." In *Performance Studies: KeyWords, Concepts, and Theories*, edited by Bryan Reynolds. New York: Palgrave 2013

Hunter, Lynette, and Desmond Murray. Forthcoming. *Moving Like Water*

Hunter, Lynette, and Rebecca O'Rourke. 1996. *Creative Writing Strategies for English Studies.* Leeds: University of Leeds

– 1999. "The Values of Community Writing." In *Transversal Politics*, edited by Cynthia Cockburn and Lynette Hunter, 144–52. London: Lawrence and Wishart

Hutcheon, Linda. 1988. *The Canadian Postmodern*. Toronto: Oxford University Press

Interviewing. 1999. *Interviewing Inuit Elders*, Vol. 1, *Introduction*. Edited by Nunavut Arctic College et al. Iqaluit: Nortext

Janik, Alan. 1987. "Tacit Knowledge, Working Life and Scientific 'Method.'" In *Knowledge, Skill and Artificial Intelligence*, edited by Bo Goranzon and Ingela Josefson, 53–63. London and Berlin: Springer Verlag

Jardine, Alice, and Paul Smith, eds. 1987. *Men in Feminism*. London: Methuen

Jickling, Bob, ed. 1996. *A Colloquium on Environment, Ethics and Education*. Whitehorse: Yukon College

Kamboureli, Smaro, ed. 1996. *Making a Difference: Canadian Multicultural Literature*. Toronto: Oxford University Press

– 2000. *Scandalous Bodies: Diasporic Literature in English Canada*. Toronto: Oxford University Press

Keeling, Kara. 2007. *The Witch's Flight: The Cinematic, the Black Femme, and the Image of Common Sense*. Durham: Duke University Press

Kelly, Michael, ed. 1990. *Hermeneutics and Critical Theory in Ethics and Politics*. London: MIT Press

Kester, Grant. 2004. *Conversation Pieces: Community and Communication in Modern Art*. Berkeley: University of California Press

Kitimeot. 1999. *The Origin of Death*. Illustrated by Elise Anaginak Klengenberg. Cambridge Bay: Kitimeot Heritage Society

Koehn, Daryl. 1998. *Rethinking Feminist Ethics: Care, Trust and Empathy*. London: Routledge

Kristeva, Julie. 1982. *Powers of Horror: An Essay on Abjection*. Translated by Leon Roudiez. New York: Columbia University Press

Kroetsch, Robert. 1983. *Alibi*. Toronto: General Publishing

– 1989. *Completed Field Notes: The Long Poems of Robert Kroetsch*. Toronto: McClelland and Stewart

– 1992. *The Puppeteer*. Toronto: Random House

Kulchyski, Peter. 1999. *In the Words of Our Elders*. Toronto: University of Toronto Press

– 2001. *Like the Sound of a Drum: Aboriginal Cultural Politics in Denendeh and Nunavut*. Winnipeg: University of Winnipeg Press

Kwon, Miwon. 2004. *One Place after Another: Site-Specific Art and Locational Identity*. Cambridge: MIT Press

LaRocque, Emma. 1990. "Preface." In *Writing the Circle: Native Women of Western Canada*, compiled and edited by Jeanne Perreault and Sylvia Vance. Edmonton: NeWest

Latour, Bruno, and Steve Woolgar. 1979. *Laboratory Life: The Social Construction of Scientific Facts*. London: Sage

Lave, Jean, and Etienne Wenger. 1991. *Situated Learning: Legitimate Peripheral Participation*. Learning in Doing: Social, Cognitive and Computational Perspectives. Cambridge: Cambridge University Press

Lennon, Kathleen, and Margaret Whitford. 1994. *Knowing the Difference: Feminist Perspectives in Epistemology*. London: Routledge

Lepecki, Andrew. 2004. *Of the Presence of the Body: Essays on Dance and Performance Theory*. Middletown: Wesleyan University Press

Levinas, Emmanuel. 1989. *The Levinas Reader*. Edited by Sean Hand. Oxford: Blackwell

– 1998. *Otherwise than Being: Beyond Essence*. Translated by Alphonso Lingis. Pittsburg: Duquesne University Press

Lovibond, Sabina. 1983. *Realism and Imagination in Ethics*. Oxford: Blackwell

– 1994. "The End of Morality." In Lennon and Whitford 1994, 63–78

Lyotard, Jean-François. 1986. *The Postmodern Condition: A Report on Knowledge*. Translated by Geoff Bennington and Brian Massumi. Foreword by Fredric Jameson. Manchester: Manchester University Press

Macdonell, Diane. 1986. *Theories of Discourse: An Introduction*. Oxford: Basil Blackwell

Majeske, Andrew. 2006. *Equity in English Renaissance Literature*. New York: Routledge

MAMA. 2000. *Footprint: Recipes for Life*. Edited by Amina Souleiman. Leeds: Peepal Tree Press

Mansbridge, Jane 1996. "Using Power/Fighting Power: The Polity." In Benhabib 1996, 46–66

Maracle, Lee, 1988. *I Am Woman*. Vancouver: Write-On Press

– 1990. *Sojourner's Truth and Other Stories*. Vancouver: Press Gang

Marlatt, Daphne. 1985. "Writing as Reading/Reading as Writing." *Tessera* 2 (Fall): 21–25

– 1986. "Feminist Fiction Theory." In Godard 1986, 6–12

– 1998a. "Engagement with 'We' – the Passage of Pronouns over Time." For the ACQL/ACCUTE panel "Revisiting Canadian Literary Feminism" with Gail Scott and Di Brand, 29 May 1998, Ottawa. Introduced by Barbara Godard

– 1998b. *Readings from the Labyrinth*. Edmonton: NeWest Press

– 2001. *this tremor love is*. Vancouver: Talonbooks

– 2002. "Poetics/ Feminism/ Buddhism: Their Interrelations in My Work." University of Windsor discussion group. Spring

Marriott, David. 2007. *Haunted Life, Visual Culture and Black Modernity*. New Jersey: Rutgers University Press

Massey, Doreen. 2005. *For Space*. London: Sage

Mbembe, Achille. 2001. *On the Postcolony*. Berkeley: University of California Press

– 2003. "Necropolitics." *Public Culture* 15 (1): 22–40

Mezei, Kathy. 1986. "Feminist Fiction Theory." In Godard 1986, 6–12

Mohanty, Chandra. 2003. *Feminism without Borders: Decolonizing Theory, Practicing Solidarity*. Durham: Duke University Press

Moore, S. 1988. "Getting a Bit of the Other – the Pimps of Postmodernism." In Chapman and Rutherford, 165–92

Morton, Stephen. 2003. "'Workers of the World Unite' and Other Impossible Propositions." *Interventions* 5 (2): 290–8

– 2006. *Gayatri Spivak: Ethics, Subalternity and the Critique of Postcolonial Reason.* London: Polity

– 2007. "Poststructuralist Formulations." In *The Routledge Companion to Postcolonial Studies*, edited by John McLeod, 161–72. London: Routledge

Mouffe, Chantal. 1993. *The Return of the Political.* London: Verso

Mouffe, Chantal, and Ernesto Laclau. 1985. *Hegemony and Socialist Strategy: Towards a Radical Democratic Politics.* Translated by Winston Moore and Paul Cammack. London: Verso

Narayan, Uma. 1997. *Dislocating Cultures: Identities, Traditions, and Third World Feminism.* London: Routledge

Nichol, bp. 1988. *Selected Organs: Parts of an Autobiography.* Windsor: Black Moss Press

– 2002. *Meanwhile: The Critical Writings of bpNichol.* Edited by Roy Miki. Vancouver: Talonbooks

Noé, Ilya. 2009. "Site Particular." In *Mapping Landscapes for Performance as Research*, edited by Shannon Riley and Lynette Hunter, 207–9. London: Palgrave

Owens, Louis. 2001. *I Hear the Train: Reflections, Inventions, Refractions.* Norman: University of Oklahoma Press

Pateman, Carol. 1979. *The Problem of Political Obligation: A Critique of Liberal Theory.* London: Polity

– 1991. "'God Hath Ordained to Man a Helper': Hobbes, Patriarchy and Conjugal Right." In Shanley and Pateman 1991, 53–73

– 1995. *Democracy, Freedom and Special Rights.* Swansea: University of Wales Press

Pauktuutit. 1991. *Arnait: The Views of Inuit Women on Contemporary Issues.* Ottawa: Pauktuutit Inuit Women's Association

Perreault, Jeanne. 1995. *Writing Selves: Contemporary Feminist Autography.* Minneapolis: University of Minnesota Press

Perreault, Jeanne, and Sylvia Vance, eds. 1993. *Writing the Circle: Native Women of Western Canada.* Norman: University of Oklahoma Press

Petrone, Pennu, ed. 1988. *Northern Voices: Inuit Writing in English.* Toronto: University of Toronto Press

Phelan, Peggy. 1993. *Unmarked: The Politics of Performance.* London: Routledge

Profeit-Leblanc, Louise. 2002. "Four Faces of Story." *Canadian Journal of Environmental Education* 7 (Spring): 47–53

Quinn, Michael. 1995. *The Semiotic Stage: Prague School Theatre Theory.* London: Peter Lang

Ramazanoglu, Caroline, ed. 1993. *Up against Foucault: Explanations of Some Tensions between Foucault and Feminism.* London: Routledge

Rancière, Jacques, and Gabriel Rockhill. 2006. *The Politics of Aesthetics.* New York: Continuum

Rasmussen, David, ed. 1990. *Universalism vs Communitarianism: Contemporary Debates in Ethics.* Cambridge: MIT Press

Read, Alan. 1995. *Theatre and Everyday Life: An Ethics of Performance.* London: Routledge

Reid, Christopher, and Michael Edwards, eds. 2004. *Oratory in Action.* Manchester: Manchester University Press

Rich, Adrienne. 1986. *Of Woman Born: Motherhood as Experience and Institution.* New York: W.W. Norton

Rieff, Mark. 2007. "The Attack on Liberalism." *Law and Philosophy* 10: 173–210

Rorty, Richard. 1991. *Objectivity, Relativism and Truth.* Cambridge: Cambridge University Press

Rose, Hilary. 1994. *Love, Power and Knowledge: Towards a Feminist Transformation of the Sciences.* London: Polity

– 1998. "Risk, Trust and Scepticism in the Age of the New Genetics." In *The Risk Society and Beyond*, edited by Barbara Adam, Ulrich Beck, and Joost Van Loon, 63–77. London: Sage 2000

Russo, Ann. 1991. "We Cannot Live without Our Lives." In *Third World Women and the Politics of Feminism*, edited by Chandra Mohanty, Ann Russo, and Lourdes Torres, 297–313. Bloomington: Indiana University Press

Saltz, Jerry. 2007. "Conspicuous Consumption." *The New York Times Magazine*, 7 May

Scott, Gail. 1986. "Feminist Fiction Theory." In Godard 1986, 6–12

Sedgwick, Eve Kosofsky. 2003. *Touching, Feeling: Affect, Pedagogy, Performativity.* Durham: Duke University Press

Segal, Lynn. 1990. *Slow Motion: Changing Masculinities, Changing Men.* London: Virago

– 1994. *Straight Sex: The Politics of Pleasure.* London: Virago

Sexton, Jared. 2008. *Amalgamation Schemes: Antiblackness and the Critique of Multiracialism.* Minneapolis: University of Minnesota Press

Shanley, Mary, and Carole Pateman. 1991. *Feminist Interpretation and Political Theory.* London: Polity

Sharoni, Simona. 1995. *Gender and the Israeli-Palestine Conflict.* Syracuse: Syracuse University Press

Sidney, Angela, Kitty Smith, and Annie Ned. 1992. *Life Lived Like a Story*, edited by Julie Cruikshank. Vancouver: University of British Columbia Press

Simpson, Mark. 1992. *Male Impersonators: Men Performing Masculinity.* London: Routledge

Smith, Dorothy. 1987. *The Everyday World as Problematic.* Lebanon, NH: Northeastern University Press

– 1990. *Texts, Facts and Femininity: Exploring the Relations of Ruling.* London: Routledge

Spillers, Hortense. 1983. "A Hateful Passion, A Lost Love." *Feminist Studies* 9 (2): 293–323

– 1987. "Mama's Baby, Papa's Maybe: An American Grammar Book." *Diacritics, Culture and Countermemory* 17 (Summer): 64–81

– 2003. *Black, White and in Color*. Chicago: University of Chicago Press

Spivak, Gayatri Chakravorty. 2001. *A Critique of Postcolonial Reason: Toward a History of the Vanishing Present*. Cambridge: Harvard University Press

Stallybrass, Peter, and Allon White, eds. 1986. *The Politics and Poetics of Transgression*. London: Methuen

Taylor, Diana. 2003. *The Archive and the Repertoire: Performing Cultural Memory in the Americas*. Durham: Duke University Press

Thompson, Ann, and John O. Thompson. 1987. *Shakespeare: Meaning and Metaphor*. Brighton: Harvester

Traub, Valerie. 1992. *Desire and Anxiety: Circulations of Sexuality in Shakespearean Drama*. London: Routledge

Trinh, T. Minh-ha. 2010. *Elsewhere within Here*. New York: Routledge

Vizenor, Gerald. 2000. *Fugitive Poses*. Lincoln: University of Nebraska Press

– ed. 2008. *Narratives of Native Presence*. Lincoln: University of Nebraska Press

Walby, Sylvia. 2011. *The Future of Feminism*. London: Polity

Walker, Margaret. 1998. *Moral Understandings: A Feminist Study in Ethics*. London: Routledge

Wieringa, Saskia. 2006. *Subversive Women*. London: Zed Books

Wilderson III, Frank. 2005. "Gramsci's Black Marx: Whither the Slave in Civil Society?" *We Write* 2 (1): 1–17

– 2010. *Red, White, and Black: Cinema and the Structure of U.S. Antagonisms*. Durham: Duke University Press

Wolin, Sheldon. 1996. "Fugitive Democracy." In Benhabib 1996, 31–45

Woolf, Janet. 1990. *Feminine Sentences: Essays on Women and Culture*. Berkeley: University of California Press

Young, Iris. 1996. "Communication and the Other." In Benhabib 1996, 120–35

– 1997. *Intersecting Voices: Dilemmas of Gender, Political Philosophy, and Policy*. Ithaca: Princeton University Press

Yukon First Nations, Council of. 2000. *Traditional Knowledge Research Guidelines: A Guide for Researchers in the Yukon*. Whitehorse: Council of Yukon First Nations

Yuval-Davis, Nira. 1997. *Gender and Nation*. London: Sage

index